Reclaiming Information and Communication Technologies for Development

Reclaiming Information and Communication Technologies for Development

Tim Unwin

OXFORD
UNIVERSITY PRESS

OXFORD

UNIVERSITY PRESS

Great Clarendon Street, Oxford, OX2 6DP,
United Kingdom

Oxford University Press is a department of the University of Oxford.
It furthers the University's objective of excellence in research, scholarship,
and education by publishing worldwide. Oxford is a registered trade mark of
Oxford University Press in the UK and in certain other countries

First Edition published in 2017
Impression: 1

Published in the United States of America by Oxford University Press
198 Madison Avenue, New York, NY 10016, United States of America

British Library Cataloguing in Publication Data
Data available

Library of Congress Control Number: 2016958031

ISBN 978–0–19–879529–2

Printed in Great Britain by
Clays Ltd, St Ives plc

Preface and Acknowledgements

This book is about the reasons why poor and marginalized people have not yet benefited sufficiently from the widespread and pervasive expansion of Information and Communication Technologies (ICTs) into most aspects of human life over the last quarter century. It is about the inequalities that the use of these technologies has enhanced, and the risks to us all that these are creating. However, it remains a book of hope; hope that by better understanding the interests underlying these increasing inequalities, wise people of good will may be able to work collectively together to help the poorest and most marginalized use ICTs to enhance and improve their lives.

Much has changed in the use of ICTs for 'development' (ICT4D) since my last edited book on the subject was published in 2009. In that book I laid out the case for why the focus of ICT4D should be on reducing inequalities as well as increasing economic growth, and this remains a core theme of this new book. However, I was much more optimistic a decade ago that ICTs would be used effectively to enhance the lives of poor people. My previous book thus included chapters by leading authorities in their fields about the many ways through which ICTs were helping to improve the quality and quantity of education, to transform health delivery, to enhance rural and agricultural incomes, and to enable better government. Most of those examples remain valid, and there is indeed much good work continuing to be done by civil society, governments, and the private sector to benefit the poor. This has been widely reported in the many books and papers that have been published over the last decade on the subject. However, as the present book argues, in this period the rich have got very much richer through the use of ICTs, and the poor have become relatively poorer. I am impatient and frustrated by this increasing inequality, and so rather than emphasizing all of the oft-cited examples of the benefits of ICTs, I concentrate here on the interests underlying why ICTs are being used in this way. Yet, I still retain a belief that these technologies can indeed help empower poor people and this must never be forgotten through the darker sections of the book.

The book draws on Critical Theory to help understand these interests, and is explicit about the particular relationships between theory and practice that this implies. I have been privileged and honoured to cross many boundaries in my own journey of understanding ICT4D, and the use of two fonts is intended to emphasize this distinction between more personal practical reflections and the conceptual arguments. I have tried hard not to overburden the text with too many references, but the ideas of so many other people have influenced me in writing this book that I have wanted to pay tribute to their work and to provide links that will enable readers readily to explore this body of literature themselves. To facilitate this further, I have used footnotes to provide URLs for key material mentioned in the text, and also to enable easy access to references at the end of the book online where this is possible. Although accessed at various times, these links were all checked on 22 August 2016, and earlier dates of access are only given when they were not live at this date, or included time-specific information.

Very many people have influenced my ideas and my practice since I first undertook research in India and learnt to program in Fortran in the mid-1970s, and I have been truly privileged to learn from and be inspired by them. I would especially like to recognize and thank the following, all of whom have had a very particular influence on this book: Adrian Godfrey, who has taught me much about the personal attributes that are important in implementing ICT4D partnerships; Alex Wong, with whom I have had many enjoyable hours working together on ICT4D for the World Economic Forum, and from whom I have learnt so much; Anusha Palpita, for his generous kindness in introducing me to Sri Lanka, and for his insights into regulation; Anusha Rahman Khan, who has done much to help me to understand the role of women in politics in Pakistan; Astrid Dufborg, who so sadly died in January 2016, for her depth of insight and humanity, especially about ICT4D policy matters; Belinda Exelby, who so kindly introduced me to the world of the GSMA; Boubakar Barry, who welcomed me to Sénégal, and helped me better understand African universities; Bushra Hassan Malik, for her inspiration, kindness, and care in helping me appreciate the place of women in patriarchal Islamic societies, and for all that she has done to help me complete this book; Carla Licciardello, for her boundless enthusiasm in driving forward cyber-security and gender-related issues in the ITU; Caroline Stratton, for her helpful comments on a draft of Chapter 1; Chris Painter, for his deep insights into ICT policy and the US Department of State; Cris Seecheran, for all of his advice while I led the CTO, and especially for his comments as a regulator on a draft of Chapter 5; David Hollow, for all the fun we have had working together especially on monitoring and evaluation, and the use of ICTs for education; Derek Gregory for first introducing me to Critical Theory; Erik Hersman, for his friendship and undiminished passion for technological innovation in the interest of the poor; Erkki Sutinen, for welcoming me into the world of computer science; Fadi Chehadé, for sharing his leadership insights with me; Francis Wangusi, for guiding me through the political complexities of

Kenya, and the gift of an elephant statue; Gavin Dykes, for his modesty, moderating skills, and deep understanding of technology and education; Godfrey Mutabazi, for his generous hospitality in Uganda, and all I have learnt from him about diplomacy and regulation; Gunnar Olsson, for his generosity of spirit and challenging intellectual acuity; Hamadoun Touré, for his inspirational leadership of the ITU, and his warm friendship; Ineke Buskens, for her passionate commitment to gender issues, her support for my intellectual adventures, and for her comments on a draft of Chapter 1; Ivo Ivanovski for his unfailing belief in the power of ICTs to drive economic growth; Jean Louis Beh Mengue, for helping me better understand Cameroon, and for his soft, kind, and thoughtful diplomacy; Jean Philbert Nsengimana, for the passionate and inspirational way he has driven forward ICT initiatives in Rwanda, for the warmth of his smile, and for the generosity of his friendship; Jim Wynn, for his ability to get things done, and for all I have learnt from him about ICTs and education; John Garrity for helpful comments on Chapter 6; Jose Maria Diaz Batanero and his team at the ITU for involving me in so much of their conference-related work; Joss Gillet and the GSMA for kindly preparing Figure 2.3 for me; Juma Kandie, for his generosity and warm friendship as Chair of the CTO when I was Secretary General; Ken Banks, for his boundless entrepreneurial spirit, and the many anarchic conversations we have had together; Lídia Brito for her inspiration, passion, and commitment, as well as her generous hospitality in Mozambique and Paris; Lorenzo Cantoni, for his innovative, open mind and intellectual ICT4D leadership at the Università della Svizzera italiana in Lugano; Marco Zennaro for his passionate commitment to ICTs and the Internet of Things, as well as his comments on aspects of spectrum management in Chapter 2; Marianne Treschow for all of the advice and the support that she gave me while I was at the CTO, as well as for her insights on regulation; Mariemme Jamme, for all of her generous encouragement, and for her commitment and enthusiasm for African technological entrepreneurship; Marije Geldof, for her friendship and everything that I have learnt from her about PhD supervision and practical delivery of ICT initiatives in Africa; Mark Weber, for teaching me about running software companies, and so much more; Matt Perault, for his astuteness, and for opening doors that have enabled me to learn so much; Michelle Selinger, for the great times we had working together on ICT for education partnerships; Mike Best, for sharing so many ideas with me, and for all I have learnt from his research; Mike Trucano, who is so amazingly generous with his time, and has such an understanding of the ways through which ICTs should be used in educational contexts; Mohamed Abida, for his Tunisian friendship and his political and funding insights; Mohamed Sharil Tarmizi, for his passion and understanding of regulatory affairs; Nigel Hickson, for persuading me to join the CTO, and for all of his subsequent support; Omobola Johnson for providing so much advice, for her warm welcomes to Nigeria, and for her insights about the section on app development and incubators; Owen Barder, for his original leadership of Imfundo, and his recollections; Rebecca Stromeyer, who has taught me so much about conference organization, and for everything she has done to encourage e-learning in Africa; Robert Pepper for the joy of our many fun discussions, albeit from very different perspectives; Samantha Dickenson, for her very helpful comments on parts of Chapter 3, and all she does to report on international conferences; Sarah Taylor, for being one of the very best civil servants in the UK, and for helping to put the world to rights; Sudhir Wanmali, for introducing me to India, and having patience with my attempts to understand development over the last forty years; Sunil Bose, for his insights about regulation, and his gentle, warm hospitality in Bangladesh; Thari Pheko, for his welcoming friendship in Botswana and insights about regulation; Torbjörn Fredriksson, for our many conversations about ICTs, as well as wine; and Zhao Houlin, for his continued friendship and insights about the ITU. I am also very grateful to those people at Oxford University Press, and in the production process, for having confidence in this book, and helping to bring it to publication, especially David Musson, Adam Swallow, Clare Kennedy, Joanna North, and Raj Clement.

The following have kindly granted permission for works undertaken for, or reproduced in full or in part, in this book: the Computer Laboratory at the University of Cambridge for Figure 1.1, which is reproduced by permission and remains copyright of the Computer Laboratory, University of Cambridge; The International Telecommunications Union for Figure 2.1 and parts of Table 2.1; Joss Gillett and GSMA for Figure 2.3; Next Generation Mobile Networks Ltd. for Figure 2.4; and Giles Walker, for Figure 7.2.

Contents

List of Figures

List of Tables

List of Boxes

1

A Critical Reflection on ICTs and 'Development'

This book is about the ways through which Information and Communication Technologies (ICTs) have become entwined with both the theory and the practice of 'development'. Its central argument is that although the design and introduction of such technologies has immense potential to do good, all too often this potential has had negative outcomes for poor and marginalized people, sometimes intended but more often than not unintended. Over the last twenty years, rather than reducing poverty, ICTs have actually increased inequality, and if 'development' is seen as being about the relative differences between people and between communities, then it has had an overwhelming negative impact on development. Despite the evidence to the contrary, I nevertheless retain a deep belief in the potential for ICTs to be used to transform the lives of the world's poorest and most marginalized for the better. The challenge is that this requires a fundamental change in the ways that all stakeholders think about and implement ICT policies and practices. This book is intended to convince these stakeholders of the need to change their approaches.

It has its origins in the mid-1970s, when I learnt to program in Fortran, and also had the privilege of undertaking field research in rural India. The conjuncture of these two experiences laid the foundations for my later career, which over the last twenty years has become increasingly focused on the interface between ICTs on the one hand, and the idea of 'development' on the other. The book tells personal stories and anecdotes (shown in a separate font). It draws on large empirical data sets, but also on the personal qualitative accounts of others. It tries to make the complex theoretical arguments upon which it is based easy to understand. Above all, it has a practical intent in reversing the inequalities that the transformative impacts of ICTs have led to across the world.

* * *

I still remember the enjoyment, but also the frustrations, of using punch cards, with eighty columns, each of which had twelve punch locations, to write my simple programs in Fortran. The frustration was obvious. If you made just one tiny mistake in punching a card, the program would not run, and you would have to take your deck of cards away, make the changes, and then submit the revised deck for processing the next day. However, there was also something exciting about doing this. We were using machines to generate new knowledge. They were modern. They were the future, and we dreamt that they might be able to change the world, to make it a better place (Figure 1.1). Furthermore, there was something very pleasing in the purity and accuracy that they required. It was my fault if I made a mistake; the machine would always be precise and correct. These self-same comments also apply to the use of ICTs today. Yes, they can be frustrating, as when one's immensely powerful laptop or mobile phone crashes, or when one receives unwanted e-mails that extend the working day far into time better spent doing other things, but at the same time the interface between machines and modernity conjures up a belief that we can use them to do great things—such as reducing poverty.

In 1976 and 1977 I had the immense privilege of undertaking field research in the Singbhum District of what was then South Bihar, now Jharkhand, with an amazing Indian scholar, Sudhir Wanmali, who was undertaking his PhD about the 'hats', or periodic markets, where rural trade and exchange occurred in different places on each day of the week

Figure 1.1 Modernity and the machine: Cambridge University Computer Laboratory in the early 1970s
Source: University of Cambridge Computer Laboratory (1999).

Figure 1.2 *Hat,* or rural periodic market at Hat Gamharia, in what was then South Bihar, 1977
Source: Author.

(Figure 1.2). Being 'in the field' with him taught me so much: the haze and smell of the woodsmoke in the evenings; the intense colours of rural India; the rice beer served in leaf cups at the edges of the markets towards the end of the day; the palpable tensions caused by the ongoing Naxalite rising (Singh, 1995); the profits made by mainly Muslim traders from the labour of *Adivasi*, tribal villagers, in the beautiful forests and fields of Singbhum; the creaking oxcarts; and the wonderful names of the towns and villages such as Hat Gamharia, Chakradharpur, Jagannathpur, and Sonua. Most of all, though, it taught me that 'development' had something powerful to do with inequality. I still vividly recall seeing rich people picnicking in the lush green gardens of the steel town of Jamshedpur nearby, coming in their smart cars from their plush houses, and then a short distance away watching and smelling blind beggars shuffling along the streets in the hope of receiving some pittance to appease their hunger. The ever so smart, neatly pressed, clothes of the urban elite at the weekends contrasted markedly with the mainly white saris, trimmed with bright colours, that scarcely covered the frail bodies of the old rural women in the villages where we worked during the week. Any development that would take place here had to be about reducing the inequalities that existed between these two different worlds within the world of South Bihar. This made me look at my own country, at the rich countries of Europe, and it made me all the more aware of two things: not only that inequality and poverty existed in the midst of our rich societies; but also that the connections between different countries in the world had something to do with the depth of poverty, however defined, in places such as the village of Sonua, or the town of Ranchi in South Bihar.

Between the mid-1970s and the mid-2010s my interests in ICTs, on the one hand, and 'development' on the other, have increasingly fascinated and preoccupied me. This book is about that fascination. It shares stories about how they are connected, how they impinge on and shape each other. I have been fortunate to have been involved in many initiatives that have sought to involve ICTs in various aspects of 'development'. In the first instance, my love of computing and engineering, even though I am a geographer, has always led me to explore the latest technological developments, from electronic typewriters that could store a limited number of words, through the first Apple computers, to the Acorn BBC micro school and home computer launched in 1981, using its simple BASIC program-ming language, and now more recently to the use of mobile phones for development. I was fascinated by the potential for computers to be used in schools and universities, and I learnt much from being involved with the innovative Computers in Teaching Initiative Centre for Geography in the 1990s (see Unwin and Maguire, 1990). During the 2000s, I then had the privilege of leading two challenging international initiatives that built on these experiences. First, between 2001 and 2004 I led the UK Prime Minister's *Imfundo: Partnership for IT in Education* initiative, based within the Department for International Development (UK Government Web Archive, 2007), which created a partnership of some forty governments, private sector and civil society organizations committed to using ICTs to enhance the quality and quantity of education in Africa, particularly in Kenya, South Africa, and Ghana. Then in the latter 2000s, I led the World Economic Forum's Partner-ships for Education initiative with UNESCO, which sought to draw out and extend the experiences gained through the Forum's Global Education Initiative's work on creating ICT-based educational partnerships in Jordan, Egypt, Rajasthan, and Palestine (Unwin and Wong, 2012). Meanwhile, between these I created the ICT4D (ICT for Development) Collective, based primarily at Royal Holloway, University of London, which was specifically designed to encourage the highest possible quality of research in support of the poorest and most marginalized. Typical of the work we encouraged was another partnership-based initiative, this time to develop collaborative research and teaching in European and African universities both on and through the use of ICTs. More recently, between 2011 and 2015 I had the privilege of being Secretary General of the Commonwealth Telecommunications Organisation,[1] which is the membership organization of governments and people in the fifty-two countries of the Commonwealth, enhancing the use of ICTs for development.

* * *

Two things have been central to all of these initiatives: first a passionate belief in the practical role of academics and universities in the societies of which they are a part, at all scales from the local to the international; and second,

---

[1] <http://www.cto.int>.

recognition of the need for governments, the private sector, and civil society to work collaboratively together in partnerships to help deliver effective development impacts. The first of these builds fundamentally on the notion of Critical Theory developed by the Frankfurt School (Held, 1980), and particularly the work of Jürgen Habermas (1974, 1978) concerning the notion of knowledge constitutive interests and the complex interrelationships between theory and practice. Section 1.1 therefore explores why this book explicitly draws on Critical Theory in seeking to understand the complex role and potential of ICTs in and for development. Section 1.2 thereafter then draws on the account above about rural life in India in the 1970s to explore in further detail some of the many ways in which the term 'development' has been, and indeed still is, used in association with technology.

1.1 A Critical Approach to ICTs for Development

Many early accounts of the use of ICTs for development focused largely uncritically on describing the diverse ways in which technology was being implemented in poorer countries of the world to contribute to their development (see for example, Weigel and Waldburger, 2004). This has remained true of much recent work over the last decade, which has usually sought to provide positive narratives of the evolution of ICT initiatives that have been implemented in support of global development objectives (Dutton, 2013; Cantoni and Danowski, 2015; Hanna with Summer, 2015; Mansell and Ang, 2015; Proenza, 2015). Others, though, have been less positive. Toyama (2015), for example, has provided a critical account of what he sees as the manic rhetoric of digital utopians, highlighting the failures of many ICT initiatives, and arguing that there needs to be a people-centric view of social change if technology is to be used effectively to deliver on development goals. Likewise, there is some feminist and action-oriented critical research (see, for example, Buskens and Webb, 2009; Lennie and Tacchi, 2013; Buskens and Webb, 2014), that has drawn attention to the divisive ways through which technology has shaped inequalities within societies, and what might be done to change this (see also Avgerou, 2010).

However, although many such accounts can indeed be called critical in the sense that they present a contrasting, or disapproving, view of otherwise accepted arguments, the present book argues for a rather different approach to the notion of being 'critical'. It does so by drawing explicitly on the ideas of members of the Frankfurt School of Critical Theorists, and particularly the work of Jürgen Habermas (1974, 1978, 1984, 1987). The word 'critical' is therefore not used here so much in the sense of being negative or disapproving of any particular ICT4D initiative or approach, but rather as a means to embed my arguments within the conceptual, and indeed practical, tradition of such Critical Theory. I adopt this approach in part because of a belief that these ideas provide valuable insights into ways through which poor people might be able to benefit from such technologies, but also because they have become central to my own life over the last forty years, and it is impossible to understand my arguments without at least some insight into Habermas's writings (for an earlier version of some of these notions, see Unwin, 2009).

Many substantial accounts of the school of social theory and philosophy developed initially under Grunberg in the 1920s at the Institut für Sozial-forschung (Institute for Social Research) at the Johann Wolfgang Goethe University in Frankfurt, and then taken much further by Marcuse, Adorno, Horkheimer, Benjamin, Fromm, and others from the 1930s onwards have already been published (see for example, Jay, 1973; Tar, 1977; Held, 1980; Bottomore, 2002), as have overviews of the work of Habermas himself (McCarthy, 1978; Geuss, 1981; Anon., 2014). This is not therefore the place to provide a detailed account of the evolution of these ideas (see Unwin, 1992 for an overview), but it is important to draw out five themes that have specific and direct relevance to the arguments that follow with respect to the use of ICTs for 'development': the interplay between *theory and praxis*; the notion of *knowledge-constitutive interests*; a *normative*, as against a positive, approach to knowledge construction and enquiry; the potential *emancipatory* and empowering character of some types of knowledge; and a particular view of the relationships between *technology and society*. These draw especially on two of Habermas's substantive early works, *Theorie und Praxis*, first published in 1963 (Habermas, 1974 for English translation), and *Erkenntnis und Interesse*, first published in 1968 (Habermas, 1978 for English translation of the second edition).[2]

1.1.1 *A Specific Connection between Theory and Praxis*

At the heart of Habermas's (1974) work was his exploration of the profound interconnectedness between theory and praxis. By tracing the relations between philosophy, science, and politics from Aristotle to the modern era, he shows clearly how the relations between theory and praxis have changed over time. Although 'praxis' is usually translated merely as 'practice', inherent in Habermas's arguments is the notion that it is something very much more complex than just action based upon an idea. This has been summarized particularly well by Carr and Kemmis (1986, p. 190) in the context of action-oriented research in education, where they emphasize that:

---

[2] Habermas's (1984, 1987) later works on communicative competence are also of relevance, but the core arguments used in this book derive primarily from his earlier work.

> *Praxis* has its roots in the commitment of the practitioner to wise and prudent action in a practical, concrete, historical situation. It is action which is considered and consciously theorized, and which may reflexively inform and transform the theory which informed it. *Praxis* cannot be understood as mere behaviour; it can only be understood in terms of the understandings and commitments which inform it. Moreover, *praxis* is always risky; it requires that the practitioner makes a wise and prudent practical judgment about how to act in *this* situation.

There are many implications of such arguments for research and practical action in the field of ICT4D, but three are of particular significance. First, it recognizes that there is a crucial reciprocal connection between any theoretical conceptualization and practical action, and that this should be clearly articulated. Whilst some may argue that good academic research can be conducted solely within the confines of a university environment, and that it is somehow 'free' and 'pure', my own experience has convinced me otherwise that universities themselves are but a construct built and maintained to deliver certain kinds of knowledge. It is impossible to grasp fully the complexities of any dimension of life, be it implementing a development initiative, working in the private sector, or engaging in the political reality of government, without actually having engaged practically in such a context. The constraints of normal academic life do not usually enable those working in universities to cross such boundaries. Moreover, far too many ICT4D initiatives have been concocted in a university or corporate research and development laboratory, far from the reality of the lived world of poor and marginalized people, and although often well-intentioned they have invariably failed to deliver their anticipated outcomes. As the account with which this chapter opens indicates, I have therefore deliberately sought to engage in different working contexts and environments, and this book draws on the richness of these experiences to share what I hope are valuable insights at both a conceptual and a practical level into the ways through which ICTs are being used in development.

Second, though, Habermas's work implies a particular kind of practice, one that is not only built on deep understanding and critical reflection, but is also committed to a certain kind of action. Built within his notion of praxis is the idea of intentionality, that the person engaged in Critical Theory is intent on taking wise actions that will in their turn also inform the theory that gave rise to them in the first place. The process of being critical is thus a reciprocal one in which both theory and practice are informed by each other. This book is thus a historically situated product of my interpretations and actions particularly over the last fifteen years, and seeks to be explicit about this in the hope that the lessons I have learnt can be shared more widely amongst all those with a commitment to serving the interests of the poor and marginalized.

Third, and closely building on this, is the notion that Critical Theory is profoundly about making change happen. One of the key notions underlying the work of the Frankfurt School was that both Marx and Freud provided exemplars of this new kind of approach to critical thinking, one in which the development of theory and understanding was intended to change the behaviours of those in whom such knowledge was developed. Central to this is a profoundly moral process, designed to enable societies to be improved, or if necessarily radically changed, through the practices of enlightened citizens. Hence, Critical Theory retains the optimism of the Enlightenment, in its commitment to the idea that the continual interplay between theory and praxis may indeed lead to wiser decisions being made, in the interests of all members of society. Academics are a hugely privileged group of people, set apart by society in university institutions in the interests of better understanding and changing that society; in a sense, they are the psychoanalysts of society, whose role is to help society overcome the systematic distortions within it. Again, as the introductory accounts at the start of this chapter indicated, this book is built on the fundamental belief that ICTs have been instrumental in the creation of greater inequality across the world in the twenty-first century. Yet, in the spirit of the Enlightenment, those who believe in ICT4D must believe that it is possible to use technology to improve the lives of the poorest and most marginalized in our local, national, regional, and indeed global societies.

1.1.2 *Knowledge-Constitutive Interests*

One of Habermas's (1978) most important contributions in *Knowledge and Human Interests* was his argument that different kinds of intellectual enquiry, or forms of science, are associated with particular knowledge-constitutive interests, which 'take form in the medium of work, language and power' (Habermas, 1978, p. 313). According to Habermas (1978, p. 309) the cognitive interest of *empirical-analytic science*, derived from its hypothetico-deductive explanatory method, is 'in technical control over objectified processes' that are inherent in manual labour; *historical-hermeneutic science*, in which 'access to the facts is provided by the understanding of meaning' has a practical interest in reaching 'a possible consensus among actors in the framework of a self-understanding derived from tradition' (Habermas, 1978, p. 310); and *critical science* has an emancipatory interest which leads to self-reflection and is expressed through a consideration of relations of domination and constraint. These arguments are of great importance for understanding the evolution of the use of ICTs in development practice.

At a general level, they emphasize the need always to seek to understand the interests underlying the specific ways in which a phenomenon is explained, understood, or transformed. Descriptive accounts of the expansion of ICTs in developing countries, for example, have far too often ignored these interests, and have had a tendency to see the global spread of ICTs as being in some way a natural and positively progressive process. The reality is that technologies have always been developed to serve particular interests, and these have most usually been to enable those in power to retain their positions of power. A fundamental question addressed in this book is thus whether ICTs are but a continuation of this process whereby the rich and powerful can maintain their control, or whether there is indeed something potentially disruptive about them that could enable the poor and marginalized to benefit.

In the early to mid-2000s, there was considerable optimism about the potential of ICTs to lead to positive change for the poorest peoples and countries in the world, especially with the emergence of disruptive technologies such as mobile devices and the rapid expansion of social media (Unwin, 2009). However, the reality is that the expansion of ICTs has usually been associated with increasing inequality in the world, and despite many well-intentioned initiatives, there is uncertainty as to precisely how much the very poorest have indeed benefited. It is thus encouraging to see that the *World Development Report 2016: Digital Dividends* (World Bank, 2016a) clearly recognizes that the benefits of the digital economy have been less than expected and have not been equally distributed. Sadly, the World Bank fails sufficiently to explore the interests that have underlain this increased inequality, but it is not in its own interest to do so. One of the purposes of the present book is therefore to reveal these interests, and suggest what remains to be done if ICTs are indeed to be used to change the social and political structures that create poverty. Indeed, increasingly the very idea of 'development' has become subverted to the interests of those who wish to expand and extend the reach of ICTs; positive 'development' outcomes are no longer the end purpose, if ever they were, but are rather a means through which technology is being embedded in the daily lives of everyone in the world. Instead of 'ICTs for Development' (ICT4D) we have become increasingly and surreptitiously enmeshed in a world of 'Development for ICTs' (D4ICT), where governments, the private sector, and civil society are all tending to use the idea of 'development' to promote their own ICT interests.

A second important insight that can be drawn from Habermas's (1978) work is the specific connection between different kinds of science and the interests underlying them. Although his framework can be criticized for being difficult to interpret, overly prescriptive, and insufficiently flexible, it does prove useful in helping to understand the ways in which different people have approached the subject of ICTs for development (see Section 1.3 for further detail). Much work in ICT4D has been led by engineers, computer scientists, and technologists, rooted in traditional positivist science. As Habermas (1978, p. 315) comments with respect to such empirical-analytic sciences, 'The glory of the sciences is their unswerving application of their methods without reflecting on knowledge-constitutive interests', and that they therefore 'lack the means of dealing with the risks that appear once the connection of knowledge and human interest has been comprehended on the level of self-reflection'. All too often, ICT4D research and practice has been technologically driven, and has therefore tended to replicate existing social and economic structures, thereby failing sufficiently to explore, interpret, or change the very conditions that have given rise to them. Habermas (1978, p. 316), though, is equally clear about the limits of historical-hermeneutic science, with its prime focus on the understanding of meaning, noting that 'It defends sterilized knowledge against the reflected appropriation of active traditions and locks up history in a museum.' In essence, for Habermas, neither empirical-analytic science nor historical-hermeneutic science can enable us fundamentally to change society for the better. Accordingly, it is only through the self-reflection that lies at the heart of critical science that people can truly become emancipated, and thereby realize their full potential in creating a fairer and more just world (see Section 1.1.4 for a fuller discussion). The present book is therefore firmly grounded in the tradition of critical science, seeking to offer insights that will encourage all stakeholders involved at the interface between ICTs and development to reflect both on their theories and on their practices, in the firm belief that by so doing people may indeed be able to change practices and use technology to help shape that fairer and more just world.

1.1.3 *Reclaiming the Normative*

Much academic enquiry during the second half of the twentieth century relating to broadly defined 'development', particularly in the context of economics and policy-making, tended to focus on the *positive*, on what is thought to be objective and fact-based (Lipsey and Chrystal, 1995). Large data sets, the ability to test hypotheses and thus to predict outcomes came to dominate research and practice. The empirical-analytic model of enquiry, rooted in the physical and natural sciences and grounded in the belief that there really are value-free 'facts', played an ever increasing role in shaping political decision-making. Value-based, subjective approaches were frequently condemned as lacking in rigour. Hence, in the field of 'development' policy, increasing emphasis has been placed over the last twenty years on evidence-based policy-making, drawing largely on an empirical-analytic and quantitative approach to enquiry (Behague et al., 2009; Dhaliwal and Tulloch, 2012). Today, the way in which Big Data is being seen as offering enormous new opportunities for resolving development issues (Spratt and Baker, 2015) is but a continuation of this dominant trend (see Section 6.4). Habermas's (1974,

1978). Critical Theory provides an important reminder that many such approaches have focused on the *positive*, 'what is', rather than the *normative*, 'what should be'.

To be sure, there have been other approaches to enquiry into the meaning of development, and many in the humanities and social sciences have continued to argue for the value of historical-hermeneutic approaches that focus on the subjective, qualitative, and value-laden aspects of life (Camfield, 2014; Skovdal and Cornish, 2015). Nevertheless, many of these approaches can be seen as open to the same criticisms that Habermas applied more generally to historical-hermeneutic science, namely that it has a tendency to focus on understanding to the exclusion of action that might change the conditions of inequality that exist (although, see Chambers, 2014). Understanding is crucially important, but is insufficient by itself. Much qualitative research has failed to go beyond describing and interpreting 'what is', to take the normative leap into 'what should be'.

Throughout the last half-century there have, though, also been proponents of more radical alternatives to the dominant mode of theory and practice in international development drawing particularly on Marxist and feminist traditions (Momsen and Townsend, 1987; Sachs, 1992; Escobar, 1995; Kothari, 2005; Chambers, 2014; Buskens, 2015). Many of these have laid claim to a critical stance, and some have drawn in part on Critical Theory, with its clear concern for advocating alternative models of society. However, since the failure of the radical Left, particularly in Europe following the collapse of the Soviet Union in the early 1990s, the dominant mode of empirical-analytic led 'development' has reasserted itself (for further discussion, see Section 1.3). There now needs to be a reassertion of the normative into development theory and practice. This is especially true of ICT4D, and this book advocates that all stakeholders need to reflect closely on how such technologies have been used in 'development' in the past, so as to adopt a much more radical normative stance that might permit them to use ICTs for the betterment of humanity in the future.

What Habermas (1974, 1978) reminds us is that *positive* approaches by themselves are insufficient, and that they need to be countered by *normative* approaches, grounded in particular values and theories, if the world is to be transformed into a better place. While some feminist and postmodern approaches have explicitly sought to question 'the "grand theories" of the past and the idea that rational thinking and technological solutions will bring "progress" to the world' (Hunt, 2012, p. 284; see also Keith, 1997), Habermas (1996) remains tied to the Enlightenment project and its view that progress can be achieved through the human potential for reason to create a more equal, fair, peaceful, and just world. Despite the failings of the twentieth century, reflected in the wars and oppression that characterized it, Habermas remains an optimist, and has provided a rigorous defence of the intentions of the Enlightenment in the face of the postmodern challenges of the latter part of the century (Habermas, 1981).

1.1.4 *Emancipation and Empowerment*

> In self-reflection knowledge for the sake of knowledge attains congruence with the interest in autonomy and responsibility. The emancipatory cognitive interest aims at the pursuit of self-reflection as such. My *fourth thesis* is thus that *in the power of self-reflection, knowledge and interest are one.*
>
> (Habermas, 1978, p. 314, italics in original)

At the centre of Habermas's (1974, 1978) early work was the notion, drawn largely from his interpretation of the work of Marx and Freud, that self-reflection was the means through which emancipation could be achieved; at the heart of his idea of Critical Theory is that it has an emancipatory interest, not least with respect to freeing science from its positivist illusions. While his early accounts of this were subject to much criticism, his later *Theory of Communicative Action* (Habermas, 1984, 1987) developed them further through an analysis of communicative rationality and a theory of modernization and society, but still with the aim of establishing the grounds upon which society could be truly emancipated (Raiti, 2006; Anon., 2014). This commitment was already apparent in his earlier work, where he argued that 'only in an emancipated society, whose members' autonomy and responsibility had been realized, would communication have developed into the non-authoritarian and universally practiced dialogue from which both our model of reciprocally constituted ego identity and our idea of true consensus are always implicitly derived' (Habermas, 1978, p. 314).

A detailed examination of the relevance of Habermas's work on communicative rationality, and its relevance for *communication technologies* would be an interesting intellectual project in its own right, but lies beyond the remit of this book. Suffice it to say here that the emphasis in much ICT research has previously often been more on the *information* dimensions of ICTs rather than on their role in *communication*, and so Habermas provides a reminder of the importance of redressing this balance. What matters more for present purposes, though, is his focus on self-reflection driven by an emancipatory interest that lies at the heart of his critical science. As Caspersz and Olaru (2014, p. 226) have commented in an educational context, 'Developing an emancipatory interest enables individuals to free themselves from the intersubjective or commonly held meanings that dominate their understanding of their current world, and subsequently change their practices.... developing an emancipatory interest is critical to learning to create social change, that is, wanting to create a better world and society for self and others'. Given the complexity of notions of emancipation and empowerment, Section 1.3.4 of this chapter explores the specific implications of this for ICT4D in more detail.

1.1.5 Power and the Technical Interests of Science

The final element of Habermas's arguments that is of particular relevance to this work is his exploration of ideas surrounding modernity, technology, and science. The important points to grasp from this for the argument in this book are the following: (1) technology is not something neutral with a power of its own, but is rather a deliberate product, suffused with interests, that is designed for a particular purpose; (2) there is an intricate relationship between technology and modernity, through which, for example, ICTs can be seen as a powerful symbol of 'the modern' in developing countries; and (3) the empirical-analytic science that underlies most such technological develop-ment does not yet have the critical acuity to be able to escape its powerful claim to be the only knowledge that is acceptable as truth.

Habermas's (1971) critique of technology has not been without its critics, especially under the influence of Foucault and Marcuse, and as Feenberg (1996, p. 45) has argued, 'his defense of modernity now seems to concede far too much to the claims of autonomous technology'. By combining Haber-mas's arguments with Marcuse's claim that technology is socially determined, Feenberg (1991, 1996) offers a new framework for a critique of technology that emphasizes its historicity and reflexivity as any form of social institution, thereby asserting that it is always implemented in value-biased forms that are subject to political critique. The notions that technology is constructed as a result of a specific set of interests, and that these have historically been driven by those in power, raise challenging questions for those who wish to claim that ICTs can be used to change those power relationships and thereby create a fairer and more equal world.

1.2 Understanding 'Development'

The previous section has outlined five elements drawn from Critical Theory that underlie the arguments that follow: a particular conceptualization of the relationship between theory and practice; the interests underlying the role of ICTs in development; the importance of adopting a normative stance that considers not only what is but also what should be; the potential emancipa-tory and empowering character of some types of knowledge and technology; and a particular view of the relationships between technology and society.

However, it is impossible to consider any aspects of the relationships between ICTs and 'development' without a clear understanding of what is meant by the notion of 'development' (Unwin, 1994, 2009, 2013). One technology might, for example, contribute positively to 'development' defined in one particular way, but be damaging to 'development' defined in an alternative way. How 'development' is defined is thus crucial to any notion of 'ICTs for development'. All too often, though, this fundamental distinction seems to be forgotten or ignored both in theoretical and in practical ICT4D interventions.

As the previous section has also noted, there have been many different approaches to the theories and practices of 'development' over the last century, and numerous diverse accounts and interpretations of these have been published (see, for example, Sachs, 1992; Escobar, 1995; Cowen and Shenton, 1996; Crewe and Harrison, 1998; Sen, 1999; Forsyth, 2004; Kothari, 2005; Easterly, 2006; McMichael, 2012; Desai and Potter, 2014).

1.2.1 Diverse Meanings of 'Development'

At the basis of any understanding of 'development' is usually a sense of evolution and change, most often in the positive sense of growth or expansion. In normal parlance, development is associated with advancement and progress. Although it is possible to trace this notion of development back to antiquity (Unwin, 1994, 2009), it is most often considered to have received a distinctive impetus in the European Enlightenment of the seventeenth and eighteenth centuries (Bronner, 2004; Sachs, 2005). Importantly, it should be stressed that 'development' is therefore a profoundly European concept, and that technology has always played a significant part in its evolution, as with the so-called industrial revolution in the nineteenth century, or indeed what some see as the third or fourth industrial revolution occurring today (Schwab, 2016). The pursuit of 'development' has also been one of the main ways through which European views and practices have come to dominate other peoples and regions through the many processes that have shaped an increasingly modern and interconnected world (Castells, 2000). Much more research therefore needs to be done in exploring the wider relevance of alternative cultural conceptualizations of 'development', such as Bhutan's 'Gross National Happiness Index', coined by the fourth Dragon King, Jigme Singye Wangchuck, in 1972 (Gross National Happiness Commission, Royal Government of Bhutan (n.d.).

Elsewhere I have traced the historical evolution of the interface between technology and different conceptualizations of 'development' (Unwin, 2009, 2013), paying particular attention to the differences between the concepts of absolute and relative poverty (Unwin, 2004, 2007), and focusing especially on the distinction between notions of 'development' as economic growth and 'development' as reducing inequality. Drawing on these, I have argued

Figure 1.3 Women farming in South Bihar, India (1977): what kind of development?
Source: Author.

passionately that poverty will always be with us, and that most contemporary development rhetoric that focuses on economic growth actually leads to an increase in relative poverty. This has been greatly exacerbated by the use of ICTs over the last twenty years. Such arguments were developed from my practical experiences in Singbhum in the 1970s recounted earlier in the chapter (Figures 1.2 and 1.3), but have also been reinforced strongly by my subsequent practical work especially in Africa and Asia. Rather than recounting such histories of 'development' once again, I focus here especially on the ways in which 'development' has been theorized and practised during the twenty-first century, to provide a context for the exploration of ICTs and development in the pages that follow. Before doing so, though, it is important to draw out five main principles from the previous century of theory and practice in international development that are pertinent to this exploration.

First, it must be stressed that academic *theorizing* of 'development' has often followed very different trajectories to the *practice* of 'development' by governments and international agencies. Many university-based academics have challenged existing practices, but have usually done so 'from a distance' without having immersed themselves for any length of time in the challenges of actually trying to 'do development'. There are some notable exceptions, as with explicit action-research (see for example Tacchi et al., 2003; Chambers, 2014), and also with the practical engagement of many economists, who often tend to dominate the practice of bilateral and multilateral donors. Throughout my recent career, though, I have sought to cross and transgress such boundaries, deliberately seeking to combine the theory and practice of 'development', and am acutely aware not only of the challenges that this creates, but also of the immense richness of understanding that it can provide. Although I had written previously about development, I now realize that until I started working for the UK's Department for International Development in 2001, I had little real understanding of the complexity of actually 'doing development'. It is far easier to criticize than it is actually to deliver.

Second, there have always tended to be *dominant theories and practices* of development, but the strength of alternative propositions has tended to vary in prominence at different periods (Cowen and Shenton, 1996). The ground-breaking model of economic growth proposed in the 1960s by Rostow (1960), for example, was of both theoretical and practical importance, but despite the appeal of radical feminist and Marxist academic critiques in the 1970s and 1980s, most proponents of such critiques explicitly sought to distance themselves from traditionally defined development practice (Sachs, 1992; Escobar, 1995; Harris, 2005; Kabeer, 2015). This left neoclassical economists to dominate in the 1990s, and economic growth once again reached overwhelming prominence as the prevailing rhetoric of the first decade of the twenty-first century. Closely linked to this has been the tendency for there to be particular fashions in views of how 'development' practice should be delivered. Thus, from a world where structural adjustment programmes dominated in the 1990s, subsequent years saw a particular focus on budget support mechanisms and poverty reduction strategy papers (Ranis et al., 2006). Likewise, in recent years the log-frame approach to development delivery has often been replaced by a focus on business cases and theories of change (Vogel, 2012).

Third, despite the ebb and flow of particular ideas, the *discipline of economics* in all its diversity, has retained unparalleled power in both the theoretical and practical arenas. This is exemplified not only by the high prestige of economists within the broad field of international development research and publication, but also by their concentration in positions of power in aid agencies and international organizations such as the World Bank and International Monetary Fund (IMF). Moreover, although there are indeed alternative radical economic positions, as with the post-autistic economics movement launched in Paris in 2000,[3] the dominant mode of development economics, especially drawing on neoclassical theory, has been supportive of the economic growth agenda, and is thus inherently unlikely to be able to serve the interests of the poorest and most marginalized (although, see Easterly, 2006).

---

[3] <http://www.paecon.net/HistoryPAE.htm>.

Fourth, there has been a remarkable increase in the strength and influence of *international multilateral development institutions* over the last half century. This is reflected not only in the power of UN agencies, despite the frequent criticisms thereof, but also in the work of the World Bank, and especially the coordinating role of the Organisation for Economic Co-operation and Development (OECD), through its Development Assistance Committee (DAC). As the world has become more interconnected, in large part as a result of the processes set in motion by new ICTs, there has been an increasingly important need for international coordination, which has been reflected, for example, in the highly influential Millennium Development Goals (MDGs) launched in 2000,[4] and the new Sustainable Development Goals (SDGs) set in motion in 2015.[5]

A final strand has been the increasing role played by the *private sector* in international governance relating to development, expressed particularly through the public–private partnerships (PPPs) that have achieved such prominence over the last twenty years. This has been of particular importance in the arena of ICTs in development, with the efforts of major global technology companies in the latter part of the 1990s finding fruition in Target 8F of the MDGs: 'In cooperation with the private sector, make available the benefits of new technologies, especially information and communications technologies' (Millennium Project, 2006). This subsequently found expression in the substantial involvement of the private sector in the World Summit on the Information Society, held in Geneva in 2003 and Tunis in 2005, the first time that companies played such a significant role in a major UN Summit (Unwin, 2009) (see Section 3.2).

There is no single definition of what 'development' is, but rather the term has been shaped and crafted in different ways to serve the contrasting interests of those using it, whether as a theoretical concept or as a practical heuristic device. In the twenty-first century, though, one conceptualization of 'development' has come to achieve a hegemonic position, and this is the notion that development above all else should be concerned with economic growth. It is no coincidence that this has happened at a time when the pace of growth of the ICT sector has expanded dramatically, and when companies have come to play such a prominent role in the delivery of 'development'.

1.2.2 Development as 'Economic Growth' or as 'Reducing Inequality'?

The dissolution of the Soviet Union in 1991 was in many senses the replacement of post-capitalism by capitalism. The socialist dream that was meant to

---

[4] <http://mdgs.un.org/unsd/mdg/default.aspx>.
[5] <https://sustainabledevelopment.un.org/?menu=1300>.

create a better, fairer society had been overthrown by the economic system that preceded it, namely capitalism. The defeat of communism by capitalism led to a decade of disarray for the socialist left, despite attempts to advocate for a Third Way that might be able to take the best from both systems to shape a new social democratic project (Giddens, 1998). Rampant capitalism, with its driving interests in expanding markets and reducing labour costs, appeared victorious, and set in motion a series of fundamental changes in global governance that would see the economic growth mantra once again firmly embedded at the heart of international development discourse and practice.

Building on the apparently successful experiences of the previous decade in the countries of South America, officials in international institutions such as the World Bank and IMF had by the end of the 1980s reached broad agreement on the prescription that they deemed appropriate for reforming the economies of developing countries, the so-called Washington Consensus (Williamson, 1990). This consisted of a series of economic prescriptions, focusing on macro-economic discipline, a market economy, and openness to the world, and despite many criticisms (Easterly, 2002) and varying modalities of delivery this broad construct has remained dominant ever since. Three pillars have been at the heart of this hegemonic view of what 'development' has meant over the last quarter of a century: *economic growth*, *liberal democracy*, and a *free market*. Despite considerable evidence that some of the fastest growing economies have not been liberal democracies, these principles have been of fundamental importance to the work of most multilateral and bilateral agencies ever since 1990. They lay, for example, at the heart of the MDGs agreed by the UN in 2000 that were meant to be achieved by 2015, where poverty was explicitly defined in absolute terms. The first target in Goal 1 was thus the ambition simply to 'Halve, between 1990 and 2015, the proportion of people whose income is less than one dollar a day',[6] although it should be noted that absolute poverty was subsequently defined as those living on under US$1.25 a day in 2008 and then to US$1.90 a day in 2015. Given the role of the private sector in generating economic growth, and the considerable amount of lobbying of governments and international organizations done by global corporations in the late 1990s, it was not at all surprising that MDG 8 also highlighted the important role that partnerships with companies could play in achieving this objective, especially in the field of ICTs.

By the middle of the first decade of the twenty-first century, an additional pillar, that of *good governance*, was increasingly recognized as being essential for the achievement of economic growth and liberal democracy, and although this has come to play a much greater role in international development policy

---

[6] <http://www.un.org/millenniumgoals/poverty.shtml>.

(DFID, 2006), it has reinforced, rather than undermined, the fundamental emphasis that has been placed on the need for economic growth to overcome absolute poverty. Typical of the passionate expressions of the need for economic growth was the work of Sachs (2005) who headed up the Millennium Project, and was a vehement advocate of the need for far more international intervention to achieve these goals to end poverty (Sachs, 2005).

Although such positions were dominant, other diagnoses and prescriptions were advocated, amongst the most important of which was Sen's (1999) approach to welfare economics which had been conceived in the 1980s, but from the early 1990s had also become one of the underpinnings of the United Nations Development Programme's (UNDP) Human Development Index. This was intended to shift the emphasis away from indices such as Gross Domestic Product (GDP) to more people-centred policies (Alkire, 2010). For Sen (1999; see also Sen, 1983) the freedoms that people have to achieve their capabilities are central to any effective development, and his ideas have attracted an increasing amount of attention, particularly in the field of ICT4D where the potential for such technologies to increase freedoms and capabilities can be seen as having some relevance (Kleine, 2013). However, it is important to recognize that Sen's work was itself broadly situated within a framework that envisaged economic growth as still being central to development. For him, growth is a necessity for development, but other things are also necessary if the real freedoms that people can enjoy are to be expanded. Despite these, and other alternative offerings, such as the Human Happiness Index mentioned in Section 1.2.1, a focus on economic growth as being the dominant modality through which poverty can be eliminated remains a powerful influence in both development theory and practice, with the SDGs of 2015 (UN, 2016), for example, continuing to place heavy emphasis on a belief that poverty can indeed be ended everywhere through economic growth.

This conceptual and practical agenda to eliminate poverty through economic growth is not only theoretically flawed, but has also been shown to have failed practically. As highlighted in the introductory part of this chapter, a completely different approach to poverty is that which places an emphasis on inequality and relative, rather than absolute, poverty (Ravallion, 1997, 2001; O'Boyle, 1999; Unwin, 2004, 2007; Davis and Sanchez-Martinez, 2014). O'Boyle (1999) has suggested that those who advocate for absolute and relative notions of poverty do so from fundamentally different moral and ideological principles: the former have a worldview based on the individual, on competition and freedoms; the latter on human sociality, cooperation, and values of solidarity. In contrast to absolute poverty, which refers to a set universal standard, relative poverty situates it within the context where an individual lives, which can be at a variety of scales from the local to the global. Relative poverty is often used to refer to poverty in the richer countries of the world, once a basic level of prosperity has been achieved, but it has equally important relevance at a global scale, not only in differentiating between individuals in various parts of the world, but also between the prosperity of different countries. Despite the appeal of relative poverty as a concept (Unwin, 2004, 2007), it is definitions of absolute poverty that have until recently dominated the theory and practice of international development.

However, there is increasing empirical evidence showing that the recent focus on economic growth as a solution to poverty is associated with an unparalleled increase in inequality and thus relative poverty. In the nineteenth century, Marx (1976) had highlighted that economic growth at the expense of others lay at the heart of the capitalist mode of production during the so-called industrial revolution, and with the rampant reassertion of capitalism in the threefold guise of liberal democracy, a free market, and economic growth in the post-Soviet era, such inequality has reasserted itself. The OECD (2014, p. 1; see also OECD 2015a) has thus noted that 'The gap between rich and poor is at its highest level in most OECD countries in 30 years. Today, the richest 10% of the population in the OECD area earn 9.5 times more than the poorest 10%. By contrast, in the 1980s the ratio stood at 7:1.'

Increasing inequality within countries, as reflected by indices such as the Gini coefficient (Beddoes, 2012), is matched by increasing inequality at a global scale (Milanovic, 2003). A report by Oxfam (2016) suggests that in 2015 the richest sixty-two people in the world owned the same as the total amount owned by the poorest half of the world's population, and that this inequality is increasing; the wealth of the richest sixty-two people rose 45 per cent between 2010 and 2015, at a time when the wealth of the bottom half fell by 38 per cent. Moreover, international agencies are at last increasingly now recognizing that an untrammelled emphasis on economic growth has damaging effects on human societies, and that this increase in inequalities must be addressed. The UNDP (2015, p. 24) in its latest Human Development Report thus focuses especially on this increasing inequality, commenting that:

> Even with all the economic and technological advancements at the world's disposal, people do not have equitable benefits from progress, human capabilities and opportunities do not always flourish, human security is at stake, human rights and freedoms are not always protected, gender inequalities remain a challenge, and future generations' choices do not get the attention they deserve.

Likewise, the World Bank's (2016a, p. 2) *World Development Report*, for the first time offers a more balanced view of the impact of digital technologies, noting, for example that 'Although there are many individual success stories, the effect of technology on global productivity, expansion of opportunity for the poor and the middle classes, and the spread of accountable governance has so far been less than expected.' Whilst the World Bank's analysis focuses, not surprisingly, primarily on the economic aspects of digital technologies, and does not sufficiently address the interests underlying their recent expansion, the recognition that such usage has not yet delivered on intended development outcomes is an important one. Also important is the Bank's emphasis on what it terms 'analog complements', such as an appropriate business environment, people having the right skills to take advantage of the digital world, and the need for there to be an accountable government, which are necessary for effective digital development to be achieved.

There is thus increasingly accepted evidence that the hegemonic model of international development that sees economic growth as the prime driver in reducing absolute poverty has increased relative poverty, and that this has the potential to increase social and political tension in the future. ICTs have played a crucial role in driving such economic growth, but they also have a darker side, not least in creating greater inequalities through the considerable differential access to them that exists both spatially and socially across the world.

Two important conclusions can be drawn from this section. First, it has emphasized that there are very different concepts of 'development' in both theory and practice. There can never be a single notion of ICT4D; it depends fundamentally on what kind of development is intended. One of the central themes of this book is thus to argue that most uses of ICTs in development have been focused on delivering the hegemonic agenda of economic growth, but because ICTs are an accelerator this has also led to much greater inequalities in the world. For those who see development in a *relative* sense, and focus instead on reducing inequalities, the challenge is to identify ways through which ICTs can be used to support the poorest and most marginalized. Second, it must be recognized that whilst the private sector has played an important role as the engine of economic growth, its necessity to generate profit means that it cannot be expected to deliver services to the unprofitable poorest and most marginalized people. Hence, states have a crucial role in ensuring fairer and more equitable use of ICTs. The four pillars of economic growth, a free market, liberal democracy, and good governance have all tended to be associated with a reduction in the role of the state. If inequality is to be addressed effectively, particularly in the field of ICTs, states must step up to the mark, reassert their importance, and play a much greater role in helping to ensure that these amazing technologies are used to reduce inequality, as much as to increase economic growth (Unwin, 2013).

1.3 ICT4D in Theory and Practice

The theoretical context in the previous two sections has four particularly important ramifications for understanding and changing the relationships between ICTs and development: (1) the diversity of ways through which academics have sought to engage at this interface; (2) the tendency for technology to be considered and used primarily in an instrumental way; (3) the interests of the various stakeholders involved; and (4) the challenges of empowerment and emancipation.

1.3.1 *Multi-Disciplinary Challenges*

ICTs have pervaded all aspects of society in most parts of the world (Mansell and Wehn, 1998; Castells, 2000, 2012; Walsham, 2001). One important consequence of this has been that academics from many different disciplines have increasingly sought to understand the interface between ICTs and development from diverse intellectual traditions, and with many different interests underlying them. In one sense, this diversity is exciting and stimulating, since innovative ideas are often shaped and formulated at the edges between disciplines. Indeed, I have long argued that we should not seek to create a new discipline out of ICT4D, with its own rules, structures, and constraints, but should rather leave it as a fluid concept that incorporates different flows and currents.

However, the plurality of approaches and ideas in the field has led to three main challenges (Unwin, 2013). First, there has been a tendency for academics to focus inwards on the priorities of their own disciplines, and not be sufficiently outward-looking and collaborative. Far too often, there is duplication and overlap in research and practice, with little recognition of the creative and valuable work done in other disciplines. This is not surprising given the vast amount of research and publication on technology and development now occurring and the impossibility of any one person being able to grasp its full diversity, but it is important that academics continually explore outside the boundaries of their own disciplines to gain new ideas and insights. Second, there has been somewhat unhealthy competition between groups of academics and 'their' journals, each seeking a position of pre-eminence, and wishing to impose their own particular imprint on what the field should be like. In this context, Heeks (2010) has provided a useful listing of relevant ICT4D journals, which also notes in passing that such specialist journals do not have as high an impact score as more established journals in particular disciplines. There is therefore a tendency for academics to publish their best papers in more traditional journals, which reinforces the trend towards an inward-looking, rather than truly multi-disciplinary approach. Third, there remains a problematic dominance of English language publications in the field (Unwin, 2011). Although this is typical of academic publishing as a whole, it is critically important that diverse voices, from contrasting cultural backgrounds, are also heard in the field of ICT4D (see for example, Universidad Rey Juan Carlos y Fundación EHAS, 2010).

Linking this discussion to Habermas's (1978) distinction between empirical-analytic, historical-hermeneutic, and critical sciences, it is salient to note that most research at the interface between ICTs and development has been predominantly from an empirical-analytic background, reflected not only in the physical scientific traditions of computer science and engineering (see the excellent work of the TIER group at Berkeley, for example), but also in systems sciences (Walsham, 2012) and the dominant mode of economics. It is no coincidence that such technological disciplinary perspectives have come to dominate, given their interests in technical control over objectified processes, and the use to which such research can be put by those advocating the value of technology to achieving economic growth (Heeks, 2008; Sutinen and Tedre, 2010; Steyn and Johansen, 2011; Toyama, 2015). To be sure, there are those from a social science background who adopt a more historical-hermeneutic perspective and indeed sometimes a critical stance (for example, Tacchi et al., 2003), but these have been less influential than they should be in practice.

Whatever approach to development is advocated, it remains important that researchers interested in the use of ICTs in development retain an open mind, work together with colleagues across traditional boundaries, seek to understand each other's disciplinary languages, and above all focus on addressing the aspirations of the poor and the marginalized. As Walsham (2012, p. 87) has eloquently emphasized, there needs to be 'a focus on ethical goals, increased use of critical approaches, welcoming other disciplines with open arms, widening our field of study to many non-traditional settings and rejecting a dominant methodological paradigm'.

1.3.2 *Against an Instrumentalist Perspective*

One outcome of the empirical-analytic emphasis in ICT4D noted earlier has been that much theory and practice in the field has adopted an instrumental view of technology (Tiles and Oberdiek, 1995). As I have argued elsewhere, 'An instrumental view that ICTs are somehow autonomous, value free, "things" that can automatically do good, or be seen as a "silver bullet" to "fight poverty", is fundamentally problematic' (Unwin, 2015, p. 195). ICTs are technologies that have been created by particular individuals and companies, each with very specific interests, to achieve particular objectives. They are imbued with social, cultural, economic, and political value (Mackenzie and Wajcman, 1999). There is nothing inherently good in them. Once created, they can be used for a whole range of both anticipated and unexpected 'results', many of which may be negative, and far removed from the original aspirations of their designers. As Green (2001) has argued, technology is never neutral, but is always closely linked with culture, society, and government policies (see also Lanier, 2011).

The belief that ICTs are inherently good, and will therefore undoubtedly contribute effectively to development practice, is all-pervasive and implicit in most ICT4D initiatives. Few people deliberately seek to develop technologies that would deliberately damage the lives of poor and marginalized peoples, although as later chapters of this book illustrate, many do so inadvertently. As noted earlier, the close connection between technology and modernity, linked to general notions of social and economic development formulated in the Enlightenment, has been deep-seated in European thought from at least the seventeenth century onwards. The crux of the matter has already been highlighted. If development is defined as economic growth, and technologies can enhance economic growth, then surely they can be used effectively for development. However, if by so doing they lead to an increase in inequality, and development is defined in terms of a more equal and fairer society, then they can indeed be seen as having a negative impact on development. This highlights once again the important moral and ethical dimensions of ICT4D.

A first step in a critical understanding of ICT4D is thus to recognize that technologies by themselves cannot contribute effectively to development. It is the interests underlying them, and the intent for which they are used that matter. It is therefore crucially important that any analysis of ICTs in development begins with an understanding of such interests. Only when more technologies are designed and utilized effectively and explicitly in the interests of the poor and the marginalized may the aspiration of a more equal and thus better society be achieved. However, even here, by postulating that technologies can be used by poor people to enhance their lives, there is an implicit suggestion of an instrumental view of technology. A resolution of this tension is explored through the notions of emancipation and empowerment in Section 1.3.4 of this chapter.

A particularly important aspect of the instrumental view of technology is the role of ICTs as symbols of modernity. Some of the appeal of ICTs in development has undoubtedly been a result of their symbolic and physical value, as much as any potential to deliver practical development outcomes, such as enhanced health or education. The arrival of bright new computers in schools in the 2000s, and the many laptop and tablet initiatives that have been introduced for children in the 2010s, are classic examples of the power of ICTs as symbols of modernity. Even if the technology does nothing practical at all, it can give hope and inspiration for change.

*   *   *

I distinctly recall visiting schools in Africa in the 2000s, when all too often there would be a bright new computer donated by a well-meaning civil society organization or company. The computer was so important that it would be placed in a position of prominence on the head teacher's desk, but because the head teacher had not been trained effectively in its use, it remained under its dust cover, used rarely if at all. Many ICTs are physical objects, and their presence can be a clear symbol of a government's attempt to implement development goals. The creation of telecentres in small towns, giving tablets or mobile phones to school children, and the laying of fibre optic cables to rural areas, are all visible symbols of progress, and for politicians seeking re-election, they can be very enticing projects to implement, especially if private sector companies are willing to contribute to the costs. One of the most graphic indications of this has been the way in which some Indian politicians have recently given out laptops with their images and logos on the desktop or cover.[7]

* * *

None of this is to deny the potential beneficial effects of ICTs for development, but it is to stress that the symbolic value of such technologies as indicators of modernity has an important role to play in interpreting the significance of ICTs in development.

1.3.3 *The Stakeholders and Their Interests*

The previous subsection highlights the importance of understanding the diverse interests underlying the use of ICTs in development. Chapters 3 and 4 examine in detail the role of partnerships and 'multi-stakeholderism' in ICT4D, but it is important at this stage to underline the diversity of actors engaged in ICT4D initiatives, and to emphasize the very different interests that underlie their engagements.

In the broadest terms, three main groups of actors, or stakeholders, have usually been identified in connection with ICT4D initiatives (Unwin, 2005): the *private sector*, referring to the part of the economy run by individuals and companies for profit; the *public sector* run by states to deliver government services; and *civil society* referring to entities involved in un-coerced collective actions around shared interests, purposes, and values (see Chapter 3 for more detail). The notion of the private sector is sometimes seen as including both the business sector and the voluntary sector, but given the fundamental different organizational structures and intentions of these, I prefer to follow the practice of including voluntary not-for-profit organizations within civil society (Lewis, 2002). The meanings of these terms, and the changing roles of these actors, or stakeholders, have nevertheless varied significantly over time (see Chapter 3). Moreover, the continuing use of the term public–private partnerships (PPPs) implies that many governments and companies involved

---

[7] <http://www.firstpost.com/politics/freebies-culture-in-tamil-nadu-reeks-of-a-guilty-conscious-neta-who-doesnt-really-care-2781472.html>; <http://graphics8.nytimes.com/images/2014/04/29/world/asia/29-gift-indiaink/29-gift-indiaink-tmagArticle.jpg>.

in ICT4D initiatives have strong interests in excluding civil society (see Chapter 4). The private sector has a particular interest in retaining such terminology, since it privileges its position with respect to other types of entity. Hence, for those who advocate a more pluralistic stance, it is particularly important to change such terminology, and refer instead to multi-stakeholder, or better still multi-sector, partnerships (MSPs) that include civil society entities and others.

Such a threefold distinction, while having the advantage of simplicity and clarity in terms of interests and values, is nevertheless a simplification, and becomes blurred around the edges when trying to fit into it many different kinds of organization, such as social enterprises or research institutes. Traditionally, the role of the state and governments, as derived from Hobbes's and Locke's social contract theory, has been to maintain a balance between the desires of people for peace, and power; citizens' political and moral obligations are dependent on a contract in which they cede some of their rights to governments in return for protection (Beehler and Drengson, 1978; Unwin, 2010). As such, ultimately, governments have a duty to serve the interests of all of their citizens. In contrast, the private sector has no such obligations, and the interests of companies and individuals are primarily driven by the need to generate profit, either for their own benefit or for those of their shareholders. Since the rise of neoliberalism, particularly in the USA and the UK in the 1970s (Chomsky, 1998) the balance of roles between these two main sectors has changed considerably, with the sell-off of state companies to the private sector reducing the role of the state, and transforming its function into that of overseeing the regulation of former public utilities. Chapter 5 examines the privatization of the telecommunications sector, and its implications for regulation as well as its impact on the potential of ICTs to be used by and for the poorest people in society (see also Chapters 3 and 4).

The stakeholders involved in ICT for development initiatives are more diverse than this threefold structure readily permits. For example, whilst many universities and research institutions were once in the public sector, the increasing privatization of higher education and research across the globe now makes such a distinction problematic. Whilst bilateral government donors can be included within the domain of the public sector and the state, the role of global multilateral donor institutions also does not fit easily into such a classification. Likewise, the dramatic increase in the power of private foundations, such as the Bill and Melinda Gates Foundation[8] established in 2000, raises important questions as to whether they should best be seen as civil society organizations or as part of the private sector. Furthermore, many

---

[8] <http://www.gatesfoundation.org>.

traditional civil society organizations, and particularly NGOs, have been criticized for becoming too closely allied to the private sector or governments (Hulme and Edwards, 1997; Mercer, 2002).

Hence, although it is useful to recognize the distinction between the private sector, the public sector, and civil society as a heuristic device to understand many of the changes taking place in the field of ICT4D (Chapter 3), it is also necessary when discussing ICT4D partnerships to explore a more granulated group of stakeholders, particularly including companies, civil society organizations, states, international organizations, funding agencies and research institutions, at a range of scales from the local to the international, and with each being subdivided according to local practices and traditions (Unwin, 2005; see Chapter 4 for more detail). Such a framework, though, ignores the most important people in any partnerships, namely the intended beneficiaries, and this is precisely one of the problems encountered in the failure of many ICT4D projects to deliver on their intended objectives. More often than not, they are designed externally, without sufficient consideration being given to the needs and contexts of those for whom they are intended. Hence, one of the key arguments of this book is that if ICT4D initiatives are truly intended to deliver on the needs of poor and marginalized peoples, they must begin with understanding those 'development' needs. This means that such people, be they street children, those with disabilities, or women living in patriarchal societies, must be involved in the conceptualization, design, and implementation of the projects from the start. This requires a wider consideration of some of the theoretical and practical challenges in terms of emancipation and empowerment.

1.3.4 *Challenges of Emancipation and Empowerment*

I am conscious that in my earlier book on ICT4D (Unwin, 2009) I discussed the notion that ICTs could empower poor people, without sufficiently theorizing the concept of empowerment. While this is closely linked to the danger of taking an instrumental view of ICTs, wanting to believe that ICTs can enhance the lives of poor people, it is remarkable how few texts actually address this very complex issue in any detail. The Swedish International Development Cooperation Agency's (SIDA) (2003) early report entitled *Digital Empowerment*, thus makes no mention of the word 'empowerment' beyond the title, implicitly suggesting that if ICTs deliver on democracy, human rights, and social development, then people will automatically be empowered. Even more recent reports, such as ActionAid's (Beardon et al., 2008) *ICT for Development: Empowerment or Exploitation?* report, whilst noting in particular the importance of power relations in shaping the spectrum between empowerment and exploitation, does not anywhere really define the concept of empowerment, or the challenges associated with it.

Adopting a Critical approach to science has inherently within it a practical focus on emancipation. Horkheimer (1972) thus argued that what set Critical Theory apart from traditional theory was that it sought to emancipate people from the slavery of domination and oppression and to create a world that satisfies their needs and powers. For Habermas (1974, 1978, 1984), self-reflection is critical to emancipation; just as an individual can become emancipated through psychoanalysis from the systematic distorted communication that causes depression, so too can societies and political systems be changed through an analogous process. Emancipation is freedom from illusions (Gross, 2010). Whilst at an individual level, the psychoanalyst can help a patient overcome such illusions and thereby live a happier and freer life, at a societal level it is the role of Critical social theorists and philosophers to help reveal to people more generally the illusions that keep them oppressed, thereby helping societies to become freer and fairer.

Such arguments are by no means without their problems, not least in terms of what legitimacy social theorists, and indeed academics more generally, have in performing this role, and whether understanding their conditions of oppression will necessarily enable people to change their societies for the better. In this context, Inglis (1997, p. 4) usefully differentiates between emancipation and empowerment: 'empowerment involves people developing capabilities to act successfully within the existing system and structures of power, while emancipation concerns critically analysing, resisting and challenging structures of power'. My own view, though, is that people can never be truly empowered, unless the power structures that constrain them are changed. Hence, empowerment requires political action, both by those seeking to empower and those who are intended to be empowered.

Although much action research has not been overtly influenced by Critical Theory, its focus on engaging the intended end users of development outcomes in the research process can be seen as going some way to achieving these objectives. Participatory Action Research has thus become increasingly popular in the twenty-first century, combining a diversity of approaches that seek to combine participation in society and democracy, with engagement in experience and history, and rigorous theoretical and empirical knowledge (Chevalier and Buckles, 2013; see also Reason and Bradbury, 2008). Moreover, the early work on Participatory Rural Appraisal by Chambers in the 1990s shows that such participatory research has deep roots in action-based work in international development (Chambers, 2007). Such approaches, though, have not been without their critics (Williams, 2004). In the field of ICTs and new media, for example, the work of Hearn et al. (2009) and Tacchi (Tacchi et al., 2010; Lennie and Tacchi, 2013) has revealed both the potential of such action research, but also some of its challenges.

Three particularly difficult and challenging questions remain about the possibility of poor and marginalized people being empowered or emancipated by technology. First, both the concepts of emancipation and empowerment are generally based on a premise that one group of people can, and indeed should, somehow empower others. This is itself, however, a power relationship. Although such processes may be well-intentioned, and designed to create a better life for the empowered, the legitimation for so doing is problematic. This is especially so when those seeking to do the empowering come from 'outside', as is so often the case with ICT4D initiatives. Second, there are doubts as to whether simply being knowledgeable can really enable change. Knowing that you are oppressed need not lead you to change the conditions of your oppression. The survival of brutal and oppressive regimes across the world is testimony to the fact that many people choose to try to eke out an existence under great duress rather than taking what they see as the higher risk and inevitable hardship of attempting to replace such regimes. This leads to a third challenge, which concerns how such change might be effected. Should, for example, ICTs be used to try to create consensus on difficult issues, or as a vehicle through which violence can be used to overthrow oppressive regimes? The use of digital communications and mapping technologies to direct drones to bomb so-called 'terrorists' is, for example, little different in principle from the use of such technologies by 'freedom fighters' to direct suicide bombing missions against those they see as their enemies.

Those who believe that ICTs can be used to empower or improve the lives of the poorest and most marginalized therefore have some tough questions to address. I hope that this book goes some way to suggesting a range of ways through which all stakeholders can begin to reflect on their existing practices, and thereby help craft a world where ICTs are indeed used to benefit the poorest and most marginalized, especially those with disabilities. They need ICTs far more than do the rich and powerful.

1.4 Reclaiming ICT for Development (ICT4D)

This chapter has summarized the theoretical and practical groundings for the account that follows, and has sought to make clear why this book focuses on five main aspects of the interface between ICTs and development. First, it seeks explicitly to draw on both theoretical and practical understandings of the use of technology in development. It deliberately seeks to build on insights from both *theory* and *practice*, and crosses boundaries between different stakeholder communities. This is also expressed in its style and use of language, which consciously seeks to offer different ways of reflecting on these issues.

Second, the book is built on a belief that just describing the changes that are taking place, and how technology has been used in and for development, is not enough. We must understand the *interests* behind such occurrences if we are to change what is currently happening. We must also adopt a normative stance, and be much more willing to say what should be rather than just what is. It is no coincidence that technology is being used to drive economic growth forward at the expense of those who do not have access to it, or the knowledge or interest in how to use it. This book thus has an avowedly practical intent to help poor and marginalized people gain benefits from the use of these technologies, and it does not shy away from making tough policy recommendations as to ways in which this can be achieved.

Third, it emphasizes that there are many different ways in which technology and development interact. I have previously championed the notion of ICT4D, but now fear that this has been subverted to a situation where many stakeholders are using the idea of 'development' as a means to promulgate and propagate their own specific technologies, or what might be called 'Development for ICT' (D4ICT). Hence, I wish to reclaim ICT4D from the clutches of D4ICT. This requires us above all to focus primarily on the intended development outcomes rather than the technology.

To do this, it is very important that this book concentrates on both the positive and the negative, intended and unintended, consequences of the use of ICTs in development. There has been far too much euphoric praise for the role of technology in development, and although the recent UNDP (2015) and World Bank (2016a) reports go some way in pointing to the failures, they do not go anything like far enough in highlighting the darker side of technologies and particularly the Internet (for a darker view of ICT in general see Lanier, 2011). To be sure, ICTs have transformed the lives of many poor people, often for the better, but they have not yet really structurally improved the lot of the poorest and most marginalized.

Finally, as I hope the discussion in this chapter has shown, this book argues that development should not be focused on economic growth, nor on the modernizing power of technology. Rather, development is fundamentally a moral agenda. ICT4D is about making difficult choices about what is right or wrong. It is about having the courage to be normative, rather than just positive, and it holds on to the belief that we can still use technology truly to make the world a better place.

2

Understanding the Technologies

I had still just about found it possible to distinguish between different kinds of ICTs when writing my earlier book on ICT4D in 2007 and 2008 (Unwin, 2009). Televisions, fixed-line phones, computers, radios, and laptops could still be seen as separate types of object. I had indeed emphasized that the distinction between such technologies had become increasingly blurred since the late 1990s through the replacement of analogue by digital technologies, and I distinctly remember struggling to make sense of the increasingly converged technologies that I was trying to describe. Now, such an attempt would be foolhardy, and so this chapter takes a very different approach to understanding technologies.

Looking back, I am also glad that I had made some mention of the transformations that were beginning to occur through the use of new kinds of mobile telephony in the mid- to late 2000s, noting the ways that they were transforming not only the technologies themselves but also their social and spatial use. I especially emphasized the ways through which mobile phones were beginning to transform Africa, which had previously had very low levels of fixed-line telephony (Unwin, 2009). It is salient to remember that in 2006, Africa was the continent in which mobile subscriptions represented the highest percentage of all subscriptions, at 87.2 per cent, compared with Europe's 70.5 per cent and the USA's 57.5 per cent (Unwin, 2009, p. 105).

I also commented, in a rather instrumental way, about the enormous potential that this rapid rise of mobiles had for the implementation of effective development interventions, noting the early use of mobile banking, the role of mobile phones in providing health services, and the ability of farmers to use them to gain market information. However, few people anticipated the very dramatic changes that were soon to be unleashed through the introduction of mobile broadband. In July 2007 there were only some 1.373 billion Internet users in the world (Internet Live Stats, 2016),[1] but by 2010 the 2 billion number had been passed, and there were 3 billion Internet users in 2014, representing 42 per cent of the world's population. Two key things had enabled this dramatic

---

[1] <http://www.internetlivestats.com/internet-users>.

transformation. First, General Packet Radio Service (GPRS) was commercially introduced in 2000, which enabled access to the Internet that was always on, albeit very slow (ISOC, 2015). Second, June 2007 saw the launch of the first iPhone by Apple, which enabled users to browse the Internet similarly to how they did on a personal computer. It also opened the door for the creation of software specifically designed for mobile phones, thus giving birth to the application (app) industry. Despite such dramatic changes, it must, though, be recalled that in 2016 more than half of the world's population still does not use the Internet, and the pace of growth is slowing. As the Broadband Commission (2015, p. 19) reports, 'After two decades of explosive growth, several commentators have noted that overall growth in the number of Internet users (but not traffic or volume) is slowing, as more markets reach maturity and/or saturation.'

Another fundamental change in large part resulting from the very rapid expansion of the mobile Internet has been the transformation of human interaction brought about by social media, and especially Facebook. I became a Facebook user in 2007, and have watched its evolution ever since. It is fascinating to recall that back in August 2008 there were only 100 million active Facebook users in the world. By July 2010, this had risen to 500 million, reaching 1 billion by September 2012. The important role that new forms of social interaction online would play, together with the dramatic rise in prominence of Alphabet, Google's parent company, which became the world's most valuable corporation at the start of 2016, were not things that I had necessarily seen or expected in 2009, although in creating the ICT4D group on Facebook in April 2007,[2] I had hoped that this could become a vehicle for sharing theory and practice on matters relating to the use of ICTs in development.

* * *

The distinction between hardware and software technologies remains useful despite the increasing blurring of concepts and technologies. In the simplest sense, hardware includes the physical ICTs, particularly 'things' such as satellites, cables, computers, tablets, mobile phones, routers, and integrated circuits, or chips. Hardware is essential for communication and information to be shared, but it is useless without the software to run on it. Software is the instructions, or code, that tells hardware what to do; it enables users to interact with the physical components of a system. This distinction in part relates to the traditional academic divides between the 'hard' engineering essential for hardware design and construction, and the 'softer' automation of algorithmic processes that lie at the heart of computer science, although the multidisciplinary character of computer engineering has long since fragmented this distinction (Ralston et al., 2000; Tucker, 2004).

---

[2] <https://www.facebook.com/groups/2553350463>.

More importantly, as highlighted in Chapter 1, the physical character of hardware also has particularly significant symbolic value. Simply having the latest smartphone or laptop, even if it has no software running on it, can be of value. Thus, in focus groups I held in Pakistan in 2016, young men and women commented that some people, particularly men, purchased Chinese fake copies of the latest model iPhones to show off with at social events, such as weddings, in the hope that the mothers of potential spouses would think that they were wealthy and successful. Likewise, it is relatively easy for politicians wishing to be seen as offering 'real' benefits to voters in democratic societies, to provide large amounts of hardware such as tablets or computers to schools in their constituencies at local or national scales, even if the teachers do not know how to use them effectively. Such physical and symbolic values of hardware, closely allied to its value in the rhetoric of modernity, should never be underestimated in seeking to understand and change ICT for development.

More often than not, though, users do not see a distinction between hardware and software. Mobile devices and computers ship with all of the necessary software for them to run, and this is regularly updated automatically, with mobile software applications (apps) being readily downloadable, often for free. In a practical sense, it is not the hardware or software that are really of most interest and importance to users, but rather the content or traffic that these technologies enable to flow. This is particularly important in the development context, because without appropriate content that poor and marginalized people are able to use to their advantage, the provision of fibre optic cables, computers in telecentres, or mobile phones with the latest commercial apps will never have a positive impact on poverty reduction. Furthermore, the Internet, probably the most powerful aspect of contemporary ICTs (Naughton, 1999, 2012; Zittrain, 2009; Dutton, 2013), combines both hardware and software to create a network of networks. Information and communication are accessible on the Internet through a range of protocols and languages such as SMTP (Simple Mail Transfer Protocol), FTP (File Transfer Protocol), and HTML (HyperText Markup Language). Here it should also be noted that the World Wide Web, hereafter the Web, which uses HTML for the formatting of pages, is only that portion of the Internet accessible through the use of HTTP (HyperText Transfer Protocol), with the Internet also being used, for example for e-mails through SMTP, file exchange through FTP, as well as things such as instant messaging, and USENET for user groups. Again, though, for many users, such distinctions matter little, with numerous studies replicating Galpaya's (Samarajiva, 2012) findings that for large numbers of people, Facebook literally is the Internet.

At the outset, one other key feature of modern ICTs, both hardware and software, that must be emphasized is its inherent, deliberately inbuilt unsustainability. This applies to the technologies themselves, but also in terms of their impact on the environment. A fundamental feature of the ICT sector over the last half-century has thus been that companies making both hardware and software have explicitly designed them to have a limited life-span, and that technology requires frequent replacement and upgrading. Unlike old fixed-line telephones, which lasted very many years, modern mobile phones are, for example, mostly designed to last only a couple of years and then be replaced. Moreover, there is clear symbiosis between hardware and software, because as a new generation of hardware is introduced, it is often necessary for customers to purchase new software to run on it, and vice versa. In part, this is closely allied to the socio-cultural drivers of fashion that encourage those who can afford it to purchase the latest 'modern' technology, but ICT companies have also been very adept at forcing users, who may well not necessarily want to, to upgrade their technology by ensuring that it becomes incompatible with the next generation of software or hardware. Whilst this has become a very successful and accepted business model, ensuring that there is regularly increasing demand, it has serious environmental implications. Not least, there has been a long history of dumping old ICTs in poor countries, thereby transferring to them the environmental impact of hardware disposal, or e-waste (Osibanjo and Nnorom, 2007; Boni et al., 2015), albeit also providing some limited opportunities for the development of recycling facilities.

To date, there has not been a satisfactory global environmental audit of the ICT sector, and many of the publications that have been produced on this subject are only partial (Global e-Sustainability Initiative 2008; Mingay and Pamlin, 2008; Blackman and Srivastava, 2011, p. 217; IIMB and CDP, 2014), largely reflecting the corporate interests of particular ICT companies (Ericsson, 2014). For example, the assessment framework for the environmental impact of ICTs prepared by the International Telecommunication Union (ITU, 2012) focuses primarily on existing standards, and there is no other currently global set of criteria that would, for example, include the costs and environmental impact in space of the many communication satellites in orbit around the earth. Likewise, few rigorous attempts have been made to include the increased demand for air conditioning and electricity as a result of the expansion of the ICT sector especially in poorer countries of the world. This is an area that requires substantial further research and modelling (Hilty and Aebischer, 2015), because the current approaches that usually suggest that ICTs, for example in the form of video-conferencing, are actually environmentally more efficient than other modalities of communication may be vastly inaccurate.

This chapter seeks to introduce the complexity of some of the technological issues that are currently of most importance in understanding the potential of

ICTs in development practice. It is only partial, and as new technologies are developed in response to particular interests over the next decade, the list will undoubtedly change. It begins by building on the earlier definitional discussion to highlight the importance of convergence and miniaturization, as well as the challenges that this creates in the use of terminology. This is followed by a brief introduction to the technologies associated with the radio spectrum and their management, which leads into an account of the increasing importance of the mobile Internet and the technological challenges of its delivery. The next section briefly addresses the Open Movement, and particularly the different conceptualization and business models that underlie Open and Proprietary software and content. This is followed by an analysis of the rapid rise to importance of social media and 'Over The Top' (OTT) services, and the challenges that these create, particularly for mobile operators. The final sections of the chapter address the potential impacts of 5G and the Internet of Things, and the role of digital hubs and the app economy as potential drivers of economic growth in poor countries. Throughout, it seeks to combine a description of the technologies with an analysis of the interests that have underlain their implementation, and their effects on 'development'.

2.1 An Ever More Converged and Miniaturized Digital World: Terminological and Business Implications

The increasing convergence of technologies, associated with digitalization and miniaturization, has been one of the most significant changes in the field of ICTs over the last two decades. These processes have enabled a wide range of new business opportunities, but at the same time have created challenges for businesses that are unable or unwilling to change their practices. They also have important implications for the uses of terminology, all of which have particular interests that underlie them.

The convergence of technologies, whereby single devices or systems now perform the same role that multiple ones previously did, has transformed the design and usage of ICTs. This applies not only in terms of hardware, but also of software, as with social media platforms that now combine a multiplicity of functions, not least through the integration of smaller specialist companies acquired by major corporations such as Facebook and Google. Convergence also has significant implications for regulation, as the distinct technologies associated with media broadcasting or telephony that were once regulated separately are now overlapping and combined (see Chapter 5 for more detail). Pavlik (2005, p. 157) has thus highlighted both the positive and negative aspects of convergence in the field of broadcasting: on the one hand convergence has provided opportunities for 'increased operational efficiencies, more interactive and involving programming, expanded distribution or networking capabilities, and new creative avenues to be explored'; but on the other convergence needs to be systematically developed to realize its potential, it may undermine quality, it can 'create false expectations', and it brings 'cross-media and cross-border competition to new heights'.

Convergence in hardware has particularly been enabled as a result of the miniaturization benefits associated with the replacement of analogue technologies by digital ones (Unwin, 2009). Although the transistor was invented in 1947, and digital computers were developed in the 1950s, digital mobile phones were only introduced commercially in the 1990s, and digital photography only became dominant in the 2000s. The underlying emphasis in this expansion of digital technologies has been the potential that they offer, especially in miniaturized form, for personal use. The shift from large mainframe computers to personal computers was driven in large part by the realization that a very considerable market existed if computers could be made small enough and cheap enough for individuals to own them. This was enabled by the introduction of microprocessors, and particularly the innovations undertaken by Intel which dramatically reduced their size and cost of production (Malone, 2014). Likewise, the dramatic expansion in sales of digital mobile phones, especially from the late 2000s onwards, has been enabled by creating the power of earlier computers in a small device that also combines many other functionalities such as radio, television, camera, Internet access, word processors and more recently functions such as health monitors.

The experiences of the Finnish conglomerate Nokia highlight many of the challenges facing companies in this rapidly restructuring world. In 2007 it had advertised its new N95 as 'It's what computers have become', but by 2011 it needed to join forces with Microsoft to try to strengthen its position in the smartphone market, faced with growing international competition, especially from new Chinese producers of mobile phones such as Huawei and ZTE. This venture was not entirely successful, and in 2014 Nokia sold its share of the Devices and Services part of the company to Microsoft, thus effectively divesting itself of its handset business.[3] One specific development impact of this was that its Nokia Life Tools programme, which had been launched in 2009 to provide people in poorer countries with healthcare, agriculture, education, and entertainment services, was shut down at the end of 2013 because it had not been possible to find a sustainable way of maintaining the service,[4] even though by 2011 it had served more than 15 million people in four countries and had been widely praised. This indicates both the difficulties facing

---

[3] <http://company.nokia.com/en/about-us/our-company/our-story>.
[4] <https://www.microsoft.com/en-ng/mobile/support/faq/?action=singleTopic&topic=FA142264>, accessed 9 February 2016.

handset producers in ever more challenging markets, but also the impact that this can have in a development context.

A final related point to note about convergence has been the problematic confusion and conflation of meanings that it has led to with respect to technologies. Whereas in the past it was possible to conceptualize ICTs and telecommunications as separate and distinct, this is much less true today, presenting real problems, for example, to governments in trying to decide how best to structure their administrations to deal with telecommunications and ICTs. Likewise, at the global level, it raises important questions as to where the best place for reaching agreements on critical issues, such as global Internet policy, should lie (see Chapter 3). From its origin in 1865, the ITU had thus focused mainly on the telegraph and telephony as well as international agreements on spectrum allocations, but it has increasingly sought to address wider policy issues relating to the Internet and the use of ICTs in development. These have recently brought it into conflict with other stakeholders with interests in the Internet, notably at the World Conference on International Telecommunications in 2012, where many governments and civil society organizations argued that this was not the forum for international agreements on Internet policy (see Chapter 3 for more detail).

The use of the term 'cyber' as a prefix for all matters relating to computers and the Internet, not least as in '*cyber*-space', '*cyber*-governance', '*cyber*-security', and '*cyber*-crime', is also problematic. This is not only because in origin 'cyber' had nothing to do with computers, but also because different cyber-terms are used to describe the same thing; one person's 'cyber-crime' is another's 'cyber-security'. In origin, 'cyber-' is derived from the term 'cybernetics' and ultimately the ancient Greek κυβερνήτης, meaning steersman, pilot, or governor. The concept is therefore fundamentally to do with governing or steering, and the word 'cyber-governance' is thus tautological. Cybernetics, in its modern form, came to be used in the first half of the twentieth century to refer to control systems in biology, engineering, applied mathematics, electronics, and other such fields, and so was always a very much broader concept than just relating to the field of computing. However, in 1948 Norbert Wiener used the term cybernetics to refer to control and communication in both the animal and the machine, and in 1984 the novelist William Gibson coined the term cyberspace to refer to the space where online interactions take place. Interestingly, though, the term cyberspace had been used in the visual arts much earlier, in the late 1960s, when a group of Danish artists coined the term in the original sense of 'cyber', to mean 'managing spaces' (Lillemose and Kryger, 2015).

One important point to grasp about the abuse of the prefix 'cyber-' is that it tends to conflate many different notions, and is increasingly being used to serve particular interests that are concerned with control. Graham (2013, p. 177) notes with reference to cyberspace that 'The metaphor constrains, enables and structures very distinct ways of imagining the interactions between people, information, code and machines through digital networks. These distinct imaginations, in turn, have real effects on how we enact politics and bring places into being.' At an international political level, it has been fascinating to see, for example, how the series of conferences initiated in London in 2011 on the rather restricted concept of governing behaviour in cyberspace, focusing especially on cyber-security, and subsequently held in Budapest in 2012 and Seoul in 2013 also particularly focusing on cyber-security, had expanded by the time of The Hague conference in 2015 to take into account all-encompassing themes of global perspectives on security, freedom, and the economic and social benefits of cyberspace (see Section 3.3.5). The notion of 'cyber' is not only confusing, but also implies a particular notion of control in the use of technology, control by those in power wishing to maintain their control over power.

This example of convergence and conflation of terminology is but one case of the growing complexity of dealing with such issues. Another has been the increased use of the term 'digital' to refer to all aspects of information and communication technologies, not only the technology but also the content. Likewise, there has been a proliferation of usage of the prefixes 'e-' and 'm-', as in e-learning, m-health (health services supplied through mobile devices), and e-agriculture. This too has led to confusion, and endless discussions as to whether, for example, m-health is a subset of e-health. Invariably, such terms are coined to give the impression of something new, and with the interests of the person or organization promoting them uppermost in mind. Instead of engaging in such debates, the solution offered here is to be as precise as possible in referring to specific terms, and seeking to clarify the interests and meaning behind the usage of more generic terms where relevant. My preference is for the use of the inclusive term ICTs to refer to all information and communication technologies, not only digital but also analogue. In this context, it is interesting to note that the *World Development Report 2016* (World Bank, 2016a) on *Digital Dividends*, places particular importance on the need for 'analog complements' if the 'digital revolution' is to benefit more people across the world.

2.2 The Radio Spectrum and its Management

The use and management of wireless or radio spectrum is of fundamental importance to the functioning of all wireless operated ICTs, and thus particularly important in poorer countries of the world that never had substantial fixed-line telephony. Spectrum usage and management has been an integral and important aspect of telecommunications ever since the origins of wireless telegraphy in the nineteenth century (Chaduc and Pogorel, 2008; Cave et al., 2012). Although initially a national concern, it rapidly became evident that international agreements were essential, and in 1906 the first International Radiotelegraph Conference was held in Berlin with the Bureau of the ITU as its central administrator. This gave rise to the first International Radiotelegraph Convention, and the ITU has ever since taken on the role of administering international agreements in this sphere through the regularly updated Radio-communication Regulations and Standards administered by its Radiocommunication Sector (IT-R). Until the 1980s, spectrum allocation and management were relatively unproblematic, since the main concern was about radio and television broadcasting. However, with the rapid expansion of mobile phones and wireless computing that also required access to spectra from the 2000s onwards, the allocation of spectra has become much more complex and controversial.

To understand the complexity of radio regulation and spectrum allocation, its potential for uses in a development context, and the business opportunities that it provides, it is essential to understand some basic elements of wireless or radio technology (Blackman and Srivastava, 2011; ITU-*info*Dev, regularly updated). The radio frequencies used by wireless technologies are summarized in Table 2.1. Four observations about radio waves are essential for understanding their technological applications, because these properties determine how the different spectra can best be used (Alchele et al., 2006):

- as frequency increases, wavelength decreases;
- the longer the wavelength and the shorter the frequency, the further it travels;
- the longer the wavelength and the shorter the frequency, the better it travels through and around objects; and
- the shorter the wavelength and the longer the frequency, the more data it can carry.

Thus, radio broadcasting uses longer wavelengths than television, since it needs to send less data, and digital broadband uses much shorter wavelengths since it needs to transport very large amounts of data. Deciding which frequencies to use thus requires trade-offs, and for many wireless applications, especially in developing countries, the best trade-offs are in the 400 MHz-4 GHz frequency range. As technologies change, the demands for different spectra vary, and thus allocation of particularly frequencies for particular services becomes a pressing issue.

More recently, given the crowded character of the radio spectrum, and the need for more efficient data transfer, experiments have been undertaken on Li-Fi (Light Fidelity), which utilizes visible light communication (VLC, using

Table 2.1 Radio frequency propagation and use

Band	Frequency	Wavelength	Range	Use	Bandwidth*	Interference; and LOS/ NLOS**
ELF, SLF, ULF	3–30 Hz 30–300 Hz 300–3000 Hz	100,000– 100 km	100,000– 10,000 km	Communication with submarines; sonar	Extremely narrow	Widespread interference; NLOS
VLF	3–30 kHz	100–10 km	1000s km	Long-range radio navigation	Very narrow	Widespread interference; NLOS
LF	30–300 kHz	10–1 km	1000s km	Long-range radio navigation and strategic communications	Very narrow	Widespread interference; NLOS
MF	0.3–3 MHz	1 km–100 m	2000–3000 km***	Long-range radio navigation and strategic communications	Moderate	Widespread interference; NLOS
HF	3–30 MHz	100 m–10 m	< 1000 km***	Global broadcast and point to point; shortwave radio; radiotelephony	Wide	Widespread interference; NLOS
VHF	30–300 MHz	10 m–1 m	2–300 km***	TV broadcast; personal communication service; mobile; WAN	Very wide	Confined interference; LOS
UHF	0.3–3 GHz	1 m–100 mm	<100 km	TV broadcast; personal communication service; mobile; WAN	Very wide	Confined interference; LOS
SHF	3–30 GHz	100 mm–10 mm	Varies 30 km–2000 km	Broadcast; personal communication service; mobile; WAN; satellite communication	Very wide up to 1 GHz	Confined interference; LOS
EHF	30–300 GHz	10 mm–1 mm	Varies 20 km–2000 km	microcell; point to point; personal communication service; satellite; astronomy	Very wide up to 10 GHz	Confined interference; LOS

Notes: *Bandwidth, referring to range of frequencies. **LOS = Line of Sight, NLOS = Non/Near Line of Sight. *** Refraction from the ionosphere in the range of 500 kHz to 50 MHz, but mainly in HF, enables travel of radio waves over great distances and supports Non/Near Line of Sight (NLOS) radio transmission.

Source: Derived from *ITU*-info *Dev ICT Regulation Toolkit* (regularly updated), Section 5.1, <http://www.ictregulationtoolkit. org/en/home>, with additions from <http://www.sengpielaudio.com/calculator-radiofrequency.htm>.

light in the 400–800 THz range), in essence using the pulses from invisibly flickering LED bulbs to transfer data (Haas, 2013). These experiments show that Li-Fi can reach speeds of 224 GBs^{-1} which is about 100 times faster than usual Wi-Fi speeds. Pilot projects in office environments in Tallinn, Estonia, in

2015, have proved promising,[5] and it seems probable that such technology will soon become a further means through which mass communication and data transfer will be enabled, particularly since the visible light spectrum is some 10,000 times larger than the entire radio frequency spectrum.

2.3 From Fixed-Line to Wireless Communication

The impacts of the change in technologies from essentially fixed wired to mobile wireless communications over the last twenty years have been quite remarkable, liberating people from the need to be at a particular place at a specified time to make and receive phone calls (for the African context, see Skouby and Williams, 2014). Communication and data transfer are for the first time in human history now possible anywhere and anytime, provided that people have access to, and can afford, the necessary technologies. The implications of this for reducing inequalities in the world are immense, but as yet they have not been fully realized.

Until the arrival of second generation (2G) mobile phone systems in the 1990s, almost all telephony was based around fixed copper cables, but by 2002 global mobile phone subscriptions had overtaken fixed telephones. It is important to reflect on the cultural, social, economic, and political implications of this shift from fixed to mobile technologies in seeking to understand the development of the industry in recent years, and especially the approaches adopted in different states towards universal access before the wireless digital transformation began. In its earliest days, telephony was initially provided by private sector companies, but given its importance and the recognition that the private sector could not deliver a cost-effective service to everyone, many countries during the early to mid-twentieth century nationalized their industries or created specific government departments to run them. Government policies varied, but some countries explicitly sought to provide universal access, through fixed lines to every household and telephone boxes located across their territories to ensure that those who did not have their own line could access telephony services, and those away from their houses or offices could also have access to nearby phones as often as possible. Many countries in Europe, particularly those that had a strong social welfare based ethos, such as Sweden, placed great emphasis on trying to ensure that the most remote hamlets had access to telephone lines, even though this was a costly and difficult task. These efforts meant that such countries often had more than one fixed line for every two people before the advent of wireless telephony.

---

[5] <http://www.ibtimes.co.uk/lifi-internet-first-real-world-usage-boasts-speed-100-times-faster-wifi-1530021>.

The vast majority of countries, though, and especially the poorest in Africa, Asia, and South America, had very few, or no fixed-line phones, and likewise had no history that universal service was something to be valued.

This old ethos that every household should have access to a phone was often lost in the rapid privatization of the sector that took place from the 1980s onwards, coinciding with the technological transformation from fixed to wireless telephony. Although regulatory authorities have sought to devise a range of mechanisms to ensure universal access, and despite estimates that three-quarters of the world's population had access to a mobile phone by 2012 (World Bank, 2012), the poorest and most marginalized still do not benefit, and there remains a fundamental tension between the need for private sector companies to generate profit and the attempts by some governments to ensure that universal access is achieved (see Chapter 5).

The desire by private sector interests to expand their markets and reduce costs in order to drive profits has led to the introduction of numerous different technologies and standards to ensure inter-operability over the last decade. It is important, though, to recognize that there are many different technological options for providing a range of digital services including satellites, Wi-Fi (since 1997), WiMAX (since 2001), and new types of fixed fibre optic cables (with the first transatlantic fibre optic cable, TAT-8, going into operation in 1988). In essence, all wireless solutions require a signal transmitter, or antenna, and a receiver. Given the parameters summarized in Table 2.1, it becomes clear that the longer wavelength spectrum allocated to television broadcasting enables it to pass round objects and through buildings, whereas the shorter wavelengths for Wi-Fi have required line-of-sight visibility, and thus the construction of numerous radio masts for the antennae, transceivers, amplifiers, and switches necessary to create a network.

Satellites have become a crucial technology for communications since their first launches in the early 1960s, and can be classified into three main types of orbit: Geostationary (35,786 km above the earth), Medium Earth (2,000–35,786 km above the earth), and Low Earth (c.160–2,000 km above the earth). Satellites in Medium and Low Earth orbits move relative to the earth, and so several satellites are required to provide constant coverage in any one place. However, since they are nearer the earth, their signals are stronger. New entrants to the market, such as O3b (Other 3 billion), whose satellites orbit at 8,062 km from the earth, can thus claim that their 'next generation satellite constellation brings our customers better, faster and more affordable connectivity and gives 70% of the world's population fiber-quality Internet services'.[6] Satellites have always played a major role in broadcast television and international

---

[6] <http://www.o3bnetworks.com/>.

telephony, and although the increased use of submarine cables from the late twentieth century has challenged that role, satellites are still important for providing access to people living in places far from such cables, particularly on isolated islands and in remote places in the interior of land-locked countries, as well as for international shipping. Depending on location and type of demand, satellite companies seek to use different bandwidths to provide relevant services (Table 2.2). C-Band for example requires large antennae, whereas Ku- and Ka-Band use smaller antennae, but these are subject to rain-fade and so are more challenging for use in tropical areas.

The rapid expansion in construction of submarine cables, and terrestrial wireless networks has offered a range of alternative solutions for digital communications, often meaning that operators and indeed governments have difficult choices to make in deciding what technology to employ to deliver services to as many people as possible. Although the western and southern coasts of Africa were connected as early as 2001 with the SAT 3 cable, it was not until 2009 that SEACOM first provided direct submarine cable connectivity to East Africa, and the subsequent rapid increase in the number of cables has now transformed connectivity in the coastal regions of the continent.[7]

Table 2.2 Satellite frequencies, characteristics, and uses

Band	Frequency	Characteristics	Usage
L-Band	1–2 GHz	Easy to process; wide beam; less expensive	GPS; satellite mobile phones
S-Band	2–4 GHz	Crosses the conventional UHF/SHF boundary	Weather radar; some communications
C-Band	4–8 GHz Uplink: 5.925–6.425 GHz Downlink: 3.7–4.2 GHz	Requires higher power and thus larger antennae than L- and S-Bands; less susceptible to rain fade than higher frequency bands, so used in tropics; hardware more expensive; but cheaper bandwidth	Satellite communications; TV networks
X-Band	8–12 GHz Uplink: 7.9–8.4 GHz Downlink: 7.25–7.75 GHz	Smaller antennae; more cost efficient than C-Band	Mainly military use; air traffic control
Ku-Band	12–18 GHz Uplink: 14 GHz Downlink: 10.9–12.75 GHz	Needs less power so smaller dishes than C-Band; suffers from rain fade, but less than Ka-Band; less expensive hardware; but capacity more expensive	Satellite communications
Ka-Band	26.5–40 GHz Uplink: 26.5–40 GHz Downlink: 18–20 GHz	Permits higher speed communication; but suffers from rain fade; smaller antennae than Ku-Band, so cheaper to install	Satellite communications

Source: Derived mainly from European Space Agency: Telecommunications and integrated applications, <http://www.esa.int/Our_Activities/Telecommunications_Integrated_Applications/Satellite_frequency_bands>.

---

[7] <https://manypossibilities.net/african-undersea-cables/>.

The provision of optical fibre within the interior of continents, though, remains challenging and expensive. One of the most ambitious of such initiatives has been India's National Optical Fibre Network project initiated in 2011, to be funded by the Universal Service Obligation Fund. This is intended to extend fibre to more than 200,000 Gram Panchayats (centres of local self-government) in India not yet connected, at a cost of some US$3 billion.

Enormous technical challenges remain in providing comprehensive universal connectivity across the poorer countries of the world, and it is important to recognize that no one technology is best for all circumstances. The model of using different technologies to deliver services in different contexts is inherently sound. Although its genesis was controversial, Australia's National Broadband Network thus provides a good example of how such a network can be successful, with its objective of combining three elements to create a national wholesale open-access data network for phone and Internet connectivity: fibre to the premises; fixed wireless in the 2.3 GHz and 3.4 GHz frequencies for Long Term Evolution (LTE) coverage for the 4 per cent of the population outside the fibre footprint; and the use of satellites for those with otherwise limited data speeds.[8]

The global impact of these changes can be seen in the fundamental restructuring of telephone and broadband networks that has taken place in the first fifteen years of the twenty-first century as summarized in Figure 2.1. What this official ITU view of the sector clearly shows is that mobile subscriptions grew dramatically during the 2000s, but have since levelled off; fixed-line subscriptions which were just higher than mobiles in 2001, started to decline slightly from 2006 onwards; and active mobile broadband subscriptions have grown exponentially since 2007. These figures nevertheless mask the very considerable differences that there are in these indicators between different countries, with developing countries in 2015 only having 39.1 active mobile broadband subscriptions per 100 people, compared with 86.7 in the developed world. Moreover, these figures are only subscriptions, and mask real usage because of the substantial differences that exist between the number of subscriptions and the number of devices. The GSM Association (GSMA, 2015a) thus helpfully focuses on the term 'unique mobile subscriber' to refer to a single individual who has subscribed to a mobile service, and who might hold multiple mobile connections (Gillet, 2014). According to this measure, only half the world's population had one or more mobile subscriptions in 2014.

---

[8] <http://www.nbnco.com.au/>.

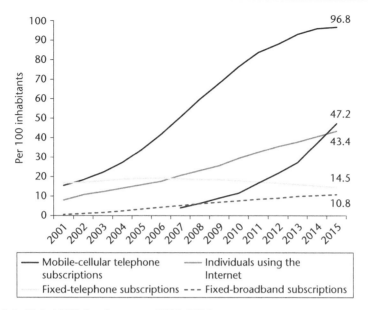

Figure 2.1 Global ICT developments 2001–2015

Source: ITU Statistics, <https://www.itu.int/en/ITU-D/Statistics/Pages/stat/default.aspx>, accessed 12 February 2016.

2.4 From Voice to Data: Impacts of the Digital Transition

The dramatic expansion of wireless technologies has not only enabled telephony to be released from its previously fixed character as indicated in Figure 2.1, but advancements in mobile technology have also had a very significant impact on what such devices are capable of being used for. The first mobile phones in the 1980s were analogue, but with the introduction of new second generation standards and technologies (2G) in the 1990s, the first digital phones were being created to deliver low speed text services (Short Message Service, SMS) alongside voice (Table 2.3). In essence, digital services break up the continuous analogue signal into discrete blocks that can be transmitted digitally. Analogue signals are continuous in amplitude and over time, but they degrade with interference over distance; digital signals lose such precision continuity, but are very much more robust in resisting noise and distortion. As with the previous analogue systems, the first digital mobile services were based on circuit switching, in which two nodes in a network first need to establish a direct dedicated channel or circuit between them before communication can take place. Data could indeed be transferred, but it was at a very low rate compared with more recent technologies. By the early 2000s, General Packet Radio Service (GPRS) technologies were introduced using

Table 2.3 Mobile phone generations

Generation	Date introduced	Speed	Standards/ technologies	Main features and uses
1G	1980 (commercial 1982)	< 2.4 Kbps	AMPS; TACS	Analogue mobile service; voice; using FDMA
2G	1991 (commercial 1992)	< 9.6 Kbps	CDMA; GSM; TDMA	Digital; mainly voice but also slow data; more efficient spectrum use; data services (SMS) permits text; circuit-switched; narrow band
2.5G (informal)	2000	< 50 Kbps	GPRS	Digital; packet-switched in addition to circuit-switched; always on; started to enable mobile Internet
2.75G (informal)	2003	< 1 Mbps	EDGE	Digital; addition of 8PSK encoding
3G	1998 (commercial 2001)	Minimum 2 Mbps stationary, 384 Kbps for moving vehicle	[ITU IMT-2000] W-CDMA; TD-SCDMA; CDMA-2000; UMTS; HSPA; WiMAX	Digital; enhanced audio and video; faster data speed; video-conferencing; broadband; location-based services; GPS
4G	2008 (commercially 2012)	100 Mbps for moving vehicles; 1 Gbps for stationary	[ITU IMT Advanced] LTE; WiMAX; HSPA+	Digital; all-IP packet switched; mobile broadband; faster speeds; inter-operability with existing standards; mobile Web access; IP telephony; HD TV; multimedia messaging; video chat
5G	Under development (likely from 2020)			Digital; much faster data rates; greater spectral efficiency; enhanced coverage; enhanced signalling efficiency; reduced latency.

Notes: AMPS = Advanced Mobile Phone Service; CDMA = Code Division Multiple Access; CDMA-2000 = Based on the Interim Standard-95 CDMA; EDGE = Enhanced Data GSM Environment (officially ITU ratified 3G technology, but usually referred to as 2.75G); FDMA = Frequency Division Multiple Access; GPRS = General Packet Radio Service; GSM = Global System for Mobile Communications; HSPA = High Speed Packet Access; HSPA+ = Evolved High Speed Packet Access; IMT-2000 = International Mobile Telecommunications-2000; LTE = Long-Term Evolution; PDC = Personal Digital Cellular; TACS = Total Access Communication System; TDMA = Time Division Multiple Access; TD-SCDMA = Time Division Synchronous Code Division Multiple Access; UMTS (Universal Mobile Telecommunications Service); W-CDMA = Wide-band Code Division Multiple Access; WiMAX= Worldwide Inter-operability for Microwave Access.

Sources: Derived mainly from Bekkers (2001) and Dahlman et al. (2014), but using many other sources.

packet switching, through which data is broken down into packages that are transmitted independently through the network. These enabled faster and more effective data transfer, thus setting in motion the dramatic changes that were to take place over the next decade, during which data would begin to outstrip voice in volume. Moreover, the introduction of Voice over Internet Protocol (VoIP) from the mid-1990s meant that digitalized voice could also be transmitted across the Internet, thus giving rise to a whole new system of telephony. By 2003, the year in which Skype (Porterfield, 2013) launched its beta software, VoIP calls represented approximately one-quarter of all voice calls. The introduction of 3G technologies for mobile phones in the 2000s, and particularly 4G commercially from 2012, has led to a very rapid acceleration of data traffic, as faster speeds, video capabilities, and true mobile broadband has been enabled. By 2010, the volume of data traffic was thus only twice that of voice, but by the first quarter (Q1) of 2015 data volume was approaching 25 times that of voice, having seen a 55 per cent growth between Q1 2014 and Q1 2015 (Ericsson, 2015).

These developments have effectively transformed mobile phones into small multifunctional devices that are no longer mainly used for voice calls, but instead are primarily means for people to access the Internet for all of their information and communication purposes. They have also disrupted traditional business models by opening up entirely new economic opportunities, most notably through the dramatic expansion of the app economy. From the release of Apple's iPhone in June 2007 and its App Store in July of 2008, followed by the launch of Google's Android Market in October 2008 (later to be renamed Google Play Store in 2012), the number of apps produced and downloaded has grown exponentially. In 2013 both Apple and Google reported that they each had more than 1 million apps available through their stores, and global mobile app revenues rose from US$8.32 billion in 2011 to around US$41.1 billion in 2015.[9] However, as discussed in more detail in Section 2.8, this growth is not something from which everyone can benefit, and is not a miraculous way through which individuals and national economies can suddenly experience dramatic growth (VisionMobile, 2014).

Three aspects of this shift from voice to data in the context of mobile technologies are of particular interest in the context of their implications for the poorest people and countries. First, there has been a transformation of the handset industry, as with the example of the changing fortunes of Nokia noted earlier. In the developed countries of the world, there was one mobile subscriber per person as early as 2007, although in 2014 there were still only 79 per cent who were unique subscribers. In countries where most people can afford smartphones that perform the functions of a computer, the competition has for over a decade been in building ever more powerful high-specification devices, that can be sold at a premium price. Once newer devices come onto the market, manufacturers have then sought to extend sales of their older models by offering them more cheaply in developing country markets, which had previously only really had lower cost 1G or 2G phones.

---

[9] <http://www.statista.com/statistics/269025/worldwide-mobile-app-revenue-forecast/>.

However, in light of the recent expansion of 3G services in many poorer countries, whereby some 70 per cent of the world's population was served by 3G networks in 2015 (GSMA, 2015a), greater attention is now being placed, particularly by Chinese producers, on serving this market directly with lower cost smartphones, often priced at as little as $50. Higher specification smart-phones nevertheless remain beyond the reach of all but the rich, and as newer technologies continue to be directed towards them, this process seem likely to continue to lead to ever increasing inequality. Even if smartphones are now much more accessible to larger numbers of people across the world today, technological developments mean that the rich continue to reap the even greater benefits of the next generation of technologies.

Second, the development of new generations of mobile technologies has important ramifications for network coverage, and the costs are considerable both for operators to roll-out next generation networks, and also to consumers who wish to purchase new devices and payment plans to run on these enhanced networks. Indeed, there is now much underutilized 3G capacity in the poorer countries of the world, and it has not always proved easy to attract consumers to use 3G-enabled services. Another interesting feature of my field research in Pakistan in 2016 was that a surprising number of people had 3G phones, but only ever used them for voice calling. For countries that do not yet have 3G networks, it also makes sense for them to move straight to 4G networks. Given the dramatic increase in demand for high speed data transfer, though, it is also important to understand some of the technological con-straints on increasing data transfer rates further. As Dahlman et al. (2014) emphasize, two fundamental factors limit the achievable data rate: the ratio of signal power to noise impairing the signal, and the available bandwidth. Hence, there are ever increasing demands on bandwidth and electrical power, both of which place wider constraints on governments and companies in implementing high quality mobile broadband services. For operators, a very considerable cost has also been the need to bid for licences for each new generation of mobile technologies. As more bandwidth has been required, regulators have sought, or been encouraged, to generate additional govern-ment revenue through spectrum auctions, and this has usually necessitated operators charging considerably higher amounts for each generation of new services, again making it increasingly difficult for poorer people to afford the resultant services. Regulators thus have a very fine balance to manage in developing appropriate policies that will encourage universal access, and these are explored in much further detail in Chapter 5.

Third, given the very considerable demand for increases in bandwidth available for mobile broadband, many of the world's richer countries began switching off their analogue TV services from the mid-2000s, and converting them to digital. The message to consumers was usually that digital TV would be of much better visual resolution, sound fidelity, and have the potential for a considerable increase in the number of channels available. However, an important underlying interest was the potential that this offered to governments and the private sector to release and reallocate bandwidth, so that it could be used for more lucrative commercial purposes associated with mobile broadband. To this end, a treaty agreement was signed in 2006 by governments at the ITU Regional Radiocommunications conference in Geneva that all countries in Europe, Africa, and the Middle East would switch over to digital broadcasting by June 2015. Eventually, some 119 countries met this target, although for many of the poorest countries this was not without considerable difficulty, and several have continued to run both analogue and digital services for a transition period. As of 2016, the ITU's portal indicating the status of countries with respect to transition[10] shows considerably more countries where the transition process has not started or is ongoing than those that have completed. Whilst there are definitely opportunities for enhancement to broadcasting, not least the potential it offers for subtitling for deaf people, it is in the area of bandwidth reallocation, known as the 'digital dividend', that at least as much impact is likely to be felt. This is discussed further in Chapter 5, but before concluding this section it is important briefly to mention the potential of TV white spaces as being another means through which increased bandwidth can be made available. In essence, TV white spaces are the parts of the licensed spectrum that are not being used by broadcasters at a particular place and time. In some countries, as in the UK, white space has been made free to use, and experiments have been undertaken to show that it can indeed be used effectively for providing broadband IP connectivity (Pietrosemoli and Zennaro, 2013). As yet, though, few countries, especially in poorer parts of the world, have permitted its use on anything approaching a widespread scale.

2.5 On Openness and Being Free

The dramatic technological changes that have taken place in the ICT sector over the last quarter of a century have reformulated one of the fundamental social, political, and indeed ethical debates at the heart of human society, namely that over the balance between *communal* and *individual* interests. This finds particularly interesting ramifications in the ICT sector where it has been expressed through the polarized differences between *Open* and *Proprietary* models of software and content (Unwin, 2009).

---

[10] <http://www.itu.int/en/ITU-D/Spectrum-Broadcasting/Pages/DSO/Default.aspx>, accessed 12 February 2016.

Figure 2.2 Imfundo's workshop on an economic evaluation of Free and Open Source Software solutions for African education, March 2004, Dakar, Senegal
Source: Author.

* * *

Struggling with the seemingly irreconcilable differences between colleagues arguing on the one hand for Open Source software and Open content solutions for African education, and on the other those who maintained that Proprietary solutions would bring better quality and value for money, I was eager that one of my last contributions to Imfundo in 2004 should be the convening of a workshop where we could explore whether there was any common ground, and how we might be able to promote sound business models for Open solutions (Figure 2.2). We did not reach any clear conclusions, but listening to the amazing people we brought together in Dakar made me aware that this issue is of fundamental importance to the ways in which different people view the role of ICTs in development, and is based not so much on logic or economic principles, but rather on deep-seated beliefs and moral values.

Then, in the latter 2000s, the ICT4D Collective working with other European and African universities, undertook some very practical research to try to find ways to develop a shared curriculum in ICT4D that could be used in both continents (funded by a DelPHE award from DFID, managed by the British Council, and an Edulink award from the ACP-EU Partnerships in Higher Education programme). I still remember the challenges that this created, not least when an African colleague asked me what incentives there were for

African academics to make their lectures notes and 'content' freely available, when many of them are used to selling their notes to students in order to supplement their incomes. This once again made me think deeply about the business models associated with Open content, and the Open Educational Resource agendas.

*   *   *

The enclosure of the large open fields of medieval Europe, which had previously provided common resources for the peasantry, is often seen as being at the heart of the origins of capitalism in the sixteenth and seventeenth centuries, since it enabled individual profit to be gained from a previously communal resource (Thompson, 1991; Neeson, 1993). Individual investment in the land, on newly enclosed fields, could provide the source of greater individual profit. However, as Hardin (1968) has also argued, such rational self-interested individual behaviour could also be detrimental to the wider community since it depletes resources that were once held communally. Likewise, particularly from the eighteenth century onwards, increasing regulations over intellectual property, including copyright, trademarks, and patents, meant that individuals were able to gain monopolies over their ideas, thereby enabling them to reap financial profit from investing time and energy in innovation (Bettig, 1996).

Both enclosure and intellectual property rights are examples of ways through which individuals are able to benefit exclusively from knowledge that was previously, or is potentially, communal. However, both also reflect a somewhat idealized view of what 'communal' life is actually like. Thus, the life of medieval feudal villeins, legally tied to the manor of their birth, was unremittingly harsh. By permitting villeins to labour in gleaning and utilizing common resources, manorial lords were able to exploit them yet further. Similar arguments lie at the heart of debates over the relative costs and benefits of Open and Proprietary technologies. They also raise important questions about the nature of freedom, which resonate with some of Sen's (1999) arguments discussed in Chapter 1.

2.5.1 *Free and Open Source Software*

The development of ICTs closely reflects such arguments, which are of fundamental importance to understanding the potential of ICTs to be of communal value in the interests of everyone, and thus in 'development'. At the origin of the Open software and content movement, though, there lay an inherent challenge, which found its expression in the conflation between the concepts of 'Open' and 'Free'. Ever since the origins of software, people had been developing code and sharing it, sometimes for individual financial benefit, and on other occasions simply sharing it for free amongst friends to help improve it. The 'Free Software Movement' was officially founded by Richard Stallman in 1983, when he initiated the GNU (GNU's not Unix) project in opposition to the dominant Unix operating system that had been developed commercially in the 1970s at Bell Labs. In 1985 Stallman created the Free Software Foundation,[11] and by 1992, when Linus Torvalds released Linux, a completely independent and free operating system, this movement had a viable alternative to the dominant Proprietary operating systems then available (Moody, 2002; Söderberg, 2008).

The Free Software Movement was, though, much more than merely software available at no cost, and in Stallman's formulation users and writers of such software had to abide by four freedoms: to run the program for any purpose; to study how it works and adapt it; to redistribute copies; and to improve it and release the improvements back into the community. Subsequently, other communities of software developers increasingly began to use the term Open Source, which had been coined by a group of academics and venture capitalists in February 1998, a month after Netscape Navigator made its browser free to the public, in opposition to what they saw as the confrontational and moralizing approach of the free software movement. Shortly afterwards they created a separate Open Source Initiative,[12] which listed ten criteria that any such software should comply with, including such things as free redistribution, the integrity of the author's source code, no discrimination, technology neutrality, and permitting modification and derived works. Although at times debates between these two communities have been acrimonious, for most users this distinction is relatively unimportant, and the generic terms FOSS (Free and Open Source Software) and FLOSS (Free-Libre/Livre/ Libero and Open Source Software, to take account of French/Spanish, Portuguese, and Italian usage) have come into common usage to refer to such software.

Advocates of FOSS usually see it as having the advantages over Proprietary software of being cheaper, giving users more control, protecting privacy, and increasing security and stability, since it is developed by a committed community of programmers. However, advocates of Proprietary software argue that paying staff to develop software means that it will be of higher quality, can be tailored to specific needs of customers, and can benefit from the reinvestment of profits in innovative design. The fundamental question facing the development of FOSS by individuals or companies, though, is how to generate revenues for something that is usually given away at no cost (Fitzgerald, 2006). Some individuals thus earn their main income from other sources, such as an academic salary, and they therefore in a sense self-exploit

---

[11] <https://www.fsf.org>.   [12] <https://opensource.org/>.

in developing FOSS in their 'out-of-office' hours in the interests of the wider community. Increasingly, though, FOSS is also released by companies, or used by them, as part of their wider agenda for harnessing the international communal expertise available in the FOSS community. Apple thus claims that it uses Open Source to make its software more robust and secure, drawing on existing software created by the Open Source community and making some of its own code available through the Apple Open Source licence. Yet others generate their revenue from the services that they can provide in support of the software that they have developed, by using advertising revenue, or by selling the details of users to third parties. Recently, more innovative models, such as crowdsourcing, where funding is generated from a community of supporters or investors, has been a popular means to fund software and app development, and some governments are also increasingly requiring that any projects funded by them, including software and content development, should be made freely available to the wider international community.

Theoretically, Open Source initiatives can provide substantially cheaper software, both operating systems and applications, that should be able to benefit poorer and more marginal communities. The Ubuntu operating system,[13] for example, first released in 2004, is an Open Source project that develops a cross-platform operating system based on Debian, which is itself a volunteer project that developed and maintains a GNU/Linux operating system. Its name derives from the Nguni Bantu notion of *Ubuntu*, which can be translated as 'human kindness' but encompasses a broader understanding of the bond of sharing that unites all humanity. It has largely been funded by the South African entrepreneur Mark Shuttleworth, through Canonical, the company that he created to promote and support free software projects. Whilst it is difficult to gain definitive figures for operating system usage, Ubuntu was used by around 11 per cent of all the websites with known operating systems in February 2016.[14] Although this is only a small share of the global market, it represents a significant number of users, and such alternative models were part of the reason why Microsoft, a bastion of the Proprietary model, announced in early 2015 that it would make its Windows 10 operating systems available for free.

2.5.2 *Open Educational Resources and Content*

In a parallel vein to the software examples just discussed, a significant debate between Open and Proprietary *content* also emerged in the mid-1990s, initially within the academic community and particularly in the field of Open and

[13] <http://www.ubuntu.com/>.
[14] <http://w3techs.com/technologies/details/os-ubuntu/all/all>, accessed 16 February 2016.

Distance Learning (ODL). The advent of the Web, innovative digital technologies, and greater connectivity, have all made the vision of freely available global digital educational resources a reality. As with the FOSS movement, there has, though, been considerable passionate debate about the relative advantages of Open Content, with advocates thereof being critical of the traditional publishing industry, which has often been caricatured as being a pariah, making profits from the labour of academic authors, whist offering little in return.

One of the fundamental underlying principles of Open Content is that access to knowledge should be available freely to everyone. The challenge then becomes how to pay authors and writers for its creation. This is particularly difficult in poorer countries, which often do not have sufficient resources to be able to support high enough salaries for teachers and academics, who therefore have to find additional ways of supplementing their incomes. In such circumstances, it is very difficult for them to find time, let alone have the aspiration, to make their content freely available to others. In publicly funded universities and schools in richer countries of the world, where academics and teachers are often paid by the state, it is much easier to justify a requirement that content should be made freely available, although even here competitive interests between different institutions can act as a deterrent for such openness.

The catalyst that ignited the Open Educational Resource (OER) movement is often seen as being the decision by the Massachusetts Institute of Technology (MIT) in 2002 to open up its course content freely through the OpenCourse-Ware project. The movement, though, has increasingly been championed by global organizations such as UNESCO (the United Nations Education, Scientific and Cultural Organization)[15] and the Commonwealth of Learning (COL)[16] (see, for example, Butcher et al., 2015; UNESCO and COL, 2015; Miao et al., 2016). The key role of the William and Flora Hewlett Foundation in supporting OER initiatives across the world should also be acknowledged and applauded. Without this support it is unlikely that many OER initiatives would have got off the ground anything like as quickly as they have done. There has been much debate as to what should be included within the definition of OER, but most definitions combine elements of content that is intended for learning and teaching, that is accessible digitally, and is available openly and freely. The Hewlett Foundation definition is that:

---

[15] <http://www.unesco.org/new/en/communication-and-information/access-to-knowledge/open-educational-resources/>.
[16] <https://www.col.org/news/speeches-presentations/open-education-resources-oer-what-why-how>.

OER are teaching, learning, and research resources that reside in the public domain or have been released under an intellectual property license that permits their free use and re-purposing by others. Open educational resources include full courses, course materials, modules, textbooks, streaming videos, tests, software, and any other tools, materials, or techniques used to support access to knowledge.[17]

The advent of virtual learning environments, both Proprietary and Open Source such as Moodle, have greatly facilitated access to such resources in a systematic way, and most authors and academics have sought to gain some protection for their ideas through public copyright licences such as those developed by Creative Commons,[18] a US-based non-profit organization founded in 2001.

Open Educational Resources are very appealing in the potential that they offer for delivering lower cost, high quality learning opportunities across the world (Jemni et al., 2016; Miao et al., 2016). However, many difficulties remain in using OER effectively in support of learning and teaching, especially in poorer countries of the world, where intuitively they might be thought to offer most potential. At least six issues present particular challenges. The first has already been noted, and concerns the need to find ways through which authors of content can be remunerated for their efforts. Many academics and teachers in poor countries simply do not have the time to devote to developing online content for free, despite the benefits that this could offer. All too often they are already vastly over-stretched trying to earn an income from their existing activities. Second, though, much of the content developed through OER initiatives has to date been of poorer quality than Proprietary content, and it is often insufficiently designed for the specific curriculum purposes of users. A common refrain from teachers is that material in existing textbooks is much better for their needs than material prepared by other teachers. Third, many such initiatives are led by people in the richer countries of the world, who are already comfortably off, and have the time to manage and deliver OER content. An insidious aspect of international OER development is that such initiatives can undercut the viability of local content providers in poor countries, thereby damaging the potential of local content industries. Fourth, and related to this, is the imperialistic character of OERs, especially in their MOOC (Massive Open Online Course) incarnation.

*   *   *

All too often across Africa I hear well-meaning people say how wonderful it is that the best quality educational material in the world from US universities is now available for anyone in Africa to use and benefit from. To such comments I usually retort with a resounding 'No!',

---

[17] <http://www.hewlett.org/programs/education/open-educational-resources>.
[18] <https://creativecommons.org/>.

adding that 'it would indeed be wonderful if students in major US universities regularly used content and MOOCs that had been developed in African universities!'

* * *

The challenge is for African educational systems to be able to match those anywhere in the world, and in so doing to provide African solutions to African problems. This requires substantial investment rather than simply accepting the offerings of an imperialist external state.

Fifth, there remain real issues with access to OERs. The increasing bandwidth requirements of much content, especially when it is in video format, still discriminate against and marginalize those who do not have access to the Internet, or only intermittently or at slow speeds. The availability of electricity also remains a very real issue, and in all ICT initiatives the need to consider this crucial requirement must be addressed, with solar power and micro-hydro projects now making off-grid solutions much more viable (Yeo, 2015). Finally, there are increasing concerns about the real costs of using digital content in classrooms, compared with traditional textbooks, and recent studies show that the cost of incorporating ICTs in education have often been vastly underestimated, especially since their impact on real educational outcomes may also have been exaggerated (OECD, 2015b).

Open Educational Resources are intuitively highly desirable, and have much to offer in terms of developing shared, communal knowledge, but only if the challenges just discussed can be overcome. Indeed, vast amounts of content are already freely available through the Web, and this has opened up a new world of information for the half of the world's population who have access to it. However, coming up with effective sustainable business models to develop content that is truly of value to poor people and communities is very challenging, as Nokia found out when it had to close Nokia Life. It must also be remembered that publishers, while undoubtedly generating profits, contribute much to the traditional publishing process in terms of editorial work, marketing, and distribution. As with the different logics of FOSS and Proprietary software, so too the balance of interests between advocates of OER and Proprietary educational content will continue to mean that there will be a lively debate in this area well into the future. At the heart of this debate lies the moral issue as to whether knowledge should be open and communal, or closed in the interests of private profit. This debate goes back at least to medieval times when open fields and communal agricultural systems were enclosed for individual gain.

2.6 Social Media and Over The Top Services

Many ICT4D initiatives have focused largely on information provision, for example developing new and more efficient ways to provide information that is seen as being beneficial to poor people, be it on education, health, agriculture, or entrepreneurship. However, as the name indicates, ICTs are also fundamentally about communication, and the emergence of new technologies has fundamentally changed the ways in which people communicate at least as much as they have altered the flow of information, data, and content. Mobile telephony has transformed where people communicate; social media has changed how they communicate.

The rise of Facebook, and with it the importance of new kinds of social media, has been one of the most remarkable business and technological achievements of the last decade. Above all, it shows the potential for new kinds of business that can be built on the technologies that have emerged over this period. Launched only in 2004, initially as a social networking service in a limited number of US universities, by 2008 it had 100 million users. By the beginning of 2011 there were 600 million Facebook users, by September 2012 1 billion users, by the end of 2014 1.39 billion users, and by the beginning of 2016 1.55 billion users.[19] For many people, the Internet literally is Facebook (Samarajiva, 2012). Despite controversies over many aspects of its activities (Kirkpatrick, 2011), this is a very considerable achievement and it reflects a fundamental change in the way that people have traditionally communicated. Instead of being largely on a one-to-one basis as before, social media has enabled individuals to compete with national top-down broadcasters and express themselves globally, thereby creating a one-to-many bottom-up broadcasting mechanism. The success of Facebook's model has been to offer users something that they see as being free, the ability to share information about themselves and to build online groups and communities, while generating its revenue primarily through advertising to those users and from the willingness of companies to pay to gain surprisingly detailed information about their users through so doing. Facebook's sheer size and frequency of use is itself a powerful force to encourage further users to participate.

* * *

I recall working with colleagues to create a communication and networking platform for our Edulink funded ICT4D community of African and European universities using the Open Source social networking engine Elgg, and becoming frustrated that it was not actually used very often.[20] I came to realize that, despite the appeal of Elgg, a colleague had been absolutely correct when he had said that it is much better to use what is successful and people are already using rather than going to the effort of developing something new that they would have to go out of their normal everyday activities to use.

---

[19] <http://www.statista.com/statistics/272014/global-social-networks-ranked-by-number-of-users/>, accessed 19 February 2016.
[20] <https://elgg.org>.

*　*　*

This concept of providing something that users see as being free, but from which a company can generate considerable revenue, also lies at the heart of the business model of the other big Internet giant, Google (Vise, 2005; Schmidt and Rosenberg, 2015). Google was founded much earlier than Facebook, in the mid-1990s, and from the early 2000s it had as its motto 'Don't be evil'. Its use of all of the data from its range of e-mail, search, and mapping services, which people could use for free, but from which it then generates revenue, led many to consider that this and other aspects of its behaviour were indeed 'evil', and so from 2015 with the restructuring of the corporation under the overall Alphabet identity the slogan was replaced by 'Do the right thing'.

There are many other search engines, social media platforms, and mapping software, but the ability of Facebook and Google to dominate their markets has also been based on an astute eye with respect to acquisitions, both to gain expertise and IPR, and also to eliminate potential opposition. By mid-2015, Google had acquired some 180 companies, including such well-known brands as Android (acquired 2005, mobile software), YouTube (acquired 2006, video sharing), DoubleClick (acquired 2007, online advertising), and Waze (acquired 2013, GPS navigational software). Likewise, Facebook had acquired more than fifty companies by mid-2015, with notable acquisitions being Instagram (acquired 2012, photo sharing) and WhatsApp (acquired 2014, instant messaging). Significantly, most of the companies acquired by Google and Facebook have been US-based, thus further emphasizing that country's dominance of the global search engine and social media industry. The growth of the Chinese social media industry should, nevertheless, also be recognized, with Sina Weibo, which has twice as many users as Twitter, Renren, which is similar to Facebook, and Youku, the second largest video sharing site in the world after YouTube, also being very significant in terms of their numbers of users.

This is but one example of the considerable spatial concentration of production and consumption within the ICT sector, not only globally but also within particular regions and countries (Zook, 2005; Cooke et al., 2013; Coe and Yeung, 2015). The USA thus clearly dominates the acquisitions by Google and Facebook, but it also continues to dominate other aspects of digital technology ranging from top-level domain names (Graham and Sabatta, 2013) to Twitter usage (see also Graham and Foster, 2016). This is despite the rise in prominence of other countries, most notably China, over the last decade, and reflects the USA's somewhat surprising flexible resilience in the sector. China's inexorable rise in the production of digital devices is nevertheless remarkable, and it is salient to note that in 2011 it produced more than 90 per cent of the world's computers and 70 per cent of phones (Swanson, 2014).

These new companies indicate the potential of technological change not only to lead to entirely new kinds of businesses, but also themselves to generate the potential for further technological change. Both Google and Facebook, frustrated with the slow pace of the expansion of the Internet into less accessible and underserved regions and ever eager to expand their own markets and thus revenues, are therefore developing innovative technical solutions and business models to expand access in poorer parts of the world. Google has set in place initiatives including Project Loon,[21] designed to provide Internet access through a network of balloons floating in the stratosphere, which was first trialled in New Zealand in 2013, and Project Link[22] to provide metro-fibre and Wi-Fi networks in Africa, beginning in Uganda and Ghana. Likewise, in 2013 Facebook launched its multifaceted internet.org initiative,[23] with its high-altitude Aquila pilotless aircraft, experiments with lasers, and agreements with operators to provide free access to basic websites through the controversial Free Basics programme (Song, 2016).

Such initiatives are an indication not only of the way in which new kinds of technology present challenges to the traditional business models of fixed-line and mobile operators, but also of the threats that they can pose by creating entirely new networks that do not even need to use the connectivity that such companies provide. The former are but one example of the perceived threat that so-called Over The Top (OTT) initiatives can create as a result of the blurring of function and technology. For traditional broadcasters, audio, video, and data can now all readily be received over the Internet without the need for a multi-system operator to be in control. Likewise, third party messaging and calling services provided by Twitter, WhatsApp, and Facebook Messenger are swiftly replacing mobile operator services. Rather than being seen as a threat, traditional operators will need to build on this opportunity to create new business models that will continue to generate profit. At their simplest, these involve new methods of charging, which focus especially on payments for data rather than calls and texts, and also moving towards monthly contract-based packages rather than pay-as-you-go or pre-paid agreements (see Figure 2.4). As the GSMA (2015a, p. 18) notes, 'Tiered data plans are an increasingly common tariff trend, especially in developed markets. A growing proportion of contract tariffs now offer unlimited voice minutes and text messages.' However, as Figure 2.3 indicates, it is only in the richer countries of the world that monthly contract-based payments dominate. At a global level, prepaid connections account for 76 per cent of all mobile connections, but this rises to 96 per cent in Africa, compared with only 43 per cent in Europe and 23 per cent in northern America. As the economic and social

---

[21] <http://www.google.com/loon>.   [22] <https://www.google.com/get/projectlink>.
[23] <https://info.internet.org/en>.

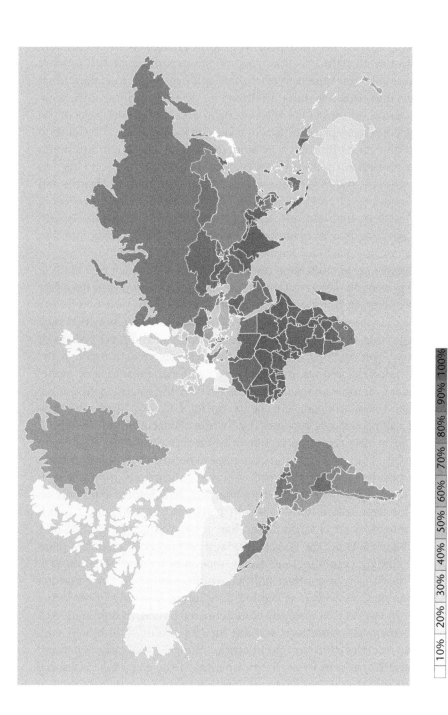

| 10% | 20% | 30% | 40% | 50% | 60% | 70% | 80% | 90% | 100% |

Figure 2.3 Prepaid connections as a percentage of total connections, (excluding cellular M2M), Q4 2015 © GSMA Intelligence

Source: GSMA.

structures of much of Africa and Asia evolve, it is likely that this balance will change substantially, and will enable new business models to emerge.

According to Kearney (2012), there are four distinct areas where different types of company are competing: mobile voice, where operators face the challenge of their revenues and profits being eroded by OTT; messaging, where there is a challenge in reversing the shift from SMS to social networking and instant messaging; media, where there is a battle for consumer mindshare and future relevance; and cloud services, which open up opportunities in consumer and enterprise businesses. These present very different challenges and options for the various stakeholders involved. For governments, concerned with universal access provision, maximizing taxation revenue, ensuring fair competition, and building technical and business capacity, OTT can offer new opportunities. However, if traditional operators are not able to generate sufficient revenue, they are less likely to pay high auction prices for access to spectra, and will not invest in the roll-out of infrastructure in areas where margins are low or non-existent, thereby delaying delivery of universal service obligations. For mobile operators, there is therefore a need to innovate with new business models, diversifying their businesses, and building new relationships with those providing services across their networks. This is becoming increasingly hard, though, especially at a time when Google and Facebook are now beginning to deliver their own networks as noted previously. The latest such initiative was the announcement by Facebook at the GSMA's Mobile World Congress in March 2016 of its Telecom Infra Project, to be developed in partnership with operators and other technology companies, to reduce the cost of deploying mobile telecom network infrastructure.[24] A further challenge for governments is the difficulty of taxing the providers of OTT services, especially if they are major international corporations that generate profits across the world, but only pay tax in countries where they are registered and which have the lowest tax rates (see Sections 5.4 and 6.4).

Social media and other OTT services offer considerable potential for the development of new businesses that develop products that can enhance the lives of the poorest and most marginalized. However, to date, they have primarily benefited those who have access to, and can afford, connectivity to mobile broadband. As I have just emphasized, the very nature of these services is threatening the future roll-out of the networks upon which they rely. Collaborative initiatives such as Facebook's Telecom Infra Project offer new partnership models that may help to resolve this paradox. However, it is also evident that in such a fluid context there is potential for innovative entrepreneurs not only to generate profits but also to serve the needs of poor

---

[24] <http://newsroom.fb.com/news/2016/02/introducing-the-telecom-infra-project>.

people (see also Banks, 2013; VisionMobile with Ericsson, 2012). Nick Hughes, who played a leading role in the development of the M-PESA mobile money service in Kenya,[25] and has now developed M-KOPA[26] as a new means of delivering cost-effective electricity in eastern Africa, for example emphasizes the need to combine new technological solutions that deliver on the real needs of poor people, commenting that:

> We have built M-KOPA based on customer needs and we use smart technology to solve problems. In Africa, over 700 million people lack access to reliable power and have no alternatives but to spend precious household income on small amounts of poor quality fuel depending on their limited available cash. Mobile money allows us to offer a new delivery model. We produce good quality solar energy systems that are connected to the mobile network using embedded GSM technology and that we can monitor remotely. We then allow customers to buy units of credit for a specific solar device by making small payments to us.[27]

2.7 5G and the Internet of Things

Looking to the future, there is much discussion about the next generation of mobile technology (5G), and the potential of the Internet of Things (IoT) to transform yet again the ways through which people interact with technology, or indeed through which technologies interact with people (Tafazolli, 2006; David, 2008; Prasad, 2014; Rodriguez, 2015). The future is explored in more detail in Chapter 6, but it is important here to summarize briefly some of the technological aspects associated with these two new, and closely interrelated, clusters of technologies. Both of them have enormous potential to open up the Internet to everyone, and especially the poorest and the most marginalized. For them to benefit from such technologies, though, their interests must be built into the technological considerations at an early stage.

There is much debate about what 5G technologies will actually look like. However, most agree that it represents a fundamentally different way of thinking about digital communication, with organizations such as the Wireless World Research Forum (WWRF, 2015) and Next Generation Mobile Networks (NGMN, 2015) each promoting their own particular vision of what this future might be. At the heart of 5G is the view that everyone and everything should be connected digitally. While not all of the necessary technologies have been invented, this ambitious agenda focuses around six main principles: that data rates will be significantly enhanced to the level of tens of

---

[25] <http://www.safaricom.co.ke/personal/m-pesa>.   [26] <http://www.m-kopa.com>.
[27] <http://www.leadersleague.com/en/news/nick-hughes-father-of-m-pesa-and-co-founder-of-m-kopa>.

megabits per second; that massive sensor networks will require hundreds of thousands of simultaneous connections; that coverage will become universal; that efficiency in the use of spectra will be substantially improved; that signalling efficiency should be enhanced; and that latency, the time delay a signal takes to get from its source to a destination, will also be improved. Figure 2.4 illustrates the NGMN's definition of use categories in their 5G

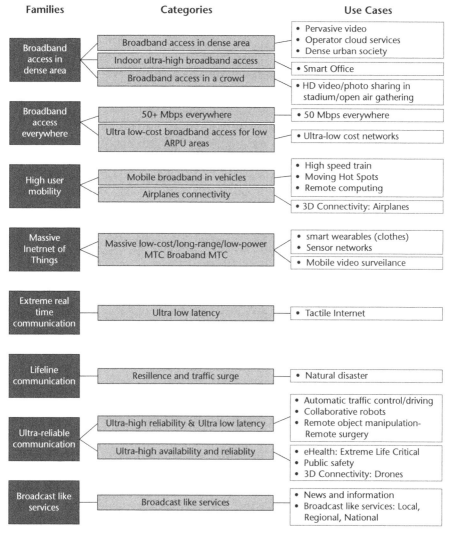

Figure 2.4 The Next Generation Mobile Networks' definition of 5G use categories
Source: Next Generation Mobile Networks (2015, p. 25).

vision, and highlights the pervasive nature of 5G. As the WWRF (2015, p. 4) puts it:

> Wireless communications are expected to dominate everything, everywhere, mainly empowered by revolutionary 5G radio network technologies. Accelerated by the dramatic impact of applications of the kinds of social networking (currently accounting for 10% of total data traffic), and machine-to-machine (M2M) communications (600–800 million active cellular M2M devices by 2019), the centre of gravity for 5G will be shifted further to application-driven connectivity, transparently deployed over various technologies, infrastructures, users and devices, towards realizing the concept of Internet of Everything.

The concept of an interconnected network of devices has been discussed for many years, although the term the 'Internet of Things' was only coined by Kevin Ashton in 1999 in connection with his work on radio-frequency identification (RFID) (Hersent et al., 2012; Colina et al., 2015; Greengard, 2015). It is now an integral part of the 5G vision. Demand for connectivity has previously been limited broadly to the number of people in the world, but the addition of communicating 'things' multiplies that demand dramatically. This offers huge potential for new revenue streams and the interest of companies wishing to exploit this potential is clear. However, to realize this potential it is essential for new technologies to be developed that can manage the resultant manifold increases in data as well as the required speeds and universality of connectivity. Although there is much research, for example, on smart driverless cars, they cannot be introduced unless the volumes of data that need to be transmitted can be handled everywhere that the cars wish to go.

One key impact of this has already been recognized, namely the need to introduce a new Internet Protocol to enable the vast number of new devices to be identified and thus connected. The existing Internet Protocol that identifies and locates computers on a network (IPv4) uses 32-bit addresses, and by the late 1990s it was apparent that this would be insufficient to handle the rapidly increasing number of devices. Consequently, a new system, IPv6, was developed which uses 128-bit addresses, theoretically permitting approximately 3.4×10^{38} addresses. It also has other advantages, such as permitting hierarchical address allocation methods, and it simplifies and improves multicast addressing. One of the challenges in the roll-out of IPv6, though, has been that it is not inter-operable with IPv4, and this has meant that people have been reluctant to make the transition while their existing equipment is functioning.

The potential of the Internet of Things is vast, both for things that most people would see as being positive, but also for negative purposes (see also Chapter 6). In essence, the Internet of Things makes use of embedded devices or sensors that have limited processing capacity, memory, or power requirements and are connected to wireless networks. These have potential in all works of life, although to date most attention has been paid to their use in urban environments (smart cities) and in the automotive industry (smart cars). The technology behind driverless smart cars, though, could readily be adapted to enable people with disabilities, and especially the blind, to move around in complex environments. Some other relevant applications of wireless networks in a development context include the following: their use in environmental monitoring, where such things as water quality measurements can be taken, and warnings given of potential landslides; in agriculture, where sensor networks can be used to monitor pasture quality for nomads, or the condition of crops stored in barns or silos; in health, through such things as fitness devices, and ensuring that medicines are genuine; and in disaster management and the delivery of relief services (ITU and Cisco, 2016). Nevertheless, to date, as with so many other examples of ICTs, maps of sensor nodes show that the vast majority are in the richer countries of the world, and even in poorer countries they are to be found mainly in urban rather than rural contexts (Zennaro and Bagula, 2015).

2.8 Incubators, Digital Hubs, and App Development

App development, and the associated digital hubs and incubators where it is often encouraged to take place, are one other area of technology that is often seen as particularly significant for development in poorer countries. This is a field in which there are ardent advocates (Southwood and Tijani, 2012; De Bastion, 2013), and equally ardent critics, both of which rely largely on rhetoric and sometimes wishful thinking in their assertions. It is indeed hard to make clear judgements as to the potential role of hubs, incubators, and app development in any one country or region, in large part because of the diversity of experiences and the lack of rigorous systematic evaluations of their role.

Whilst some initiatives, such as the iHub in Nairobi (Figure 2.5)[28] are often cited as successful examples of African innovation, these are few in number and often owe as much to particularly charismatic individuals such as the iHub's founders Erik Hersman and Juliana Rotich as they do to the concept of an incubator or digital hub. Nairobi's iHub has indeed spawned software innovations such as Ushahidi, which developed crowdsourcing mapping

---

[28] <http://www.ihub.co.ke>.

Figure 2.5 BRCK and the iHub in Nairobi
Source: Author, November 2014.

software after the post-election violence in 2008[29] and hardware such as the BRCK, which is 'a rugged, self-powered, mobile WiFi device which connects people and things to the Internet in areas of the world with poor infrastructure'.[30] However, there is little evidence yet to suggest that app development will contribute more widely to the economic growth of poor countries in the short term, apart from in a small number of particularly well-suited instances.

VisionMobile (2014, p. 17) has provided some salutary warnings about the potential of app development to play a leading role in economic growth in poor countries, noting that 'The revenue distribution is so heavily skewed towards the top that just 1.6% of developers make multiples of the other 98.4% combined. It seems extremely unlikely that the market can sustain anything like the current level of developers for many more years.' Moreover, the authors go on to point out that:

At the bottom of the app revenue pile, 24% of all developers that are interested in making money make nothing at all. A further 23% of developers make something but less than $100 per app per month. This level of revenue is unlikely to cover the

---

[29] <https://www.ushahidi.com>.   [30] <http://www.brck.com>.

basic costs of a desktop machine for development, test devices and an account to publish apps. (VisionMobile, 2014, p. 17)

Likewise, as Pon (2016, p. 6) has argued:

> despite its egalitarian appeal, developer participation in the app economy is heavily skewed toward the largest and richest economies, with the United States, Japan and China dominant. Because the app markets function as winner-take-all markets, the top-ranked apps in the most lucrative markets earn multiple orders of magnitude more revenue than low-ranked apps in markets of the Global South . . . . For lower-income countries, the outlook is relatively bleak: Most have very few developers, and even those who had significant numbers of developers—for example, India—earned very little revenue.

The reality therefore is that whilst some people will undoubtedly make a good living out of app development, this can never be a secure foundation for the economies of most poorer countries.

It is therefore interesting to consider why such emphasis has been placed on app development in the context of digital hubs, some 314 of which were active in Africa, and 287 in South and South-East Asia in 2016 (Du Boucher, 2016). Part of the answer would seem to lie in the role that international organizations, donors, and the private sector have played in encouraging their development. Incubator initiatives have been widely promoted by external agencies, such as the World Bank's *info*Dev programme[31] (see also *info*Dev, 2009; Kelly and Firestone, 2016), which has long championed the important role of entrepreneurship, and developed what it claimed was the world's one-stop shop for know-how on business incubators in its incubation toolkit.[32] As *info*Dev argues: 'Entrepreneurs in developing countries face many challenges in their journey to launch high-growth companies. Yet when they succeed, entrepreneurs can act as powerful agents of change—creating jobs, boosting economic development, and delivering essential products and services to those who need them most.'[33] Over the years, *info*Dev has undoubtedly supported some exciting and ground-breaking work, but as this quotation indicates, its focus has become increasingly influenced by the flawed economic growth agenda that has dominated development rhetoric in recent years (see Chapter 1). The trouble is that there is very little evidence in the form of rigorous monitoring and evaluation that such initiatives have succeeded in bringing substantial benefits to the poorest people and countries.

In addition to the power of multilateral donors such as the World Bank in providing financial support for incubators, the growing influence of the private sector in development governance has also played a major role in leading

---

[31] <http://www.infodev.org>.   [32] <http://www.infodev.org/about>.
[33] <http://www.infodev.org/about>.

to the promotion of such initiatives (Du Boucher, 2016; Kelly and Firestone, 2016). The logic is clear. If incubators can help to enhance entrepreneurial skills and encourage relevant technological development, then companies that support such initiatives have an opportunity to benefit directly from their 'outputs'. Invariably, companies that support digital hubs and incubators make lucrative employment offers to the most able participants, thereby neatly removing them as potential competitors, or at the very least preventing them from developing the small and medium-sized enterprises that are so often seen as being the life blood of a vibrant economy. Another key failing of the incubator model is that, while providing a locus for techies to come together in a supportive and innovative environment, they often fail to provide the necessary business skills to enable such potential entrepreneurs to build their own businesses.

Meanwhile, other interests are also at work in shaping and exploiting such incubator initiatives. This is perhaps most apparent in the promotion of the larger concept of smart cities in Africa and Asia, such as Kigali Innovation City,[34] Ethiopia's Ethio ICT Village,[35] and Modi's promise to build 100 smart cities in India by 2022.[36] Despite there being little evidence that these can transform the economic vitality of a country by themselves, international consultants leap at the opportunity to promote them, especially when supported by the donor community. A typical example was the decision by the Government of Kenya in 2008 to create the Konza Technology City as a flagship of its Vision 2030 project. The initial concept was that this would enable Kenya to benefit from the global Business Process Outsourcing and Information Technology Enabled Services sector (BPO/ITES).[37] The initiative was supported by the International Finance Corporation, and a master plan was developed by international consultants, who encouraged the belief that the city would create 20,000 new jobs, and position Kenya firmly on the international BPO/ITES map. As with so many similar initiatives across the world, progress has been slower than anticipated, and there has been little impact yet on the ground. Numerous other smaller scale digital city initiatives have been promoted across developing countries, with as yet few practical results. If international agencies and companies are in part responsible for the promotion of such initiatives, local factors also undoubtedly come into play, not least the potential windfalls that individuals can make through land speculation, and the wider financial benefits that can be gained especially for the construction industry.

None of this is to suggest that encouraging ICT-based entrepreneurial development is always mistaken, but it is to argue that more often than not the

---

[34] <http://www.focus.rw/wp/2016/05/government-of-rwanda-launches-kigali-innovation-city-flagship-project>.
[35] <http://www.ethioictvillage.gov.et/index.php/en/about-ethio-ict-village/background>.
[36] <http://tribune.com.pk/story/870190/india-builds-first-smart-city-as-urban-population-swells>.
[37] <http://www.konzacity.go.ke/the-vision/history>.

Box 2.1 SUCCESS FACTORS FOR INCUBATORS AND DIGITAL HUBS

- Organic in design and growth, building upon existing expertise and skills, located in a particular place; they will rarely succeed if they are simply 'planted' in a new location without the necessary preconditions being in place.
- A well-educated population with the necessary technical skill sets, particularly in computer science and business; co-location in proximity with high quality universities can be beneficial.
- The necessary physical infrastructure, particularly high speed broadband and reliable electricity, must be available.
- An environment in which both technical and business skills can be learnt and developed; far too often digital hubs focus on the former, with insufficient attention being paid to the latter.
- Internally driven, rather than externally imposed; whilst foreign investment is beneficial, there has to be sufficient enthusiasm, leadership, and commitment within the country to enable them to thrive.
- High-level, politically savvy and passionate champions to drive such initiatives forward and build confidence and trust in their potential success.
- A supportive policy environment, which provides the necessary financial and taxation incentives to attract investment.

---

necessary conditions are not in place in most countries for such initiatives to deliver the ambitious transformations that their advocates promote. Box 2.1 highlights seven important interrelated factors that need to be in place for incubators and digital hubs to succeed.

Overall, the evidence suggests that the much-hyped potential of app development, digital hubs, and smart cities in poorer countries is unlikely to be a major driver of economic growth. Indeed, they might often be more of a drain on scarce government resources that could better be used to support poor people directly in other ways. In some instances, where the right constellation of factors comes together, they may generate some business opportunities, but these are unlikely to do much to reduce inequalities, either between poor and rich countries, or between the rich and the marginalized within poor countries, unless specific initiatives are put in place for local developers to generate apps that are relevant to the needs of the poorest and most marginalized in their countries. The challenge, though, is to find ways that they can generate appropriate financial compensation for so doing.

2.9 The Importance of a Technical Understanding

A rigorous understanding of the technical aspects of ICTs is essential for the introduction of any effective interventions in the interests of the poor and marginalized. This chapter has provided a short introduction to some of the more important technical issues that are of specific relevance for reducing the inequalities caused by the past use of ICTs for development. By understanding their impact, and realizing the potential that these technologies have, those committed to effecting change in the interest of the poorest may be able to introduce initiatives that truly use ICTs to reduce global inequalities. Building on this framework, the remaining chapters of the book address some of the wider cross-cutting themes, particularly in the political and cultural spheres, that are influencing the roll-out of ICT4D interventions, including the challenges of partnerships, regulation, and security. Chapter 3 begins this task by exploring key aspects of the promotion of ICT initiatives in the international arena, focusing especially on some of the fraught discussions that have occurred over the last decade with respect to Internet governance.

It is important to conclude this chapter by reflecting on some of the key systemic and overarching dimensions of the technologies discussed earlier. Four conclusions seem particularly pertinent. First, it cannot be stressed enough that technology is not neutral, and is developed with particular interests and intent in mind. Certainly, it often has unintended consequences, and these must be taken into account in any evaluation of their impact, but it must always be recalled that it is the profit motive that has been the core private sector interest in driving the global expansion and pervasiveness of ICTs. It is also very important that practitioners and academics alike should recognize that far too many ICT4D initiatives have been built on an instrumental view of technology, and that if initiatives are truly going to benefit the poor and the marginalized, they must deliver on the real needs of poor people within the wider structural contexts that shape their lives. ICTs are very effective accelerators, and unless structural changes can be made in the societies within which they are used such technologies will only increase existing inequalities.

Second, much greater attention needs to be paid to the sustainability of ICTs in the broadest sense. To date, most ICT initiatives have been based on inbuilt redundancy; hardware and software products are designed to last for only a limited time, to be replaced by newer and better solutions within a relatively short period, thus ensuring that customers continue to purchase these products on a regular basis every two to three years. This business model has been very successful for the companies manufacturing and selling ICTs, but it is diametrically opposed to the increasingly prominent rhetoric of sustainability associated, for example, with the SDGs. Moreover, there are also wider concerns about the energy demands of ICTs, and the impact on the environment of their production that still require addressing more comprehensively. In this context, it should be noted that simpler, older, and more sustainable ICTs, such as radios, are still often the most effective way of providing information and entertainment to poor people.

Third, this chapter has emphasized the very different approaches of Proprietary and Open technological initiatives, suggesting that the fundamental principle underlying their differences is an ethical one, namely whether individual or communal interests are of most importance. Whilst Open solutions are indeed appealing if ICTs are to be used to support poor people and marginalized communities, appropriate business models need to be developed that enable their effective production and dissemination. Governments have a key role to play in promoting and supporting Open solutions, since they are the only entity specifically intended to serve the interests of all of their citizens. However, the choice to do so will depend largely on whether their societies are built primarily on individualistic or communal interests, and the present global dominance of fundamentally selfish individual interests suggests that those advocating Open solutions will continue to struggle.

Finally, the chapter has emphasized the great importance of wireless communication and spectrum management in influencing the availability and quality of mobile communication and information sharing. The ever-increasing role of the Internet in the daily lives of everyone in the world means that access to its benefits at an affordable price is of paramount importance. To be sure, there has to be appropriate content for these benefits to be realized, but without basic connectivity the inequalities between rich and poor will accelerate at an even faster rate than has been the case over the last two decades. Hence, the following chapters pay particular attention to such things as Internet governance and the importance of regulation and spectrum allocation. The benefits of the Internet, though, must also be considered alongside the challenges that it poses, most notably on issues relating to privacy and security, and these are explored specifically in Chapter 6.

3

The International Policy Arena

ICTs and Internet Governance

Over the last decade, the notion of multi-stakeholderism has become one of the core leitmotifs of discussions about ICTs in the international arena. This chapter explores why this has been the case, how and why different organizations define multi-stakeholderism in particular ways, and what the implications of this focus have been, especially in the context of Internet governance and the ways in which the poorest and most marginalized might benefit from using ICTs. The concept of multi-stakeholderism is grounded upon the increasing recognition and acceptance that it is useful to divide organizations into three key types or sectors: governments, the private sector, and civil society. Each of these groupings contributes in specific and different ways to debates over the delivery of ICT initiatives. They all have different interests. All too often, though, these concepts, and indeed the notion of multi-stakeholderism itself, are taken for granted, with their meanings being insufficiently dissected and discussed (although, see Martens, 2007; DeNardis, 2014; Hofmann, 2016). This chapter seeks to problematize these issues, and explore their implications for development outcomes.

The chapter begins with a summary of the characteristics and interests of the various organizational sectors represented in international discussions and debates relating to the use of ICTs. This is important, because far too often they have been seen as 'natural', or obvious categories, rather than being constructed as particular entities with specific interests. Unless these interests are recognized, it is impossible to understand their implications for ICT4D. The chapter then briefly explores the evolution of international discussions about the role of ICTs in development over the last decade, especially with respect to the post-WSIS discussions (for a review of the earlier period, see Unwin, 2009) and the low profile of ICTs in the formulation of the UN's Sustainable Development Goals in 2015. The discussions leading to international agreements are particularly important, not only because they consume very significant amounts of time, and thus expense, on behalf of those who participate, but also because they seek to set the broad parameters and legal structures within which initiatives that promote the use of ICTs in different parts of the world must function. This is a highly contested field, with many different organizations, each with their own interests, competing for prominence in determining the global agenda, particularly on Internet governance. To illustrate this, the very different approaches and styles of the International Telecommunication Union (ITU), the Internet Corporation for Assigned Names and Numbers (ICANN), and the Internet Governance Forum (IGF) are used to exemplify the interests of governments, the private sector, and civil society respectively. Chapter 4 then builds on this framework to explore the implementation of ICT4D multi-sector partnership initiatives in practice on the ground in poor countries.

3.1 Stakeholders in the International ICT Arena

Historically, people have sought to understand the organization of their lives in many different ways, not least through their religious and cultural belief systems. However, as Europeans increasingly came to dominate the world from the sixteenth century onwards, so too did their particular way of thinking about the organization of communities and states. These ideas were largely derived from ancient Greek views, and especially those of Plato who conceptualized and differentiated communities in terms of their economies, societies, political systems, and religions or cultures (Unwin, 1998). Regardless of the particular theoretical or philosophical framework adopted, the view that there are social, political, cultural, and economic dimensions to people's lives has become all pervasive (Howard and King, 1985). Cutting across these dimensions, and again largely building on European ideas that were shaped in the early Enlightenment of the seventeenth century (Unwin, 1998, 2009), are governments, the private sector, and civil society. Chapter 1 emphasized the importance of these sectors in any society, and that the balance of power and influence between them has ebbed and flowed throughout history. The following subsections provide a brief account of the roles and interests of each of these different sectors so that their contributions in the international ICT4D arena may be better understood in the sections that follow.

3.1.1 *Governments and ICTs*

In their simplest form, governments are the people or entities that exercise political authority over a state, and can take many different forms depending on the character of the political system. Of crucial importance, governments are the only one of the three sectors that should, at least theoretically, have the interests of all of their citizens, and thus particularly the poor and the marginalized, at their heart. However, complexities arise with such a simple definition of government, not least in terms of the regional and international agreements to which governments assent. For the purpose of this discussion, the UN system and regional groupings of countries such as the European Union (EU), CARICOM in the Caribbean, or the African Union (AU) are also included under the heading of government. The most important international organization in the field of ICTs is the ITU, but it must be recognized that many other UN bodies, such as UNESCO, the FAO (Food and Agriculture Organization), UNDP (United Nations Development Programme), and the UN's Department of Economic and Social Affairs (UN DESA) also have interests in ICTs, which all too often have led to competition rather than cooperation between these organizations. Indeed, when regional bodies are also taken into consideration the potential for duplication, overlap, and confusion in policy-making and practical delivery escalates considerably. Regional international organizations, such as the Commonwealth Telecommunications Organisation (CTO) with its fifty-three member countries,[1] or the Caribbean Telecommunications Union (CTU), with twenty members,[2] can nevertheless play a crucial role in helping reach consensus on key ICT issues, and are important for the effective delivery of policies and good practices on the ground.

It is also important to consider the different agencies of governments that are involved in the field of ICTs, and represent their countries in international forums and negotiations. In general, most countries have a Ministry of Telecommunications or ICT, often emanating from the old national post and telecommunications organizations. Following privatization of their telecommunications sectors, many then also created regulatory agencies that operate at various degrees of independence from the ministries (see Chapter 5). This can create challenges in terms of representation of governments in international forums, although in general regulators tend to be the representatives in regulatory forums, and ministers at ministerial events. Another challenge is that the ICT or telecommunications portfolio is often quite a minor one in terms of government priorities, and relatively junior, albeit often highly able people, tend to be appointed to these posts. Power structures within governments across the world play an important role in shaping the efficacy of ICT policy development and implementation (Adomi, 2011). It is often only when senior government figures take a leadership role, as with President Paul Kagame in Rwanda who also has the benefit of being ably assisted by a young and charismatic minister, Jean Philbert Nsengimana, that effective action takes

---

[1] <http://www.cto.int>.   [2] <http://www.ctu.int>.

place in the ICT sector. Moreover, an important lesson that still needs to be learnt is that many different ministries have to be involved across government if successful ICT initiatives are to be deployed, including not only the ICT ministry, but also the respective sectoral ministry, such as health or education, the finance ministry, and the infrastructure or power ministry especially with its responsible for electricity (ITU, 2015a). Another important dimension of government in the context of ICTs is the role that bilateral and multilateral donors play in contributing finance to the development of ICT initiatives.

For much of the twentieth century, governments also played an important economic role through public sector companies or corporations, although the extent of these varied, and continues to vary, between different political and economic systems. As Chapter 1 emphasized, a key feature of the rise of neoliberalism over the last thirty years has been the rapid privatization of many of these public sector companies, and particularly utility companies, such as telecommunications operators (Naughton, 2016). Hence, the relative balance of power between governments and the private sector has shifted towards the latter. This has in turn led to much greater demands by private sector companies to be engaged in international governance, and these are addressed later in this chapter as well as in Chapter 4 (see also Martens, 2007). A further important role of many governments in the context of development has been their role as either donors or recipients of Official Development Assistance (ODA), both bilaterally and multilaterally.

It is also important to distinguish clearly between government and governance, because all too often in the context of ICTs the term e-governance is used when what is actually meant is e-government. In contrast to the notion of 'government' as defined above, 'governance' refers to the processes and structures whereby social norms and institutions are maintained, and it can be used to refer not only to governments, but also to other types of organization (see Bevir, 2012, for a useful discussion). Thus, e-government should properly be used to refer only to the delivery of government services through ICTs, whereas e-governance is a much more radical concept concerned with organizing the processes and relationships between governments and citizens through the use of ICTs. The delivery of identity cards, passports, voting mechanisms, and taxation forms through digital means is part of e-government, whereas the ways through which these technologies might be used to create a different kind of society, hopefully one that is fairer, more open, and transparent is what e-governance is about (Guida and Crow, 2009; Unwin, 2009).

3.1.2 The Private Sector: Companies and Businesses

Definitions of the private sector vary, with it often being considered as everything other than the public sector. However, such a definition would include voluntary organizations, and I prefer to include voluntary organizations as an integral part of civil society, rather than the private sector, for the reasons outlined in Section 3.1.3. Hence, for present purposes, the private sector is defined in a more restricted manner as companies or businesses that are usually intended to generate a profit. In essence, the private sector is about making money for its owners, employees, and shareholders. However, there are many different types of company, established by varying legal instruments across the world. Social enterprises, which are designed to use commercial methods to enhance human well-being, can for example be either for-profit or non-profit.

An increasingly important group of stakeholders in international ICT forums is also the growing number of private foundations that seek to use the wealth generated by families and individuals to do what their founders deem to be beneficial. Typical of these are the Bill and Melinda Gates Foundation,[3] and the William and Flora Hewlett Foundation,[4] but they also include foundations such as the World Economic Forum,[5] which is now seeking to play a greater role in discussions on the governance of the Internet through its Internet for All initiative. Significantly, the wealth and power of many of these foundations mean that they can bypass, and sometimes undermine, much traditional bilateral and multilateral aid delivery, having both positive but also negative effects (Pratt et al., 2012). Because of their very diverse nature and governance arrangements, it is not easy to situate foundations within the threefold structure of government, private sector, and civil society, but for present purposes they will mainly be included under the private sector heading, primarily because most of their wealth has been generated from the corporate business sector, and accrued in private hands. One real problem with development initiatives supported by such foundations, though, is that the source of their wealth, as well as the business acumen and interests of many of their founders, mean that they generally come to the table with a particular private sector business approach to development. Whilst this can indeed have many positive benefits in terms of management style and efficiency, it is an approach based largely on economic growth and the profit motive, and is thus closely allied to the hegemonic economic growth agenda for development outlined in Chapter 1. All too often such foundations fail to understand the real needs of poor and marginalized people, and focus insufficiently on the reduction of the inequalities that the businesses of their founders initially helped to create through their focus on profit and growth.

Within private sector companies it is also important to distinguish between the business parts of their activities and their Corporate Social and/or Environmental

---

[3] <http://www.gatesfoundation.org>.   [4] <http://www.hewlett.org>.
[5] <https://www.weforum.org/>.

Responsibility agendas (CSR/CSER) (Campbell, 2012; Williams, 2015). Many small-scale ICT initiatives have been funded by usually well-intentioned CSR programme, but these have often not gone to scale or been sustainable, because of a failure to build a sustainable business model into their approach, expecting other donors or governments to pay for the wider roll-out, which is frequently beyond their means or interest (see Chapter 4 for further discussion of partnerships). A key lesson to be learnt is therefore that for sustainable ICT4D initiatives, which are more than just proof-of-concept or pilot projects, it is essential for the business end of corporations, rather than just their CSR departments, to be actively involved in their planning and implementation.

A plethora of companies at all scales and in many different sectors are important for the effective implementation of ICT4D initiatives, and seek to play an increasingly powerful role in international forums (ITU, 2015a). Size, however, matters considerably in enabling participation in such activities. Small companies simply cannot afford to engage in the very considerable number of international ICT meetings that take place regularly throughout the year. Those companies that do consider such engagement worthwhile are also drawn from remarkably few countries. Thus, 198 of the 431, or 46 per cent of the Sector Members of the ITU in 2016, are drawn from only nine countries, dominated by the USA (62), Japan (30), and the UK (23).[6] It is no coincidence that the major ICT companies of the global capitalist economy, such as Google, Facebook, Cisco, Microsoft, Intel, Ericsson, Huawei, and ZTE are seeking to ensure that their voice is heard in such forums as they attempt to shape the world economy in their own interests (Martens, 2007).

Another particularly important ICT private sector category is the business associations that represent industry within international forums, one of the most important and influential of which is the GSM Association (GSMA)[7] which represents the interests of mobile operators and unites nearly 800 operators with more than 250 companies in the broader mobile system. Universities and research institutes should also be included within the broad heading of the private sector, since they are increasingly now run primarily as devolved private businesses for individual profit rather than as state-run institutions for the advancement of knowledge in the common interest, despite many theoretically still being state administered. All too often, academic research serves the established power structures and interests of the private sector, rather than those of the poorest and most marginalized people and communities.

---

[6] <https://www.itu.int/online/mm/scripts/gensel11>, accessed 20 April 2016.
[7] <http://www.gsma.com>.

3.1.3 *Civil Society*

There are those who persist in seeing civil society as being part of the private sector (see for example, Government of the Netherlands, 2016), on the ground that it includes the private sphere of the family. However, most global multi-stakeholder forums now specifically recognize the existence of civil society as a separate and distinct voice, and this is itself justification for its inclusion here as a separate category or sector. However, a distinct civil society contribution is also fundamentally important in its own right. The notion of civil society is complex, and has evolved through many different forms since its emergence in early Greek thought (Glasius et al., 2002). It was given new impetus following the collapse of the Soviet Union in the late 1980s and early 1990s, alongside the growing dominance of neoliberal ideology, which reduced the role of the state. Whilst some aspects of the state were devolved to the private sector, other aspects of the welfare system were increasingly expected to be delivered by civil society, or what was sometimes called the third sector (Etzioni, 1973).

The meaning, identity, and role of civil society have long been contested, but a useful starting point is the definition proposed by the London School of Economics' Centre for Civil Society, which describes it as 'the arena of uncoerced collective action around shared interests, purposes and values. In theory, its institutional forms are distinct from those of the state, family and market, though in practice, the boundaries between state, civil society, family and market are often complex, blurred and negotiated'[8] (for a longer discussion, see Unwin, 2009, 2015). Fukuyama (2001, p. 11) provides a somewhat simpler definition of its role, noting that 'Civil society serves to balance the power of the state and to protect individuals from the state's power.' This highlights an important role that civil society is seen as serving on the international ICT stage, where it can act to balance some of the excesses resulting from unfettered private sector expansion of ICTs that drive inequality, by reminding governments of their responsibilities in serving the interests of the world's poorest and most marginalized peoples.

There has long been a belief that civil society has a broadly more positive role than either governments or the private sector. Chandhoke (2002, p. 36) has summarized this nicely, noting that 'contemporary thinking gives us a picture of a global civil society that seems to be supremely uncontaminated by either the power of states or that of markets'. However, the reality is often rather different. Civil society organizations are themselves fraught with the internal political dynamics that are encountered in the other two sectors, and in their pursuit of continued funding often become self-seeking entities that are more concerned with their own survival than with the purpose for which they were

---

[8] <http://www.lse.ac.uk/collections/CCS/what_is_civil_society.htm>, accessed 21 April 2005.

originally created. Moreover, whether they have any real power to transform the existing global governance agenda that has become dominated by the alliance between governments and the private sector seems very unlikely.

Broadly speaking, civil society includes non-governmental organizations (NGOs), trades unions, religious organizations, voluntary organizations, charities, disabilities groups, and community organizations. As noted earlier, the boundaries between the private sector and civil society do blur, especially with respect to foundations and social enterprises, but this reflects the fluidity and evolving nature of society. The idea of civil society as distinct from government and the for-profit private sector is nevertheless important, particularly because of the opportunities that it offers for alternative voices, and for practical actions that can be implemented for the benefit of the poor and marginalized. The role of civil society in ICT4D is discussed further later in this chapter, particularly with respect to the Internet Governance Forum (IGF) and the post-WSIS agenda, but it is worth emphasizing here that, as with companies and governments, civil society operates at different scales and has its own particular set of interests.

At the global scale, organizations such as the Internet Society[9] and the Association for Progressive Communications[10] have played crucial roles in helping to shape and influence international ICT policy over the last decade, particularly through the role of charismatic individuals within such organizations. Scale, however, matters, because most small civil society organizations do not have the financial wherewithal to participate in such dialogues, despite attempts by some international organizations to encourage this through the use of ICT-enabled remote-participation facilities. Where small civil society organizations have, though, played important roles is in funding and supporting innovative ICT-based interventions, many in the interests of the poorest peoples (Weigel and Waldburger, 2004; Unwin, 2009). However, all too often such small-scale initiatives have failed to go to scale or be sustainable, and once a particular external funding source, be it from governments, foundations, or crowdsourcing, has dried up, such organizations frequently turn to new avenues of funding and new ICT projects to continue to support their activities. As Fukuyama (2001, p. 18) has also noted more generically, 'it is difficult for outsiders to foster civil society in countries where it has no local roots. Foundations and government aid agencies seeking to promote voluntary associations have often simply managed to create a stratum of local elites who become skilled at writing grant proposals; the organisations they found tend to have little durability once the outside source of funds dries up.'

Such failures are also evident at a larger scale, and interestingly some of the more important and active civil society organizations working in ICT4D in the

---

[9] <http://www.internetsociety.org>.   [10] <https://www.apc.org>.

first decade of the 2000s have now closed or been restructured, often turning themselves into network-based entities in poorer countries in the southern hemisphere. It is appropriate here to recognize the important work in terms of research, advice, and implementation undertaken by organizations such as Panos,[11] based in London, which between 1987 and 2013 worked in the field of media and communication for development, and the International Institute for Communication and Development (IICD)[12] operating from The Hague between 1996 and 2016, which very much championed the use of bottom-up roundtable discussions to help shape ICT4D initiatives.

Finally, it is once again important to re-emphasize that size and wealth are crucial factors in determining the ability of civil society organizations to participate in the multitude of international ICT forums; despite the attempted use of online consultations in reaching agreements and consensus, it is mainly those at the upper levels of the hierarchy of international civil society organizations that have a voice at the top table. Hence, much responsibility is placed on the shoulders of those who lead such organizations, and have the extremely difficult task of balancing the need for visionary leadership with consensus building and participatory discussion.

3.1.4 *Voices of the Poor and Marginalized: Questions of Representation*

As will be clear from this account, the voices of the poorest and most marginalized are rarely if ever directly present in international ICT4D forums. There is therefore a very real challenge of representation in such meetings. Few participants at international ICT gatherings have anything other than a relatively shallow understanding of what poverty is really like, or have ever engaged deeply in trying to understand the needs of the poor, and how these might be delivered through ICTs. To be sure, much research has been undertaken on ICTs and poverty, and some policy-makers may have read a little of this literature, but global ICT forums remain forums of the elite and the powerful. Some civil society representatives, with their supposedly strong involvement with community groups, are most likely to be closest to understanding the needs of the poorest and the most marginalized, but even then their senior representatives at international meetings are often far removed from the reality of poverty on the ground. Theoretically, government officials, with their responsibility for all of their citizens, should be mindful of the needs of their poorest and most marginalized citizens, but all too often government representatives are drawn from ruling elites, in both rich and poor countries alike, and again do not necessarily understand or care about how ICTs might

---

[11] <http://panoslondon.panosnetwork.org>.   [12] <http://www.iicd.org>.

be able to empower poor people. Their interests often lie primarily in being re-elected. Moreover, the increasingly close relationships between governments and private sector companies mean that all too often governments favour the interests of the private sector over those of the most marginalized, in the mistaken belief that economic growth will necessarily eliminate poverty. Additionally, many of the most capable ICT ministers in poor countries are themselves drawn from the private sector, thereby reinforcing this private sector view of how to reduce poverty through the use of ICTs. The private sector itself, including the supposedly munificent founders of foundations, is primarily interested in driving economic growth and profits, and tends to see the poor and the marginalized largely as potential customers or an enhanced market. Few representative of the private sector at international ICT4D forums can lay claim to being poor. To be sure, it is inevitable that international forums are populated by elites, and many people who attend them do like to think that they have the interests of the marginalized at heart. Nevertheless, it is important that further consideration is given to this issue, and innovative ways are sought through which the balance of conversation and debate is changed. This short section highlights challenges with three particular areas: the involvement of young people, the highly sexist male-dominated character of the ICT sector itself, and the voices of those with disabilities. It does so, drawing very much on personal experience.

There is much global rhetoric about the engagement of young people in decision-making, and increasingly 'token' young people are invited to participate in international forums. Around half the world's population is under the age of 25, and this is often seen as being sufficient justification for their involvement.

* * *

As a practising academic for many years, I know that young people can indeed teach us and inspire us. Hence, during my time at the CTO, I was eager to involve young people in some relevant activities. We initiated workshops on ICTs and entrepreneurship for young people in Trinidad in 2014, and included a Hackathon as part of our Annual Forum in Mauritius in 2012. Perhaps most innovatively for an international forum, we also held a young people's panel at our e-government conference in Botswana in March 2012, instead of a ministerial panel. The ministers were in the audience, listening to the views of young people. I remember being widely criticized in advance for what was seen as a rash move, and so it was with some relief that at the end of the session one of the ministers present stood up to lead the applause.

* * *

However, my participation in meetings in which young people have been involved, particularly in various Commonwealth forums, has highlighted three particular challenges in engaging young people in global decision-making. First, there is once again a challenge of representation in the select-ion of young people to participate in such events. In most instances, the selection process leads to already privileged young people being involved, more often than not including those who aspire to positions of political leadership in their own countries. They are already active in the processes, democratic or otherwise, that lead to this hierarchical structuring of society. Second, even when they participate in international forums, many young people are simply too eager to get on and do things, particularly in the ICT sector; sitting through tedious presentations and debates that often make little progress is frequently seen as being a waste of their time. They are often quite correct in this, and we must all do more to restructure the format of such events. Third, though, whilst there is no doubt that the future belongs to younger generations, and their vision and enthusiasm is indeed often refresh-ing, their lack of experience of the issues being discussed often means that they do not have the breadth and depth of understanding to contribute proactively to the discussions. To be sure, this can be an argument for revising the topics of discussion at such forums, but the complexities of international treaty negotiations, for example, do require comprehensive knowledge of the issues and processes involved that usually benefit from an accumulation of experience and wisdom.

A second area of particular concern is the participation and representation of women in international ICT forums. This, of course, reflects in part the male dominance of the ICT sector more generally, and also the low representation of women in senior positions in government in many countries as well as in many civil society organizations. However, two aspects of this are particularly striking, and indeed concerning. First, the representation of women as speakers on panels or as moderators of such events is far too low. Convenors of such forums need to do much more to ensure that women are represented appropriately, and not just treated as symbols or tokenistically, often relegated to special sessions on 'Gender and ICTs'.

* * *

This is by no means easy, and I am sure that all of us involved in delivering such forums could do much more to achieve a better balance. Nevertheless, it was with a tiny feeling of satisfaction that the organizers of the CTO's Annual Forum in Abuja in 2014 achieved a figure of more than 40 per cent of the panellists and speakers being women.

* * *

Even more worrying than this, though, is the misogyny and behaviour of some men in the ICT sector.

Figure 3.1 Women marketing The Cloud at Telecom World, Bangkok, 2013
Source: Author, November 2013 <http://phandroid.s3.amazonaws.com/wp-content/uploads/2013/02/zte-grand-memo-girls-1.jpg>.

* * *

The main role of women at international ICT forums all too frequently appears to be dancing in the opening ceremonies or trying to attract male visitors to stands on the exhibition floor (Figure 3.1). However, this is just the tip of the iceberg. Often, there is inappropriate behaviour by men at these events, and many senior women in the sector with whom I have spoken have told me stories about experiences from which they have suffered. Understanding such behaviour is difficult, and in part it is a microcosm of wider social behaviour, reflecting cultural attitudes in different countries. However, some organizations do have codes of behaviour at conferences, and this is a practice that should be instituted much more widely. To challenge such behaviour, it is also important that cases are identified and addressed, not just hidden under the carpet. This takes great courage on behalf of the women who have been harassed, and leaders in the sector need to do much more to address this complex and highly charged issue.

* * *

A recent incident at ICANN's 2016 meeting in Morocco, where a female researcher from the Centre of Internet and Society (CIS, 2016) alleged that she had been sexually harassed is but one visible example of a much wider issue that the ICT4D community needs to address, and the challenges involved in resolving such issues. It is incumbent on everyone to act in an individual, collective, and institutional capacity to address such matters.

In the 1990s, the slogan 'Nothing about us without us' (Charlton, 1998) gradually came into use as a powerful statement by people with disabilities, demanding their participation in international discussions about matters that affect their lives.

* * *

In 2002, when working for Imfundo in Ghana, in part to explore ways through which ICTs could support people with disabilities, I remember seeing a poster on the wall of a government office that seemed to capture very well the challenges faced by people with disabilities with respect to the perceptions that others have of them (Figure 3.2). In many countries, people with disabilities are often seen as being cursed, and are sometimes still even killed at birth. Yet people with more disabilities have far more to gain from the use of ICTs than do those with fewer disabilities. To me, this seems so obvious and so important, and yet invariably people with disabilities are absent from most international forums concerning the use of ICTs. The 10 per cent or more of the world's population with disabilities are amongst the most marginalized of all people. Whilst there has been notable progress in research and practice on ways through which people with disabilities can be empowered through their use of ICTs (Bonnah Nkansah and Unwin, 2010; UNESCO, 2013), this issue is too often ignored, or relegated to the margins of discussions. When I was at the CTO, I was therefore determined to champion the cause of the use of ICTs by people with disabilities,[13] and in 2012 we convened a Ministerial Summit that involved some people with disabilities, albeit not enough.

Moving forward, though, the CTO also convened a meeting in 2014 with the Government of Antigua and Barbuda, and with the support of the ITU, which brought together people from across the Caribbean, and particularly those with disabilities, to discuss what needed to be done to ensure that people with disabilities in the region benefited more fully from the use of ICTs (Figure 3.3). This highlighted the main challenges as being concerned with funding, training, bureaucracy and politics, people's mind-sets, and the availability of technology. To overcome these, participants suggested, amongst other things, that considerable further work needs to be done in terms of capacity development, both of people with disabilities and others in society, greater government and regulatory intervention, media campaigns to enhance awareness of the potential of ICTs to transform the lives of people with disabilities, and improvements in the availability and affordability of technology.

* * *

---

[13] <https://disabilityict4d.wordpress.com>.

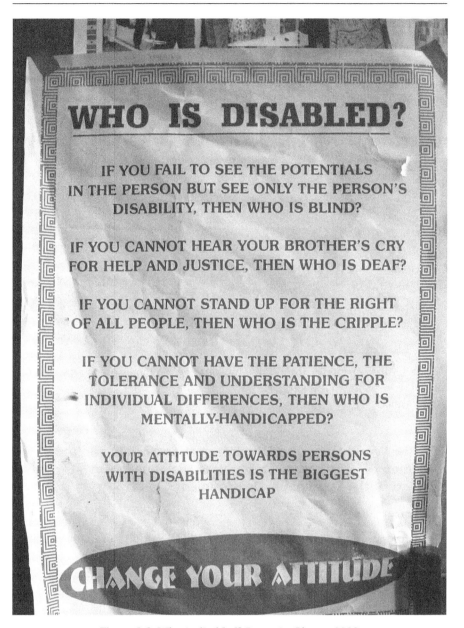

Figure 3.2 Who is disabled? Poster in Ghana, 2002
Source: Author.

Figure 3.3 Participants at the Commonwealth Telecommunications Organisation's disability workshop in Antigua, 2014
Source: Author.

3.2 The World Summit on the Information Society and the Evolution of ICT4D Multi-Stakeholder Dialogue in the Context of the Sustainable Development Goals

3.2.1 *WSIS and the SDGs*

There have been numerous accounts of the World Summit on the Information Society (WSIS) and its aftermath (ITU, 2005, 2014; Unwin, 2009; Frau-Meigs et al., 2012), many of the earlier of which wrote rather pessimistically about its likely impact (Carpentier, 2006; Souter with Jagun, 2007). Nevertheless, the WSIS process has survived, with annual update meetings, the WSIS Forums, continuing to be organized by the ITU, UNESCO, UNDP, and UNCTAD, primarily bringing together international organizations and governments, but also the private sector and civil society, to discuss matters of mutual interest with respect to the uses of ICTs for development. The Commission on Science and Technology for Development (CSTD), a subsidiary body of the UN's Economic and Social Council (ECOSOC), is charged with undertaking annual formal reviews of the WSIS outcomes, seeking inputs from all relevant facilitators and stakeholders (for an account of the complexity of reaching agreements within this forum, see Dickinson, 2016). Significantly, the substantial 2015 WSIS+10 review of progress made was warmly positive (GIP Digital Watch, 2015), and did sufficient for the UN General Assembly's 70th session in December 2015 to 'call for the continuation of annual reports on the outcomes' of the WSIS, linking this to the then newly agreed SDGs, and stating that the Annual Forums should also be continued (UNGA, 2015, p. 13).

There were undoubtedly challenges associated with the convening the original two-phase WSIS held in Geneva in 2003 and Tunis in 2005, notably disagreements over Internet governance, and a feeling by civil society organizations that they were insufficiently represented (Souter with Jagun, 2007; Unwin, 2009). Nevertheless, WSIS was the first major UN summit that involved such private sector participants; it formalized the idea of multi-stakeholder engagement being essential for effective ICT4D, it gave birth to the Internet Governance Forum (Malcolm, 2008), and with its creation of the eleven WSIS Action Lines it set in place the structure that has subsequently dominated the UN framework for the consideration of ICT4D. Whilst subsequent processes have slowly led to the US government being willing to give up its controlling influence over the Internet (see Section 3.3.3), the difficulties of finding appropriate financing mechanisms to ensure that all of the world's people can indeed benefit from access to ICTs and the Internet remain.

The UNGA (2015) high-level review provides a global perspective on the achievements of the WSIS process. It is significant that, following the usual rigmarole of recalling, welcoming, and building on and reaffirming previous resolutions, it begins by focusing explicitly on 'Information and Communication Technology for Development'. This is of note because of its explicit use of the word 'for', rather than 'and' or 'with', thereby recognizing ICT4D as the preferred UN concept, instead of the oft-used ICTD acronym. It then discusses this notion in terms of bridging the digital divide (paras 21–7), the enabling environment (paras 28–33), and financial mechanisms (paras 34–40). Nevertheless, the discussion focuses very much on economic agendas and technological inputs rather than on development outcomes, although there is indeed a welcome paragraph (16) on social benefits and inclusion. Whilst it notes that there remain significant inequalities in access to ICTs, it is remarkable how little it actually says about the specific ways through which ICTs can contribute to reducing these inequalities and contributing to development. Instead, it points to the SDGs agreed in September 2015 as replacements for the MDGs of 2000, and encourages all stakeholders to ensure that they contribute to their achievement. Three substantive sections of the report then address: Human Rights in the Information Society (paras 41–7), which ties work on ICT4D closely to the principles of the Universal Declaration of Human Rights[14] (although for a critique see Unwin, 2014); building confidence and security in the use of ICTs (paras 48–54), which addresses cyber-security challenges; and Internet governance (paras 55–63), which also touches on enhanced cooperation (paras 64–5).

As the UNGA review makes clear, the future of ICT4D, at least in terms of a UN and governmental perspective, is to be allied closely to the SDGs. However, there was a collective failure by the global community of those interested in ICT4D to ensure that ICTs featured sufficiently prominently in those Goals. As pointed out in Chapter 1, ICTs were profiled surprisingly strongly in the MDGs of 2000, where they were specifically identified in one of the eighteen targets, but they feature minimally in the SDGs, being mentioned in only four of the 169 targets. Furthermore, only one of these (Target 9c) focuses directly on ICTs, encouraging members significantly to increase access to ICTs; the other three only mention ICTs in an enabling role in the context of scholarships (4b), the empowerment of women (5b), and technology and science (17.8). The target of increasing access to ICTs is indeed to be welcomed, but given the crucial role that ICTs are playing in contemporary economic and social life it is very disappointing that such access was not elevated to a goal in its own right, or indeed mentioned specifically in the context of SDG 10 on reducing inequality. This represents a serious failing of relevant UN agencies and international organizations to raise the profile of ICT4D sufficiently strongly during the SDG lobbying process, despite the efforts of Commonwealth countries which did issue a statement on the role of ICTs in the post-2015 development goals (CTO, 2015). With hindsight, it may be that the complexity of the seventeen goals and 169 targets of the SDGs, as well as the cumbersome bureaucracies being developed around them, will mean that they fade into insignificance in terms of delivering real development impact for poor people, but the collective failure to address ICT4D appropriately therein is indeed disappointing. At the WSIS Forum in May 2015, convened some four months before the Sustainable Development Summit, there was already resignation that ICTs would not feature as one of the Goals, and so the UN agencies involved hastily put together a matrix showing how the WSIS Action Lines could contribute to each of the emerging Goals. This later reached fruition in the full WSIS-SDG Matrix (ITU, 2015b), which does little more than indicate the rather obvious point that ICTs can contribute to all aspects of development; its real significance seems to be primarily to justify the continued role of the various UN agencies in leading on each of the Action Lines.

---

[14] <http://www.un.org/en/universal-declaration-human-rights>.

3.2.2 *WSIS and Internet Governance*

The subject of Internet governance was one of the most fraught issues prior to and during the original WSIS process between 2003 and 2005, and has remained so ever since (Kleinwächter, 2004; MacLean, 2004; Unwin, 2009; DeNardis, 2014; Laprise and Musiani, 2015; Musiani et al., 2016). This was, for example, particularly evident in the difficulties in reaching agreement on the WSIS resolution for ECOSOC at the 19th Session of the CSTD in 2016 (Dickinson, 2016). Civil society organizations, particularly through the agency of the Association for Progressive Communications, had argued strongly during the original WSIS process that the Internet should be open and accessible to all, that the voice of civil society should be heard more powerfully within a multi-stakeholder context, and that US control of the Internet should be transferred to an international body (APC, 2003). One of the outcomes of the Geneva Summit was the creation of a Working Group on Internet Governance (WGIG) to try to resolve some of these issues, and in June 2005 it developed the definition of Internet governance as being 'the development and application by Governments, the private sector and civil society, in their respective roles, of shared principles, norms, rules, decision-making procedures, and programmes that shape the evolution and use of the Internet' (WGIG, 2005; see also Esterhuysen, 2005). This in turn led to the creation of the Internet Governance Forum in July 2006, as a 'multi-stakeholder dialogue on public policy issues related to key elements of Internet governance issues',[15] which has convened annually since its first meeting in October–November 2006 (for further discussion, see Section 3.3.3).

There are, though, many differing definitions of Internet governance, and this plurality of meanings has been one of the ways through which different organizations have sought to impose their own particular vision on the future of the Internet (DeNardis, 2014). As Souter (2012, p. 5) has thus noted, alongside the WSIS outcome definition, there was also that adopted by the Internet Society, namely 'a broad term used in many different contexts, [which] applies to activities as diverse as the coordination of technical standards, the operation of critical infrastructure, development, regulation, legislation, and more'. More simply, DeNardis (2014, p. 6) has emphasized that the 'primary task of Internet governance involves the design and administration of the technologies necessary to keep the Internet operational and the enactment of substantive policy around these technologies'.

The WSIS process has been important both in recognizing the existence of the three types of multi-stakeholder entity—governments, the private sector and civil society—but also in continuing to propagate this tripartite division

---

[15] <http://www.intgovforum.org/cms/aboutigf/igffaqs>.

of actors in Internet governance. Laprise and Musiani (2015) have thus emphasized that governments, the private sector, the technical community, and civil society all have differing and at times directly opposing views and objectives with respect to Internet governance and its definitions. The WSIS Annual Forums themselves have in recent years concentrated primarily on ministerial speeches and the various Action Lines facilitated and convened by different UN agencies, rather than explicitly on matters of Internet governance, although these do feature in many of the sessions. However, as DeNardis (2014, p. 9) has rightly commented with respect to Internet governance, 'arrangements of technological architecture are also arrangements of power'. Hence, those involved in debates over the governance of the Internet are still struggling in different forums to exert their influence and power over the future of this most crucial of technologies. It is to these struggles that attention now turns, focusing especially on their implications for the poor and the marginalized.

3.3 The Differing Interests of Multi-Stakeholderism: The ITU, ICANN, and the IGF

3.3.1 *On Multi-Stakeholderism and the World of International Organizations*

I first encountered the notion of multi-stakeholderism when I was writing a monograph on ICT for education partnerships for UNESCO as one of their contributions to the original WSIS process (Unwin, 2005). I had wanted to use the term multi-sector when writing this to reflect the threefold structure of partnerships between governments, the private sector, and civil society, in line with the arguments presented in Section 3.1, and opposed to the notion of public–private partnerships that was then, and still is, so powerful (see Chapter 4 for more detail). However, I was strictly told by colleagues in UNESCO that I could not do so, because 'sector' and thus also 'multi-sector' had very specific, and different meanings within UNESCO, where it referred to the different sectors within the organization. Hence, I was encouraged to use the term 'multi-stakeholder', although to my mind this meant something rather different, merely including a variety of different stakeholders, and not specifically the threefold sectoral distinction I wanted to make. I still believe this usage to be problematic, because there is a fundamental difference in meaning between stakeholder and sector. Yet, the notion of multi-stakeholderism has now generally become synonymous, for what I had wanted to call the multi-sector collaboration of partnerships.

All too often I feel angry and frustrated attending global international gatherings on ICTs and the Internet, most of which now claim to adopt a multi-stakeholder approach. I have already commented on the frequent sexist treatment of women, and the voicelessness of the poor and marginalized at these gatherings (Section 3.1.4). However, here

Figure 3.4 Empty seats during the WSIS 2016 Annual Forum
Source: Author.

I want to highlight three further frustrations. First, there are countless parallel conversations taking place about ICTs and the Internet, often among similar groups of participants (or perhaps I should call them stakeholders) in expensive hotels, restaurants, and conference centres across the world. More often than not, the cavernous conference halls are empty (Figure 3.4) in part because most people are there to network rather than to listen to yet more tedious speeches. In part too, some of those who have been funded to attend prefer to spend their time shopping or sightseeing, giving rise to what has sometimes been termed 'Fellowship Tourism'. This is a vast waste of effort, energy, and money that could be better spent in delivering real practical change on the ground in the interests of the poor.

The second frustration concerns why this is happening, which is largely because different groups of people, or communities, wish to create their own forums to promulgate their own particular sectoral or individual interests. Rather than being truly collaborative, as they would like to see themselves in a multi-stakeholder world, these different types of organization are instead highly competitive, struggling for the power to shape global policy in the way that will serve each of them best. Where existing structures do not permit this, then new global forums, such as the NETmundial Initiative beginning in Brazil in 2014 and the so-called London Process conferences held in London (2011), Budapest (2012), Seoul (2013), and The Hague (2015), are all too often created to try to shape the character of the Internet and 'Cyber' worlds. One of the latest such adventures is the World Economic Forum's Future of the Internet Initiative, to which the former President and Chief Executive of ICANN, Fadi Chehadé, joined as Senior Advisor in April 2016. Interestingly, he had also previously claimed a major role in helping to shape the NETmundial initiative, meeting with Brazil's President Rousseff in 2013 to encourage her to adopt a multi-stakeholder approach.[16]

Third, each group tends to refer to its own model of bringing different groups of people together as 'The' multi-stakeholder model, seeking to promote its own view of the relationships between different stakeholders as being the correct one. The reality is that there are actually many different multi-stakeholder models in use, proponents of each of which are competing for a position of dominance. Participants in such closed worlds have a tendency not to recognize that there may well be alternative approaches that could actually serve the interests of the poor and marginalized in much better ways. Indeed, to continue with the use of stakeholder terminology, most of these models fail sufficiently to include one of the most important stakeholders of all, namely the intended users of the technologies, although it can be noted that ICANN does include non-commercial users as one of its constituencies. If ICTs are to be used by poor people truly to transform their lives, then they must be involved as key stakeholders.

* * *

The notion of multi-stakeholderism is highly problematic both as an idea and as a practice (see also Laprise and Musiani, 2015; Hoffman, 2016). Although its origins lie in the rising importance in the 1990s of both the private sector and civil society in delivering what had previously been seen as the responsibilities of the state, it was not until the WSIS process, and particularly the work of the UN ICT Task Force in setting up the WGIG (Unwin, 2009) that it became at all widespread in the context of ICTs. As Kummer (2013) recalls, the UNDESA collection of papers prepared for the UN ICT Task Force (MacLean, 2004) was the first document really to use the term multi-stakeholder at all widely to emphasize the open and inclusive character of the negotiations. Significantly, he also notes that this replaced the phrase 'private sector-leadership' which had been used in discussions on Internet governance in the first phase of WSIS, drawing on the language that had been used when ICANN was set up in 1998 (Mueller, 1999). In part, this reflects the clear tensions that exist between the interests of those in the three different sectors, and a realization that whilst the private sector had indeed played a significant role in the first stage of WSIS, civil society had been much less prominent than its representatives would have liked. Indeed, the APC (2003, p. 6) had specifically noted in its 2003 contribution with reference to confidence building and security in the use of

---

[16] <https://icannwiki.com/NETmundial>.

ICTs that 'Civil Society has been, in the large, absent, or denied access to current discussions' at WSIS and it proposed 'that a multi-stakeholder group be formed, tasked with developing a new value and principle framework, based on the previous work of all stakeholders, so that a cohesive and legitimate framework underpins the Action Plan'. By the conclusion of the Tunis Phase of WSIS, the term multi-stakeholder had become firmly embedded in the outcome document, the Tunis Agenda for the Information Society, which advocated that 'A multi-stakeholder approach should be adopted, as far as possible, at all levels' (WSIS, 2005, para 37). The use of 'A' is particularly significant here, because it left open the possibility for many different types of multi-stakeholder arrangements to emerge.

The Tunis Agenda also did not sufficiently problematize the roles of the different sectors in Internet governance (WSIS, 2005, para 35): states were seen as having the sovereign right over policy authority; the private sector as having an important technical and economic role in the development of the Internet; and civil society as being important, especially at the community level. The role of international organizations was considered to be in facilitating public policy discussions, and in developing technical standards and policies. It rapidly became evident over the next decade, though, that all those working in the field had to consider participation from each of the three main sectors, and this has resulted in all major international organizations shifting from their original focus, and core interests, to include participation from other sectors. This has been one of the major causes of so much duplication, overlap, and parallel discussion that has permeated the field. To understand and emphasize the different interests involved, the next subsections provide a brief overview of how this has found its expression in the work of the ITU, ICANN, and the IGF. Each of these has had a tendency to describe its own version of multi-stakeholderism as 'The' multi-stakeholder approach.

3.3.2 *The ITU: Intergovernmental Dialogue and Global Policy Formulation*

The ITU claims to be unique among UN agencies in having both public and private sector membership. This situation has arisen partly because private sector companies have played a leading role in driving the industry forward from the nineteenth century onwards. Indeed, as early as 1868, at the second International Telegraph Conference, provision was made for private companies to accede to the Convention agreed in 1865. The establishment of three International Consultative Committees in the 1920s provided new opportunities for companies to be involved in its work, but it was not until 1992 when these Committees were turned into Sectors, that companies were formally permitted to join as sector members.

The reality is that power within the ITU rests with governments, but that companies also participate as sector members in the hope not only of influencing their own governments but also the entire decision-making process of governments within the ITU. The ITU Council consists of forty-eight member countries elected from five different regions. Only member states whose credentials are in order and are not in arrears with their financial contributions can vote at Plenipotentiary Meetings, and they elect the senior officials, members of Council, and members of the Radio Regulations Board, with sector members and observers having no voting rights. The vast majority of sector members are drawn from the private sector, although Hamadoun Touré, the then Secretary General, went out of his way in 2014 to emphasize that civil society organizations can indeed join the ITU as sector members or associates (itublog, 2014), and since 2011 the ITU has also tried to engage universities as members, thereby bringing greater research capacity to its deliberations. This overall balance of membership reflects the fact that the ITU is fundamentally an intergovernmental organization whose core remit is in reaching international agreements on standards, through the work of the Telecommunication Standardization Sector (ITU-T), and radio-frequency spectrum through the Radiocommunication Sector (ITU-R). These are important matters over which it is essential to have agreement between states if ICTs are to function seamlessly across borders. The ITU's third sector, the Telecommunication Development Bureau (BDT), plays rather a different role, having been founded in 1989 following the publication of the Missing Link Report, also known as the Maitland Report after its chair, with the aim of delivering more effective technical cooperation and telecommunication development (Maitland, 1984; see also Milward-Oliver, 2005; Souter, 2005). For companies, participation in ITU conferences and meetings provides a good opportunity to exert their influence with senior government officials from many different governments, with the ultimate intent of increasing their sales, market share, and profit.

The creation of the BDT did much to raise the profile and efficacy of the ITU among the poorer countries of the world, but required a careful balancing act in terms of the ITU's relationships with other UN agencies that had a longer history of engagement in 'development'. Indeed, managing these interagency relationships to try to ensure collaboration rather than competition has been a particular challenge over the last two decades, especially so since the ITU has often been seen as weak and ineffective (Hill, 2014). One strength of the WSIS process has been that it has provided a platform for UN organizations to try to develop a more coherent approach to their collaboration, through their specific responsibilities for the different Action Lines. Hamadoun Touré, Secretary General of the ITU between 2007 and 2014, did much to strengthen the ITU's international profile during his tenure, not least through his open and charismatic style. However, UN structures have long histories, and even he was unable to avoid the fractious disagreements on Internet governance that emerged during the World Conference on International Telecommunications (WCIT) in 2012, which had been called to agree a much-needed new set of International Telecommunication Regulations (ITRs) that would reflect the new world dominated by the Internet rather than the old world of telecommunications that had existed when they were agreed in 1988. In part, these disagreements represented significantly different views over the substance of Internet governance, but they also reflected tensions over the appropriate forum in which such deliberations should be considered, as well as concerns over the expanded role that many participants thought the ITU was seeking to carve out for itself.

The tensions at WCIT were not only between different groups of states, but were also about the relationships between governments, companies, and civil society more generally in determining the future of the Internet. Civil society was very much an onlooker at WCIT, as the fundamental arguments concerned the balance of ideologies as to whether the private sector or governments should have the controlling power. WCIT also provided fascinating insights about the realpolitik of international negotiations, particularly in the way that it explicitly raised the question of whether the ITU was a fit forum for such discussions. Much has been written about this controversy (Kleinwächter, 2012; Crooks and Altamirano, 2013; Hill, 2014), which reflected two different visions of the Internet. Although in his opening remarks, Touré had explicitly said that Internet governance was not part of the ITR negotiations, the Russian Federation tabled a document on Internet governance for inclusion therein, which asserted that governments should be able to regulate their national Internet segment. These views were then largely included within a proposal (Document 47-E) by Russia, China, and six Middle Eastern countries that asserted amongst other things that 'Member States shall have the sovereign right to establish and implement public policy, including international policy, on matters of Internet governance, and to regulate the national Internet segment, as well as the activities within their territory of operating agencies providing Internet access or carrying Internet traffic.'[17] This failed to recognize the multi-stakeholder character of Internet governance that had been formulated by the WGIG and agreed in the Tunis Agenda (Kleinwächter, 2012), and a coalition of democratic states led by the USA and European countries feared that such a resolution, if passed, would give governments the right to manage and regulate the Internet. This was seen as being fundamentally damaging to the expansion of the Internet as a vehicle

---

[17] <http://files.wcitleaks.org/public/S12-WCIT12-C-0047!!MSW-E.pdf>, Article 3A, 31C.

for economic growth, and thus notably the commercial interests of US corporations, but it was couched largely in terms of the democratic importance of the Internet remaining free and open. This highlighted the polarization of opinions between states that want to control the Internet in their jurisdictions, and those that want it to remain subject to multi-stakeholder governance, that has remained unresolved ever since. Whilst eighty-nine countries signed the Final Acts of WCIT 2012, fifty-five countries including the USA, European countries, Canada, New Zealand, and a few allies, particularly from Latin America,[18] did not do so. As of July 2016, only six countries had actually ratified, acceded to, accepted, or approved the outcomes.[19] This further damaged the ITU's credibility in the international community, with many arguing that 'the ITU was trying to take over the Internet, and that certain provisions of the revised ITRs would eliminate net neutrality, usher in global content regulation and surveillance, and lead to an ITU takeover of responsibility for all cybersecurity' (Mueller, 2014, unpaginated).

3.3.3 *ICANN and the World of Domain Names*

One of the sources of tension at the WCIT was the growing frustration that countries such as China and Russia felt at the USA's continued dominant role in controlling certain key aspects of the Internet. The Internet had originally emerged from work done by the Defense Advanced Research Projects Agency (DARPA) of the US Department of State, building on the ARPANET project in the late 1960s (Leiner et al., 2012), and so it is scarcely surprising that most of the oversight of the Internet had for long remained in US hands. The ARPANET had required a system of assigning IP addresses, and the Internet Assigned Numbers Authority (IANA), funded from 1988 by the US government, was created to resolve this by allocating these addresses. In 1998, following the rapid growth of the Internet, the US government then created ICANN as a non-profit corporation to manage the IANA (Cerf, 2016). Interestingly, this followed the International Ad Hoc Committee's report in 1997 that had proposed that the ITU should be given a role in domain name management, and reflected the USA's concerns about the ITU's competence to do so. What is important for the argument here is that ICANN was created specifically as a private-sector driven organization. As Mueller (1999, p. 520) has aptly commented, 'Whether deceptively or naively, official US policy characterized the creation of ICANN as a private-sector driven process that did not affect basic political and legal rights. It described an act of imposing

---

[18] <http://www.itu.int/osg/wcit-12/highlights/signatories.html>, accessed 16 May 2016.
[19] <https://www.itu.int/online/mm/scripts/mm.final-acts.list?_languageid=1&_agrmts_type=WCIT-2012>, accessed 18 July 2016.

wholesale centralization and regulation at the internet's core as a way to avoid "government regulation".'

Although the US Department of Commerce, through the National Telecommunication and Information Agency (NTIA), had oversight of some of ICANN's functions, its structure fundamentally reflected the interests of the private sector, and ICANN has very successfully promoted a burgeoning industry around the creation and sale of domain names. Nevertheless, ICANN is keen to promote itself as being multi-stakeholder, interestingly claiming that it is 'a global multistakeholder, private sector organization that manages Internet resources for the public benefit' (ICANN, 2016, p. 1). The contradiction inherent in being both a private sector organization and a global multi-stakeholder entity seems invisible to many in ICANN. This is reflected in its complex structure. ICANN is currently managed by a sixteen-member Board of Directors, which is intended to represent all of its constituencies, but in reality consists mainly of people from a private sector background. Eight members are selected by a Nominating Committee, and a further six representatives come from its three Supporting Organizations, namely the Generic Names Supporting Organization (GNSO) dealing with generic top-level domains (gTLDs), the Country Code Names Supporting Organization (CCNSO) dealing with country-code top-level domains (ccTLDs), and the Address Supporting Organization (ASO). In 2002, an At-Large Committee (ALAC) was introduced to represent individual Internet users, and it has one position on the Board, with the final place being that of the President and CEO who is appointed by the Board. In addition to the ALAC, ICANN relies on advice from four other advisory committees: the Government Advisory Committee (GAC), the Root Server System Advisory Committee (RSSAC), the Security and Stability Advisory Committee (SSAC), and the Technical Liaison Group (TLG). The role of the GAC is particularly interesting, because although governments do not have a seat on the Board, and their role is purely advisory, it had become generally accepted practice that the Board should indeed take their advice. However, this has not always been the case, and so in contrast to the ITU where government interests predominate, at least in theory the private sector has been able to trump governments in ICANN. The new bylaws agreed in 2016 have clarified when the Board must follow GAC advice, but it remains to be seen whether these will change the balance of power within ICANN in the future.

Originally, ICANN had been intended to operate under NTIA oversight for a few years, and then become an independent organization (Cerf, 2016). However, this did not happen, and it continued to function under a contractual relationship with the NTIA until the mid-2010s. In March 2014, the US government, partly in response to increasing pressure to give up its dominant position of control over the Internet, and also to emphasize its commitment to a multi-stakeholder model, announced that it intended to transition key

Internet domain name functions to the global multi-stakeholder community. This initiated a period of considerable debate and discussion within ICANN and its constituent stakeholders as to how best this could be achieved. The NTIA in particular emphasized to ICANN that it should convene stakeholders across the global Internet community to develop a transition proposal. This had to address four basic principles: 'support and enhance the multistake-holder model; maintain the security, stability, and resiliency of the Internet DNS; meet the needs and expectation of the global customers and partners of the IANA services; and, maintain the openness of the Internet' (NTIA, 2014). Two year later, in March 2016, the ICANN Board submitted its proposal to the US government, despite several governments still having reservations about their role in the future decisions made by ICANN. Whilst most governments felt able to accept it, a small number felt strongly that they did not like certain elements of the proposal. There was not, though, a clear consensus in the GAC to object. By June 2016, the NTIA confirmed that this IANA Stewardship Transition Proposal had met the criteria that they had set, noting in particular four things: that it supported and enhanced the multi-stakeholder model; it maintained the security, stability, and resiliency of the Internet DNS; it met the needs and expectations of global customers; and it maintained the openness of the Internet (NTIA, 2016). Larry Strickling, Assistant Secretary for Communi-cations and Information in the US Government and the NTIA Administrator, highlighted the importance of the multi-stakeholder process that had achieved this, noting that 'Stakeholders spent more than 26,000 working hours on the proposal, exchanged more than 33,000 messages on mailing lists, and held more than 600 meetings and calls' (Strickling, 2016). Moreover, he went on to emphasize the importance of this process having been undertaken collabora-tively by bringing together many stakeholders, noting that 'No government or intergovernmental entity could have accomplished what this community of experts has achieved in such a relatively short period of time' (Strickling, 2016). As the former Chairman of ICANN and VP and Chief Internet Evangelist at Google, Vint Cerf (2016, p. 7) has commented, 'If I have any trepidation about the proposal it is associated with its general complexity . . . I am no stranger to the evolution of ICANN's structure and processes and their relative intricacy. The new proposal adds its own unique aspects to this tendency and it remains to be seen how well the system will work.' In this context, though, the private sector had come out clear winners in terms of the ways through which the Internet will be administered in the future.

3.3.4 *The IGF: A Voice for Civil Society*

Within the multifarious multi-stakeholder world of the Internet, the public sector thus dominates in the ITU, and the private sector in ICANN. If they can afford it, or are supported to attend, civil society organizations are indeed able to participate in ITU and ICANN events and activities, but it is in the IGF where they come more fully into their own. Indeed, in many ways the IGF was created in large part to provide a forum where the voice of civil society could be represented on more equal terms. Following the strident criticisms that civil society had been underrepresented in the original WSIS process (Esterhuysen, 2005), and that a multi-stakeholder approach was central to the future of ICTs and the Internet (see Section 3.2.2), the IGF was created in 2006 with the purpose 'to maximize the opportunity for open and inclusive dialogue and the exchange of ideas on Internet governance (IG) related issues; create opportunities to share best practices and experiences; identify emerging issues and bring them to the attention of the relevant bodies and the general public; contribute to capacity building for Internet governance'.[20]

The important thing about the IGF, though, is that it was explicitly designed as a place where multi-stakeholder *dialogue* could take place that included civil society more or less on equal terms with governments and the private sector. It had no remit actually to deliver any international agreements, or even consensus, as to Internet governance. As its name suggest, it is just a forum, created as a platform which was meant to be bottom-up and transparent, enabling anyone to speak freely on an equal footing. After a decade of its existence, though, there has been much criticism about its failure to achieve much of substantive value, other than discussion. It was renewed by the UN in 2011 for a further five-year period, and then in 2015 the UN General Assembly as part of its ten-year review of WSIS agreed, somewhat surprisingly, that the IGF should continue for another decade (see also Section 3.2). It did so in recognition that the IGF provided a 'platform for discussion of Internet governance issues', but it also recommended that 'the Forum should continue to show progress on working modalities and the participation of relevant stakeholders from developing countries' (UNGA, 2015, para 63). Most stakeholders involved in the IGF thus saw value in there being such a forum, and in spending very considerable sums of money to attend its annual meetings and other events. As hinted at by the UNGA statement, such expense has all too often excluded the involvement of poorer countries, and small civil society organizations, as is also true of their involvement in ITU and ICANN activities, despite the IGF's efforts to involve them in many activities through remote participation and subsidized participation.

As with the ITU and ICANN, the IGF has created its own particular interpretation of multi-stakeholder practice. In terms of its organization, the IGF consists of two entities: a Secretariat based in the UN Department of Economic

---

[20] <http://www.intgovforum.org/cms/aboutigf/igffaqs>.

and Social Affairs (UNDESA) in Geneva, and the Multistakeholder Advisory Group (MAG). Initially, the MAG consisted of forty-six members, but by 2016 it had fifty-seven (including the Chair) drawn from governments (twenty members), civil society (fourteen members), the private sector (twelve members), the technical community (ten members), and the media (one member).[21] Former IGF host countries, usually represented by their governments, are invited to attend and contribute to MAG meetings, and representatives of six intergovernmental organizations as well as the European Commission are also invited to be attend. The IGF thus remains dominated by governments in the MAG, although civil society is much better represented here than in other major international entities, and the private sector is rather less involved than elsewhere. Civil society is, however, much more involved in actual participation at the annual meetings of the IGF, which have been held in various countries, and which discuss a very wide range of themes, many of which extend far beyond just a focus on the Internet. In 2016, 44 per cent of the participants at the annual meeting in João Pessoa in Brazil were thus from civil society, with governments accounting for 22 per cent, and the private sector only 12 per cent. Much work is also undertaken through its dynamic coalitions, sixteen of which were active in 2016.[22]

The IGF has also promoted the development of independent regional and national IGF initiatives, and encourages these to 'follow the principles and practices of being open, inclusive and non-commercial', and states that they should involve 'multistakeholder participation ... in both formation of the Initiative and in any other Initiative related events'.[23] Although these have no direct or formal links with the global IGF, they do enable important issues of substance relating to the governance of the Internet to be discussed at different scales. There are also interregional dialogue sessions at the global IGF meetings, which bring together representatives from different regions to contribute to relevant dialogues (see, for example, Cade, 2015). However, as Epstein and Nonnecke (2016) have shown, all of these local and regional IGFs once again reflect the diversity of cultural, political, and economic settings in which they take place; yet again, multi-stakeholderism means different things in different contexts.

One of the key outputs of the IGF since 2014 have been the reports of its best practice forums held at the annual meetings and continued through online platforms, with the 2015 IGF, for example having six forums, three of which continued from the 2014 IGF (IGF Best Practice Forum's Consultants,

---

[21] <http://www.intgovforum.org/cms/mag/45-mag-membership/3030-mag-2016-membership-2>, accessed 18 May 2016.

[22] <http://www.intgovforum.org/cms/dynamiccoalitions>.

[23] <http://www.intgovforum.org/cms/igf-initiatives>, accessed 18 July 2016.

2016). These are usually seen as being useful to policy-makers, as providing important inputs to discussions on Internet governance taking place in other forums, and have also been a means for the IGF to involve a greater diversity of stakeholders in its work that was heretofore the case.

* * *

Whilst such outputs have indeed contributed to consensus building on some key issues relating to Internet governance, the notion of 'best practice', so common across the ICT sector as a whole, is one that I have railed against for many years. This term is usually advocated by a particular person or organization with the main intent of trying to persuade others to adopt their 'best practice', more often than not with a fundamental interest in profiting from that adoption, usually in monetary terms. Instead, I believe passionately that in most cases there are no such things as best practices, because of the need to adapt such practices to local contexts. Instead, we need to offer multiple examples of *good* practices so that individuals, organizations, and countries can develop their own local and context-specific solutions, practices, and initiatives that will serve their particular interests, rather than the interests of those propagating best practices!

* * *

There remains considerable debate about the role of the IGF as a global forum for developing Internet governance policy. As Malcolm (2008, pp. 517–18) has emphasized, for many powerful entities 'the transaction costs of moving to an open, democratic and multi-stakeholder process are greater than those of bypassing the IGF and continuing to act unilaterally or in narrower, less accountable governance networks'. He nevertheless still believes that it is not just a utopian dream that the IGF could indeed provide the global multi-stakeholder platform for Internet governance policy development, and that this could have far-reaching implications for the ways in which other international organizations operate. The fact that the UNGA extended the IGF's role for another decade, but only as a platform for discussion rather than as a policy-making body, reflects the uncertainty and tensions that remain in reaching global decisions about the future of the Internet.

3.3.5 *NETmundial and the London Process*

Dissatisfaction and frustration with the existing structures, as well as concerns over the key interests represented by each of the main international organizations described here, have led to the launching of several other initiatives to try to grapple with the complexity of Internet governance, and indeed the wider global policy-making impasse with respect to ICTs. Prime among these have been NETmundial and the London Process.

The immediate cause for the creation of the NETmundial initiative[24] was the frustration that Dilma Rousseff, the President of Brazil, felt over the evidence of US surveillance and control of the Internet following the leaking of National Security Agency (NSA) documents by Edward Snowden in 2013. In the light of this, she cancelled a planned visit to Washington, and launched a blistering attack on US espionage at the UNGA meeting in September 2013. Shortly afterwards, on 8 October, she met with Fadi Chehadé, then President and Chief Executive of ICANN, and she recalls that 'during that meeting ... the seminal idea surfaced of establishing the Internet governance summit meeting' that she opened in São Paulo in April 2014 (Rousseff, 2014, p. 2). From an ICANN perspective (ICANNWiki, 2014), a key feature of the meeting was that Chehadé had urged her to 'take a multi-stakeholder approach that did not revolve around government or U.N. oversight'. Controversially, though, he had also said shortly following his meeting with Rousseff that 'trust in the global Internet has been punctured and now it's time to restore this trust through leadership and institutions that can make this happen' (News24, 2013).

* * *

I distinctly recall talking with many people from governments, the private sector, and civil society at the time about the implications of this initiative. Many were initially sceptical that it would get off the ground, but the persistence of the Brazilian government, which saw it as a key opportunity to play a major role on the global stage, as well as the support from ICANN, meant that it gathered momentum. By the time of the summit itself, the World Economic Forum had also come on board as one of the Organizing Partners, thus reinforcing a tone of private sector leadership in its design. As this momentum gathered, though, many of those who had initially been sceptical, and particularly some governments that had concerns over its possible implications, decided to participate, largely for damage control reasons. In the end it attracted some 1,480 participants from 97 countries. The multi-stakeholder model adopted was heavily influenced by ICANN, with members of the Inaugural Coordination Council being drawn from four categories of stakeholder, each of which had five members: Academic, Technical Community and Foundations; Civil Society; Governments and Intergovernmental Organizations; and the Private Sector. However, despite many challenges, NETmundial did produce an outcome document (NETmundial 2014), and although it had tended to overstate its claim to being bottom-up, open, and participatory, involving thousands of people from across different stakeholder communities, this was a considerable achievement. The document itself was based on only 'more than 180' (NETmundial 2014, p. 3) contributions, and generated largely bland statements, most of which had already been agreed previously in principle by other bodies

---

[24] <https://www.netmundial.org>.

and forums. Moreover, NETmundial has no global legitimacy or authority other than the willingness of those involved to work together to achieve some consensus, and attempts to continue the initiative as the major forum where Internet governance issues should be discussed seem unlikely to be successful because of the pressure from the interests represented in other bodies to retain their influence. Perhaps its lasting impact will be that it provided an opportunity for those involved to let off steam following the Snowden revelations, and for ICANN to have time to gets its processes in order so that the IANA transition could eventually take place.

* * *

The NETmundial output document itself focused on two main areas: Internet governance principles, and a roadmap for the future evolution of Internet governance. The ten process principles were that it should be: multi-stakeholder; open, participative, consensus driven governance; transparent; accountable; inclusive and equitable; distributed; collaborative; enable meaningful participation; access and low barriers; and agile (NETmundial, 2014, pp. 6–7). The roadmap focused on key general issues that all stakeholders need to consider, issues around institutional improvements, issues relating to specific Internet governance topics, and further matters that needed discussing beyond NETmundial, and it encouraged all participants to take up these issues particularly in all other forums, but making explicit mention of the post-2015 development agenda process, WSIS+10 and the IGF. Interestingly, the ITU did not receive a single mention in the document, although ICANN was mentioned three times and the IGF nine times.

Another set of parallel discussions in extravagant surroundings, has been the series of multi-stakeholder conferences for governments, the private sector, and civil society initiated in London in 2011 and known as the Global Conference on Cyberspace, or the London Process (see also Sections 2.1 and 3.3.1). Although these conferences adopted the term 'cyberspace' to reflect a broad intent, they initially focused in practice particularly on cyber-security, emphasizing the need to build a secure, resilient, and trusted global digital environment. By the time the conference was held in The Hague in 2015 (Figure 3.5) the topics covered had become far more wide-ranging, and also sought to address matters relating to economic growth and social development.

The first conference had the objective of establishing a set of principles for governing behaviours in cyberspace (for a critique of this notion, see Section 2.1), and brought together largely like-minded governments from liberal democracies in North America and Europe with an interest in keeping the Internet free and open, in the face of what they saw as increasing pressure from other governments, such as China and Russia, to control the Internet in their countries. This was closely aligned with the USA's international strategy

Figure 3.5 The Global Conference on Cyberspace, in The Hague, April 2015
Source: Author.

on cyberspace, which had been launched earlier in 2011 and which was very explicit about the USA's agenda 'to promote an open, interoperable, secure and reliable information and communication infrastructure that supports international trade and commerce, strengthens international security, and fosters free expression and innovation' (White House, 2011, p. 8).

In his closing speech at the London conference the then UK Foreign Secretary, William Hague (2011), who had initiated the event, summarized the seven principles that he had proposed 'to govern behaviour in cyberspace', noting that there needed to be 'a focused and inclusive dialogue between all those with a stake in the Internet—civil society and industry as well as governments' on how they might be implemented. Interestingly, this statement conflates the words 'Cyberspace' and 'Internet', and if the latter is used in the principles to replace the former there is remarkably little change in meaning. By the time of the Seoul conference in 2013, attended by some 1,600 participants from eighty-seven countries, the output document known as the Seoul Framework for and Commitment to Open and Secure Cyberspace (Ministry of Foreign Affairs, Republic of Korea, 2013) was more overt about its use of the term Internet, and 'cyberspace' itself was relegated to more minor emphasis.

What is significant, though, about the London Process is that it has reflected a somewhat different group of actors, being led primarily by the foreign ministries of participating governments. Given the generally higher status of these ministries than ICT ministries, some had thought that such meetings could indeed bring greater government leadership in the field. Nevertheless, as with the NETmundial process, these conferences on cyberspace have no formal international legitimacy beyond the desire of those invited to participate, and the process seems to have stalled following the most recent conference in The Hague in 2015.

3.4 The Future of Multi-Stakeholderism and Interests in the Internet

This chapter has sought to do three main things: to explore the character of multi-stakeholderism in the international ICT arena, paying particular attention to the roles of governments, the private sector, and civil society; to focus especially on the interests underlying this engagement; and to provide an overview of the way that these have played out in some of the key international forums, notably the ITU, ICANN, and the IGF.

Four fundamental cross-cutting themes can be emphasized in conclusion. First, there is far too much overlap, duplication of effort, and lack of shared learning across all of these forums. Part of the reason that each continues to reinvent the wheel in its own way is because of the interests of the dominant entities in each organization, who fear that they will lose out if they do not continue to promote their own interests therein. Governments thus tend to dominate participation and discussion in the ITU, the private sector in ICANN, and civil society in the IGF, although they all claim to be seeking to promote a multi-stakeholder approach to ICT4D in general and Internet governance in particular. While many people say they dislike attending these events, their organizations must see value in such representation, because of the vast sums of money that they are willing to spend in convening and attending such forums. All too often, the apparent glamour of international travel is also seen as a perk for participants, be they from government departments, companies, or NGOs, and this adds further fuel to the merry-go-round of the theatre of multi-stakeholder ICT forums.

Second, and linked to this, the governments of small and poor countries simply do not have the capacity, or the financial resources, to participate in all of these forums, and as a result their voices tend either not to be heard, or to be represented by others. This also applies to small civil society organizations and companies. Despite the use of digital technologies to encourage online participation, the poor and the marginalized still tend to be further marginalized by the very processes that are meant to be designed to empower them. This is perhaps inevitable given the structure of global power, and it is indeed good to see that all of the international organizations discussed here are seeking to provide ways to support the attendance of representatives of small entities who could not otherwise afford to attend because of the costs. A very real problem nevertheless remains for the governments of small, poor countries to be appropriately represented, because of the small size of their administrations and the lack of appropriately qualified and experienced people therein.

Third, there is a complex coalition of interests underlying much of the discussion in all of these platforms. The private sector in general, and the major global corporations in particular, have increasingly sought to shape global governance in their own interests (Martens, 2007). In part they do this through their membership of these international organizations, but they also seek to lobby and influence the governments that represent them. An unbounded Internet, for example, is a prerequisite for companies to expand markets and maximize profits, particularly when broadband and the mobile Internet are seen as being key drivers of the economic growth that is meant to reduce poverty. To the benefit of the private sector, such interests coincide with those of the governments of most liberal democracies, which are keen to keep the Internet as an open, transparent medium that promotes human rights and helps to ensure free, democratic speech. This is also an agenda that is high among the interests of many civil society organizations. In contrast to such arguments, though, are those governments who wish to be able to control usage of the Internet, in large part because they are concerned about the ways in which it can be used to undermine their policies and practices. Freedom House (2015, p. 3) thus notes that 'Internet freedom around the world has declined for the fifth consecutive year, with more governments censoring information of public interest and placing greater demands on the private sector to take down offending content.'. For global corporations and liberal democratic governments alike, an increasingly fragmented Internet is a nightmare scenario, not only because it reduces the capacity for companies to generate growth and profit, but also because of the constraints that it places on some of their fundamental beliefs about human rights and freedom.

Finally, this chapter has also alluded to the problematic terminology and practice associated with the idea of multi-stakeholderism itself. Although the term has come to imply any international forum that draws participation from the three main sectors of government, the private sector, and civil society, each such organization or forum tends to adopt a rather different definition of the term and they all have varying internal governance structures. This raises fundamental normative questions about the ways in which the Internet can, and should, be managed globally and in whose interests.

Ultimately, it is the role of governments to legislate nationally, and to reach international agreements on behalf of their citizens. However, debates over Internet governance, or what others might term cyberspace policy, and particularly the role of ICANN, are of such interest because they reveal how the private sector is now increasingly shaping the future of global governance. Civil society likes to think that it virtuously holds governments and companies to account, but the reality is not only that civil society tends to suffer from the same self-seeking interests of governments and companies, but also that it remains a week third element in the trilogy of multi-stakeholderism. As Chandhoke (2002, p. 52) concludes, 'the notion that global civil society can institutionalize normative structures that run counter to the principles of powerful states or equally powerful corporations, which govern international transactions, should be treated with a fair amount of caution'.

Ultimately, of the three sectors, it is states that collectively have the responsibility for legislating for and protecting all of their citizens. Private sector companies can never do this because their prime concern is the generation of profit for shareholders. There is therefore a strong argument for states to play a much more dominant role in shaping the governance of the Internet. The trouble here is that, as the WCIT disagreements in 2012 highlighted, many states do not trust the existing UN mechanisms enshrined in the structures of the ITU. This is one of the main reasons why governments involved in the London Process have been so eager to work in a multi-stakeholder fashion to build support for their approach to cyberspace policy, and in so doing to build capacity amongst governments across the world, and especially in poorer countries, in the hope that they will follow the open, inter-operable, secure and reliable ICT agenda set by the US government (White House, 2011).

4

Partnerships in ICT4D

Rhetoric and Reality

The idea that partnerships are an important element in delivering 'international development', however defined, is not recent. As Mercer (2002, 2003) has emphasized, partnerships have featured in numerous global agenda setting reports, from the Brandt Commission in the 1980s to the work of the OECD's DAC in the 1990s. They were central to the delivery of the MDGs in the first fifteen years of the twenty-first century, and have continued to be considered important for the effective delivery of their successor SDGs. All too often, though, partnerships are seen as some kind of silver bullet that will solve all of the previous challenges in implementing development, and there has been far too little critical assessment of the interests underlying them and their real impact on the ground (although, see Martens, 2007). Whereas Chapter 3 examined aspects of multi-stakeholderism in the theatre of international negotiations relating to ICT4D, this chapter changes the scale and explores the rhetoric and reality of the use of partnerships in delivering ICT4D interventions at a practical level on the ground. It begins by examining some of the ideas that have underlain the notion of partnerships, suggesting that these are older and deeper than the idea of multi-stakeholderism, but that they are underpinned by similar principles relating to the balance between public and private interests that have become particularly powerful under the neoliberal economic growth agendas that dominate much contemporary development thinking and practice. The chapter then briefly highlights the rise to prominence of distinctive public–private partnerships (PPPs), and suggests that many of these have failed, especially in the ICT4D context, because they have not engaged sufficiently with civil society organizations. The evidence for the effectiveness of partnerships in delivering ICT4D initiatives on the ground is then reviewed, before the chapter concludes by suggesting core elements that need to be in place for partnerships to be successful in using ICTs to enhance the lives of the poorest and most marginalized.

* * *

My first practical engagement with trying to deliver effective ICT4D partnerships on the ground was the challenge of leading the UK Prime Minister, Tony Blair's Imfundo: Partnership for IT in Education initiative, based within DFID in the early 2000s[1] (see also Chapter 1). In the late 1990s the ICT sector had expanded dramatically, and was rapidly changing the lives of people living in the richer countries of the world, and particularly in North America and Europe. Blair was eager to find ways through which these modern technologies could be used to network schools across Africa, and he was also keen to explore new ways through which development could be delivered at the start of the new millennium. He therefore asked leading companies to become involved in his new partnership initiative. As Selinger (2006) has recalled, this led to the secondment of three people from Cisco, Marconi, and Virgin One to Imfundo, which was initially launched as a public–private partnership, led by Blair's economic adviser Owen Barder. On taking over the leadership in 2001, together with a new team based in DFID, we rapidly realized that any partnership seeking to use ICTs to support education in sub-Saharan Africa had to involve civil society, and so we swiftly abandoned the idea that we were just a public–private initiative. As I wrote at the time on the Imfundo website, 'Working together, we are able to achieve far more than we could alone. With DFID funding, the hardware, software and management expertise of the private sector, the research skills of universities, and the local expertise and involvement of civil society organizations, we can help to create innovative and sustainable solutions' (Unwin, 2003).

Looking back, this comment neatly captured the different contributions that we sought from organizations in various sectors and it has strongly influenced all of my subsequent work (Unwin, 2005, 2015; Unwin and Wong, 2012), although in those early days I do not recall us using the term multi-sector partnerships at all frequently. One of the most significant things about Imfundo, though, was that we did explicitly emphasize the importance of working with local partners, noting that these 'are essential for helping to ensure that Imfundo's activities are delivered appropriately, sustainably and in context. By involving local partners in our activities, we also seek to develop educational ICT skills and capacity on the ground in Africa, and thereby to contribute to enhanced local livelihoods and economic growth.'[2] There were indeed many challenges in crafting Imfundo's partnerships, not least being told by one of our potential partners that DFID knew nothing about partnerships, but instead merely told other organizations what to do! This still so often seems to be the case with bilateral donors. We nevertheless created over four years an initiative that brought together more than forty partners, and worked in eight African countries, particularly in Rwanda, South Africa, Ethiopia, Kenya, and Ghana.

---

[1] <http://web.archive.org/web/20031212195343/http://imfundo.digitalbrain.com/imfundo/frontpage/home>.

[2] <http://web.archive.org/web/20031021011055/http://imfundo.digitalbrain.com/imfundo/web/partners/rb1/?verb=view>.

With hindsight, we knew remarkably little about creating partnerships and we very much felt we were creating something new and exciting, but we did try to seek out different existing models of partnership. We could find little previous work in the ICT4D field that had explicitly sought to create a partnership model, and Imfundo's inception report (DFID, 2001) also said remarkably little about exactly how its creators had envisaged such a partnership working. So what we did was very organic, drawing on whatever evidence of good practice we could find at the time. One classic example of this was my naïve question to senior management about whether DFID had an ethical policy that we could draw on in deciding which entities we might involve as partners. This was at a time when much had been made by the UK government about its ethical foreign policy, following Blair's speech on the subject in Chicago in 1999. Suffice it to say, there was no formal ethical policy or framework in DFID, and we therefore had the great pleasure of crafting a set of ethical guidelines for the initiative ourselves as one of our earliest priorities. Despite all of the uncertainties and difficulties, it was therefore very gratifying that in their contributions to our Output to Purpose Review in 2003 some of our partners did indeed recognize what our small team had achieved:

- 'Strategic partnership approach and transparent, participative, networking processes are excellent, as is direct involvement of Imfundo with relevant expertise. Most other donors don't work like this.'
- 'Imfundo's emphasis on working with the poorest of the poor communities, and collaborating with black SMMEs [small, medium, and micro enterprises] is exemplary. It is making a difference already, and could have much greater impact as the networks grow.'

At least in the eyes of these African people, we had got something right.

A decade later, in June 2012, I found myself moderating a session at the CTO's Connecting Rural Communities conference in Sierra Leone, attended by government officials, company representatives, and people from civil society organizations. Many of the participants had been commenting that partnerships, almost exclusively public–private ones, were one of the best ways to deliver connectivity in rural parts of Africa. However, no one was articulating any specific partnerships models or processes, and most seemed yet again to be reinventing the wheel. I simply couldn't resist the temptation, and so I asked the assembly whether any of them had actually read about delivering partnerships, or had drawn on examples of good practice in creating ICT4D partnerships. There was a deathly silence, and I knew I should not have asked the question. Then, one or two people mentioned that they were vaguely aware of some examples, but they could not remember them exactly. This reinforced many things in my mind: that most practitioners had failed dismally to share their good partnership practices; that there must be strong interests at work in encouraging people not to draw on existing models; and that the rhetoric of partnership was more important than its reality.

* * *

This chapter now seeks to unravel some of these complexities.

4.1 The Idea of Partnerships in Development

A general emphasis on the value of different kinds of partnership in implementing development objectives has been evident for more than thirty years. However, the emergence in the 1990s of much closer involvement of the private sector in global governance and in delivering activities that had previously been seen as lying within the remit of states brought greater prominence to the notion of partnership in development practice. Martens (2007, p. 14) thus notes that:

> When Kofi Annan arrived as Secretary General of the United Nations in January 1997 he further opened the UN to the private sector. In the very first month, Annan travelled to Davos for the World Economic Forum, where he told hundreds of the most influential business leaders in the world that *'The close link between the private sector and the work of the United Nations is a vitally important one . . . . Strengthening the partnership between the United Nations and the private sector will be one of the priorities of my term as Secretary General.'*

By the time of Annan's 1999 speech at Davos, this theme had developed into the more formal notion of a Global Compact between the UN and the business sector. This was eventually launched at the UN headquarters in New York in July 2000 as a voluntary engagement around nine principles on human rights, labour standards, and the environment; in 2004 a tenth principle against corruption was added.[3] Annan's initiative coincided closely with the ascendancy of the neoliberal economic agenda in international development, and over the next five years there was a dramatic increase in the number of partnerships between global corporations and UN agencies. Martens (2007, p. 20) noted that, by the middle of the decade, almost all UN agencies had increased their partnerships, and that 'There is hardly any multinational corporation on the Fortune 500 list which does not run a partnership project with a UN organization.' One challenge, though, was that the notion of partnerships was very loosely defined, and almost any relationship between companies and UN organizations could be deemed to be a partnership.

Although they are closely related, the concepts of partnership and multistakeholderism, as discussed in Chapter 3, are subtly different and draw on contrasting conceptual backgrounds. The notion of partnership has become so prominent and readily accepted in large part largely because of its subliminal commercial resonance. Business partnerships in Europe date back at least to the medieval period in legally recognized entities such as the English *societas*. Whilst there are many different kinds of such partnership today, enshrined in the varied legal statutes of states across the world, their essence

---

[3] <https://www.unglobalcompact.org>.

is that of a voluntary association where two or more partners are involved in a business in which the profits and losses are shared proportionally. The concept of partnership derives from the Latin, *partitionem*, meaning a partition or division. It is thus no coincidence that 'partnership' has become a readily accepted term to use in describing the relationships not only amongst companies, but also between companies and other types of entity, such as international organizations. However, drawing on the original meaning of the word, it is important here to stress also that partnerships have an explicit practical intent; they are created when two or more partners come together actually to deliver something.

The concept of stakeholders also builds on the idea that people and organizations have a particular interest in an activity, and this is usually a financial one as indicated by the use of the word 'stake', meaning a share or financial involvement. In origin a stakeholder meant a third party who holds an asset the ownership of which was not yet determined, and it was particularly used in the context of the person who held the stakes of a wager until its outcome was known. The word apparently derives from the post or stake on which a wager was placed. It is interesting to conjecture about what the implications for multi-stakeholderism might be today of adopting this archaic definition. More recently, though, stakeholder theory, especially as developed in the 1980s by Freeman (Freeman et al., 2010), has come to prominence, not only in the business management context where it was first conceptualized, but also much more widely. One of the key features of stakeholder theory was that it was embedded within a neoliberal context and explicitly sought to provide a framework for considering the relationships between the private sector and civil society, at a time when government intervention was declining (Steurer et al., 2005). Much of its focus was therefore on the consideration of ethical practices and the concept of corporate social responsibility (CSR). Specifically within the field of ICT4D, Heeks (2013) has commented that few theories in development studies have been good at analysing the increasing complexity of such multi-stakeholder initiatives. Nevertheless, there has been a long tradition of participatory (Chambers, 1992, 2007), and action-based research (Tacchi et al., 2003; Lennie and Tacchi, 2013) that has always emphasized the need to engage with those for whom any development intervention is intended (see also Cullen et al., 2011). Without such engagement, any sense of empowerment (Sections 1.1.4 and 1.3.4) is meaningless, which is one reason why so many top-down, externally led ICT4D initiatives have failed. One of the key themes developed throughout this book is the crucial importance of developing ICTs *with*, rather than *for* poor and marginalized people. Poor and marginalized people are as much stakeholders as are the companies and governments seeking to implement ICT4D initiatives. This was one of the key things that I learnt during my work for Imfundo, and I remain perplexed and saddened that so many multi-stakeholder initiatives still persist in trying to develop ICT4D initiatives *for* the intended beneficiaries rather than trying to empower them by actually working with them (see also Section 3.1.4). The intended beneficiaries must be considered as both stakeholders and as partners for ICT4D activities to be successful and sustainable.

Stakeholders and partnerships come together in the widely used notion of ICT4D 'multi-stakeholder partnerships', but it is important to disentangle three different manifestations of this idea. Although some might say that this is largely a semantic difference, the language used by different individuals and institutions is crucially important since it provides an insight into the interests that underlie their practices. First, there is the idea of *multi-stakeholderism* as explored in the context of international organizations in Chapter 3, which brings together a diversity of stakeholders largely to discuss matters of policy. This is different from the notion of *multi-stakeholder partnerships*, which is the term generally used to refer to partners from different backgrounds working together to implement ICT4D programmes or projects on the ground. Third, though, it is clear from what has been said earlier that the idea of a stakeholder is fundamentally different from that of a sector (see Section 3.3.1). Stakeholders can be drawn from many different backgrounds, and in a strict sense, it is therefore possible to have a multi-stakeholder partnership with all of the partners drawn from a single sector, be it business, government, or civil society. This flexibility of definition is perhaps one reason why it is preferred by those who want to keep civil society at a distance in delivering ICT4D interventions. Where all three sectors are involved it is much more appropriate to use the term *multi-sector* to describe the kind of practical partnerships intended, although the term tri-sector was also used by some in the early and mid-2000s to refer to this arrangement (Business Partners for Development, 2002; Warner and Sullivan, 2004).

A final important point to note about the use of the notion of partnerships is that it is highly flexible and inclusive, so that people and organizations that actually attribute very different meanings to the term can readily reach consensus by agreeing to use it. In this sense, it is rather like the idea of sustainability used so frequently in contemporary international development rhetoric. It is relatively easy for everyone to agree to create a more sustainable world, but those reaching such agreement understand the meaning of sustainability in many different ways. The idea of partnership is equally over-defined. This is well typified, for example, in its use by the World Bank, where PPPs are frequently taken to mean a contractual relationship. Patrinos et al. (2009, p. 39), in a World Bank study on PPPs in education, thus comment that 'PPPs can be defined as a contract that a government makes with the private sector provider to achieve a specified service of a defined quantity and quality at an agreed price for a specific period.' Likewise, the World Bank's Pacific Regional

Connectivity Programme, co-funded by other international donors, is specifically referred to as a PPP in the sense that private sector companies are involved, even though they are mainly contracted to lay the submarine cables. Although, in these examples, the World Bank clearly sees contracts as partnerships, this is an extreme position that seems conceptually far removed from the notion of partnerships more usually accepted in the delivery of ICT4D programmes and projects, where a very different kind of mutuality of shared resources and commitments is intended (Unwin, 2013).

4.2 The Emergence of Public–Private Partnerships

The notion of PPPs powerfully persists, despite all of the rhetoric associated with broader definitions of stakeholders and partners discussed in the previous section. This is largely because many of those within the private sector wish to keep their tight relationships with governments closed to outsiders, and particularly to civil society. Again, language is used as a means to promote a particular interest, subtly and sometimes subconsciously. Some, though, explicitly seek to include civil society within the notion of PPPs, and the so-called Dutch Diamond Approach is but one example of this. The Government of the Netherlands (2016) has described this approach in the following terms: 'Public-Private Partnerships (PPPs) play a major role in implementing Dutch development cooperation policy. PPPs are partnerships between government, the private sector, research institutions and civil society.' Such a definition explicitly, albeit perhaps unintentionally, includes civil society within the private sector, and runs counter to the arguments of Section 3.1 that emphasized the importance of keeping these categories separate and distinct.

It is important to be aware of the origin and development of PPPs as an idea in order to understand their persistence and pervasiveness in both rhetoric and practice (Unwin, 2015). This also helps to explain why they usually fail to deliver their intended outcomes, particularly in the context of ICT4D. The emergence of PPPs was a direct outcome of the neoliberal agendas set in motion under the leadership of Prime Minister Thatcher in the UK and President Reagan in the USA during the 1980s. The privatization of what were seen as previously inefficient state-run enterprises, and a reduction in taxation to encourage investment in the new companies that were created, were central to this endeavour. For a government, the creation of PPPs was thus seen as a means not only to reduce costs of delivering what had previously been seen as public enterprises, but also as a way of reducing the risks associated with their potential failure (Grimsey and Lewis, 2004; Kappeler and Nemoz, 2010).

By the late 1990s, the apparent success of such partnerships in the richer countries of the world turned the attention of donor governments and private companies to the potential that PPPs could offer in a development context, with the creation of Imfundo being but one early example of such an initiative. Three additional factors came into play in promoting such agendas. First, development had become increasingly synonymous with economic growth (Williamson, 1990; Sachs, 2005), and the private sector as the engine of growth was therefore seen to be an essential partner in delivering it. Second, donor governments recognized the need for increased Official Development Assistance (ODA) funding, but at a time of economic recession in the early 2000s, resulting from the collapse of the dot-com bubble, they were unwilling to contribute additional sums. PPPs, having the potential to deliver additional inputs, were thus an ideal vehicle through which governments could boost their contributions from taxation and achieve this objective. The naïvety of this approach was, though, extraordinary, and in many cases bilateral donors simply approached companies with an expectation that they would co-fund such programmes, failing to recognize that the most valuable thing that the private sector could contribute was actually their technical expertise and better management practices rather than simply money. This underlies the reason why many governments and civil society organizations persist in seeing companies primarily as a source of funding, usually through CSR departments, rather than a long-term partner in developing effective ICT4D interventions. Third, the shift to PPPs also coincided with the increasing global rhetoric of partnership in development agendas, as represented in the MDGs of 2000, but also more explicitly in the work of the OECD's DAC, which in its Paris Declaration of 2005 explicitly tried to change the language of bilateral aid from one of donors and recipients to one of partnership. PPPs were thus very well aligned with this emerging rhetoric, and could readily incorporate private sector companies alongside the intended new partnership relationship between governments. ICT companies, which were the crucial engine of the increasing trend towards economic and social globalization, were an obvious candidate for engagement in this new world of development intervention in the twenty-first century focused above all on economic growth (see Section 1.2).

PPPs, though, have not been without their critics, both at a theoretical and an empirical level. Conceptually, Martens (2007, pp. 5–6) has provided a very powerful critique of the dangers of partnerships, and notes eight key risks for the UN associated with the ways in which the idea of partnerships had become a new mantra in development discourse in the mid-2000s (Box 4.1).

These issues are as pertinent today as they were a decade ago when they were first noted, and they reflect not only the increasing role of the private sector in international governance, but also in the implementation of ICT4D

Box 4.1 MARTEN'S RISKS OF PARTNERSHIPS FOR THE UN

---

1. the 'growing influence of the business sector in the political discourse and agenda-setting';
2. 'risks to reputation: choosing the wrong partner';
3. 'distorting competition and the pretence of representativeness';
4. 'proliferation of partnership initiatives and fragmentation of global governance';
5. 'unstable financing—a threat to the sufficient provision of public goods';
6. 'dubious complementarity—governments escape responsibility';
7. 'sensitivity in partnerships—governance gaps remain'; and
8. 'trends towards elite models of global governance—weakening of representative democracy'.

Source: Derived from Martens (2007, pp. 5–6).

---

initiatives, which is of particular relevance to this book (Unwin, 2013). What Martens sees as disadvantages for the UN system, are clearly positive advantages for the private sector, which is why ICT business leaders have pushed so strongly for their continued importance, and why they persist in using the term PPPs to describe such arrangements.

This is despite the increasing evidence that PPPs have frequently failed, and may well not be the best solution for delivery of services, especially for the poorest and most marginalized. In the richer countries of the world, there is sound empirical evidence that such partnerships have actually cost far more than governments had originally anticipated, and that they have become a substantial drain on public finances. The UK's National Audit Office, for example has shown that the price of financing public investments through private finance initiatives (PFI) cost more than if the government had funded them directly or borrowed on its own account (UK Treasury Commons Select Committee, 2011). As it points out, organizations interested in reducing short-term costs find them attractive because they have a smaller impact on the current budget, even though they are actually much more expensive in the longer term. Although there are therefore short-term benefits for governments in poorer countries in seeking financial partnerships with the private sector to deliver major ICT4D programmes, they build up much more significant longer-term costs. This represents a significant risk if the ICT4D investments do not yield high enough returns to enable governments to cover these costs through increased taxation.

However, there is also strong evidence that many, if not most ICT partnerships simply do not deliver their intended outcomes, at least as far as governments are concerned. To return to the example of the UK, the Public Administration Select Committee in 2011 in a report entitled 'Government and IT—"A Recipe For Rip-Offs": Time for a New Approach' (UK Public

Administration Select Committee, 2011, p. 1) noted that 'The UK has been described as "a world leader in ineffective IT schemes for government". There have been a number of high IT initiatives which have run late, under-performed or failed over the last 20 years.' Many of these were meant to be delivered through partnerships with the private sector. It seems likely that weaker governments in countries with poor governance structures will find it even more difficult to negotiate with powerful private sector companies that seek to encourage them to engage in such partnerships. Many companies thus see governments of poor countries with large markets as very real potential targets for the perpetuation of what the Select Committee described as 'rip-offs'. This is clearly visible in the practices adopted by some companies in engaging in smaller scale ICT4D partnerships in countries in Africa and Asia, very many of which have failed to deliver sustainably on their intended development outcomes.

This was particularly well typified by the demonstration schools partner-ship created between the New Partnership for Africa's Development (NEPAD) and private sector companies in the mid-2000s to identify best practices in implementing ICTs in schools across Africa, which could then be rolled out 'to equip more than 550,000 African schools with ICTs and connect them to the Internet by 2020' (Farrell et al., 2007, p. v). The initia-tive was one of NEPAD's flagship projects (Kinyanjui, 2007) and was based around five consortia, led by AMD, Cisco, HP, Microsoft, and Oracle, each of which was to implement demonstration projects in schools in a selection of African countries with the help of numerous other companies. It was very over-ambitious, and although ICT facilities were introduced in some dem-onstration schools, it did not achieve the roll-out that had been hoped for, and had little lasting impact on education across Africa (Farrell et al., 2007). It was neither scalable nor sustainable. Despite this, its partnership model was still seen as a success by some of its proponents, with Kinyanjui (2007, p. 184) claiming that 'The public–private partnership model that has worked well at the continental level should be replicated at the regional and national levels and even down to the grassroots level.' Such rhetoric seems designed more to promote a continued role for NEPAD and its e-Africa Commission, rather than offering an accurate assessment of the ability of PPPs to deliver effective development interventions.

* * *

By most stretches of the imagination, the NEPAD e-schools project failed to deliver any lasting development outcomes, and was never scaled up in the sense originally intended. However, it serves as an excellent example of some of the reasons why the private sector is so eager to engage in such pilot PPP projects. I remember, for example, being in a meeting in 2008 with representatives of various private sector companies that had been involved in the initiative. I was very critical of the project, noting the high, but unknown actual, cost of this failure to deliver much lasting real educational benefit, and suggesting that it should be used as a model of what not to do rather than as something to be copied in the future. A senior executive of one US company quietly stretched across to me and said that I had clearly not understood the purpose of the initiative. As our conversation progressed, he emphasized that the main reason his company was involved was to gain access to the senior government officials from the large number of African countries involved, and that this therefore represented a real business opportunity for his company. The initiative had indeed been a success for him because he had been able to meet influential African officials, who could open doors for his company to sell products across the continent. It did not matter that there had been little impact on education.

* * *

4.3 ICT4D Partnerships: A Good Case Still Remains

Despite the many failures of PPPs, true multi-sector partnerships do have an important role to play in implementing effective ICT4D initiatives at a range of scales. The previous sections of this chapter have highlighted that governments and the private sector have very significant interests in propagating ICT4D PPPs, which is one of the main reasons why they have become such a popular mode of delivering ICT4D projects and programmes. However, there are at least three other related cogent arguments in favour of the use of multi-sector partnerships in certain circumstances to deliver ICT4D initiatives that will really benefit the poor and marginalized. These build on the ideas that those of us working in Imfundo back in the early 2000s had grasped more than fifteen years ago, but have been articulated all too rarely since.

First, the interface between technology and development is extremely complex, and requires the combination of a wider diversity of *skills, expertise and indeed personalities* for ICT4D initiatives to be undertaken effectively. As was argued in Chapter 1, such initiatives have far too often in the past been led primarily by technologists, who often are surprised that their technological innovations do not actually have the intended impact for delivery on the ground. However, equally, until recently many development practitioners have been sceptical of the value of technology in delivering on the basic needs of poor people. A frequent refrain from such practitioners is that poor and marginalized people need such things as security, food, water, clothing, and shelter before they can think realistically about the potential benefits of technology.

* * *

One important lesson I have learnt over the last twenty years is that it is often very difficult to bring together people from these very different mind-sets. Going through the difficult, and often painful process of partnership building and consensus decision-making, is one way through which people with very different skills and ways of looking at the world can be brought together to understand perspectives other than their own and deliver mutually agreed intended outcomes in the interests of the poor.

* * *

Second, effective ICT4D programmes need a wide *variety of different inputs* for them to be successful. It is essential for governments to be involved since they should have the interests of all of their citizens in mind, and undertake the difficult task of redistributing wealth through taxation to try to ensure better life chances for everyone. This applies both within countries, but also at the international level through the work of bilateral and multilateral donors. Initiatives designed to reduce poverty and inequality will not be implementable without such basic government funding. The private sector, through the development and production of the technology, as well as its innovative research capacity, likewise has a key role to play, but it is a moot point whether this should be on a contractual or a partnership basis. The complexity and time required to invest in crafting effective partnerships mean that they are expensive to deliver well, and in many circumstances it is cheaper and easier simply to tender for companies to deliver such initiatives on a contractual basis. As well as their physical inputs, be they mobile devices, telecommunication towers, or books and medicines, the private sector also introduces valuable management skills and expertise. The profit motive is a very important driver for companies in ensuring efficiency and long-term sustainability, and this expertise is a far more significant input that the private sector can bring to ICT4D partnerships than any amount of philanthropic giving through CSR, which often leads to continued reliance on philanthropy rather than forcing initiatives to be sustainable. Civil society also has an important role to play, not only because such organizations usually have detailed local knowledge and expertise in supporting poor people and marginalized communities, but also because they have structures in place for convening people to implement practical action on the ground.

* * *

I will never forget the shock once when I heard high-level industry speakers describing the biggest factor limiting the success of ICT for education initiatives in Africa. They were unanimous in the view that it was the teachers and teaching unions who always prevented such initiatives from being successful. Instead of trying to understand the concerns of teachers, and working with them, drawing on their expertise and knowledge, to develop effective and sustainable solutions, they saw civil society as being a hindrance and ineffective. This typifies why so many partnerships that draw only on the public and private sectors, and do not incorporate the skills and expertise of civil society, have failed.

* * *

Third, partnerships are important because of the fundamental need for *ICT4D activities to be delivered holistically*. The ITU's (2015a) m-Powering Development initiative has highlighted that one of the biggest challenges facing the effective implementation of development interventions using mobile devices is that they have failed to incorporate the many different stakeholders necessary to ensure success. This is not only with respect to involving civil society and the private sector alongside government, but it is also particularly important with respect to the relationships between different government departments. Given that ICT and telecommunication ministries are often relatively junior government departments, it can be very difficult to ensure the involvement of all of the necessary government interests, not only in developing policies, but also in supporting their effective roll-out (Section 3.1.1). Likewise, it is equally important to engage the different relevant divisions within large corporations, if success is to be ensured. All too often, for example, ICT4D initiatives have become the responsibility of a CSR division, whose interests can be very different from those of a sales division. A partnership approach that consciously seeks to involve as many stakeholders as is feasible is one way to encourage the creation of a holistic and systemic approach to ICT4D implementation.

These three factors, the need for diverse skills, the requirement of a wide range of inputs, and the importance of a holistic approach, are the underlying reasons for adopting multi-sector partnerships to develop and implement ICT4D policies and practices. These issues warrant the significant amounts of effort involved in making such partnerships work effectively. In circumstances where such aspects are absent, it is much more sensible to choose alternative modalities of delivery, such as direct contractual arrangements.

4.4 Delivering Effective Multi-Sector Partnerships

The paucity of high quality, rigorous monitoring and evaluation studies of ICT4D partnerships makes it difficult to identify the critical success factors in their delivery (Wagner et al., 2005). Nevertheless, there is an increasing understanding of what is necessary to help ensure that such partnerships have a better than even chance of success, and there are some good examples of effective monitoring and evaluation that provide the basis for reaching broad conclusions about what to do, and what not to do (Unwin and Day, 2005; Farrell et al., 2007; Jigsaw Consult, 2014).

4.4.1 *Critical Success Factors in Delivering ICT4D Partnership Initiatives*

Geldof et al. (2011) have highlighted the important conclusion that much evaluation of ICT4D partnerships is based on wishful thinking and unsubstantiated assumptions rather than detailed evidence of what has actually succeeded. Moreover, it is quite possible to design rigorous research on the efficacy of ICT4D interventions, using different methods and approaches, that can produce very different results (see for example the contrast between the findings of Hollow, 2008, and Hansen et al., 2009; see also Hollow, 2010). This makes it extremely difficult to reach any firm conclusions as to the real benefits of partnerships or indeed of their critical success factors in implementing ICT4D projects and programmes. Furthermore, there is no such thing as *best* practice in ICT4D partnership delivery, because such partnerships need to be tailored to the particular local context in which they are being implemented. Box 4.2, building particularly on Geldof et al. (2011) and Unwin and Wong (2012), summarizes ten of the most important good practices in implementing ICT4D partnerships; the first five are broadly conceptual, and the second five are more practical in their orientation. They cannot guarantee success, but failure to take them into consideration is likely to detract from effective delivery.

These principles imply that effective partnerships do not just happen, but instead need to be carefully and thoughtfully crafted. Moreover, this requires a substantial amount of time and effort, which means that in practice they can cost more than might be the case in a contract-based approach to delivery. Nevertheless, most of those who have engaged in effective partnership initiatives say that the value of such partnerships, in terms of mutuality of learning and collaborative delivery, outweighs such additional costs.

4.4.2 *Models of Effective Partnerships and the Importance of Knowledgeable Partnership Brokers*

It is not only important to be aware of critical success factors in delivering effective ICT4D partnerships, but it is also useful to take into consideration evidence from the various existing models of partnership delivery. Two broad types of model exist: circular ones that primarily focus on ways of building and maintaining partnerships; and linear ones that emphasize delivery of particular outcomes. As the account at the beginning of this chapter emphasizes, however, it is remarkable that so many ICT4D partnerships fail to incorporate the shared understanding about partnership building that these models represent.

The circular model is particularly well articulated by Tennyson (2011) and The Partnering Initiative (2003). It is frequently driven primarily by a private

Box 4.2 GOOD PRACTICES IN DELIVERING ICT4D PARTNERSHIPS

1. ICT4D partnerships should have clear and agreed *intended development outcomes* at their heart. Each partner will have their own particular interests in being involved in the partnership, and these need to be shared in an open and transparent manner. However, overall, it is essential that they all agree to commit to the fundamental development outcomes of the intervention, be they, for example, in health, education, rural development, or business development.

2. Success is likely to increase when explicit attention is paid to the *local context* and the engagement of *local communities* as key stakeholders in partnership conceptualization and implementation. As argued elsewhere in this book, delivery has to be *with* the poor and marginalized rather than *for* them.

3. *Sustainability* and *scalability* of the intended development intervention need to be built into the partnership design from its very beginning. Far too many partnership initiatives are created as pilot projects, often funded in large part through CSR programmes, and fail to consider sufficiently how they might be rolled out at a national scale, or made sustainable so that they can continue once the initial philanthropic funding has dried up. This involves a realistic assessment of the total cost of ownership and implementation over a time period that extends well beyond the initial pilot project horizons. In many contexts, a realistic assessment of these costs may suggest that a partnership model is not the most effective way of delivering the intervention, and that a contract-based approach would be more appropriate.

4. Successful partnerships are built on a *moral agenda* that involves sensitive personal characteristics that include *trust, honesty, openness, empathy,* and *respect.* All too often ICT4D partnerships are driven primarily by economic and material considerations, but above all they involve people, and just as in all human relationships it is essential that there is a commitment among all partners to working collaboratively together to deliver an intended outcome. This is by no means always easy to achieve, and it requires a willingness to omit some partners that would be disruptive of the partnership style and consensus, even though they could bring material benefits to its delivery.

5. The relevant *supportive wider infrastructure* must be in place to enable ICTs to be used effectively to deliver the intended development outcomes. The pertinent physical infrastructure (Chapter 2), appropriate regulatory environment (Chapter 5), and effective policy environment must be in place if ICT4D partnerships are to have a chance of success.

6. Turning to more practical factors, it has often been found that the existence of a formally constituted and appropriately staffed *project management office* helps considerably in ensuring continuity of the partnership and effective project delivery (see Section 4.4.2).

7. *Key individuals,* with appropriate skills sets and personalities, play a critical role at all levels in delivering effective ICT4D partnerships. The World Economic Forum's Global Education Initiative, for example, showed that high level champions, such as the CEOs of major corporations or heads of state, particularly if they are charismatic and able to attract the right partners to an initiative, are of great importance, not least because they can also guarantee the necessary allocation of resources at crucial points to ensure effective implementation.

8. It is also important that as far as possible there should be substantial *continuity of individual participation and commitment* from people within the different partner organizations. All too often, as people change roles within organizations, new individuals replace or represent the original partnership makers in planning and implementation meetings. These new representatives often do not have the history of engagement and depth of understanding of those that they have replaced, unless they are very carefully briefed, which frequently does not happen. Far too many meetings thus tend to waste valuable time in going over old ground, which leads to stasis in delivery.

9. It should go without saying that partnerships should focus on ensuring that they have the *right skills and resources to deliver the intended outcomes*. Frequently, though, this does not happen, because there is a strong temptation to use the skills of a group of existing partners, when these might not be optimal for the success of an initiative. This usually occurs when the value of the partnership is higher in the minds of existing partners than are the intended development outcomes, which does not bode well for successful delivery. The original partners in an intended ICT4D initiative must be chosen with great care at the outset, and there has to be real willingness to engage new partners with specific required skills or resources at a later stage should this be necessary.

10. Finally, it is very important to have in place *clear and coherent internal and external communication strategies*. Where partnerships break down, it is frequently because of a failure of effective and regular communication between partners. It is also important for external communication strategies to be in place, not only to help ensure continued visibility of an initiative which helps in achieving sustainability, but also so that others can learn more about the successes and failures of delivering ICT4D partnerships, and thereby build on good practices rather than themselves trying to reinvent the wheel.

sector interest (see Prescott and Stibbe, 2015), although its principles apply very much more broadly. In essence, according to this model, there are four fundamental stages in successful partnership delivery, which are connected in a circular model that represents the partnering cycle. First, there is *scoping and building*, which includes the distinct elements of scoping, identifying, building, and planning. This is followed by *managing and maintaining*, divided into the separate aspects of managing, resourcing, and implanting. The third crucial stage is *reviewing and revising*, which is closely similar to what others call monitoring and evaluation, and includes measuring, reviewing, and revising. This then leads to *sustaining outcomes* that includes two separate elements, institutionalizing and moving on, which can lead either to dissolving the partnership or going back to the first stage of scoping again and initiating another cycle. One very important element that this model also includes is the role of a broker or intermediary, who can be drawn from any of the organizations or from outside the partnership to help build and strengthen it, especially in the early stages. Given the dearth of expertise in delivering effective ICT4D partnerships, the role of experienced external brokers is particularly to be recommended, especially since they can be more impartial than someone from any one of the partners, and can assist all the partners to reach consensus about the design and delivery of the partnership and its activities.

As this account has emphasized, though, these characteristics of partnership building are generic, and focus primarily on creating and maintaining the partnerships. It is thus pertinent to note that attention in the toolkit focuses on outcomes primarily in the final stage, rather than at the beginning (Tennyson, 2011). In contrast, linear models, which are well exemplified by Cassidy's (2007) account of the work of the World Economic Forum's Global Education Initiative (GEI), place the intended outcomes to the fore, and seek to identify explicitly what needs to be in place for these to be achieved; the results are uppermost in mind, and everything in the model leads in a linear fashion to their achievement. Cassidy's (2007) approach has five core parts. First, two elements need to be in place throughout the process: a clear set of leadership, governance, and decision-making mechanisms, and alongside these continuing monitoring and evaluation, so that experiences of delivering the partnership can be regularly fine-tuned and improved. He suggests that such partnerships need to have three elements in place at the beginning: core values and objectives; the vision, goals, and objectives; and organizational readiness. This emphasizes once again the explicit attention that such models place on ensuring that clear objectives and deliverables are established right at the beginning. The next crucial element is the Project Management Office that played such an important part in the delivery of the GEI's work in Jordan, Egypt, Palestine, and Rajasthan (see Section 4.4.1). Cassidy (2007) suggests that such offices have at least four important and distinct functions: managing and implementing the initiative, planning, communications, and resource mobilization. Once this is in place, the different kind of partners can be engaged, and he suggests that these can be conceptualized in two ways: the partners involved in delivering the initiatives, and the intended beneficiaries and recipients, which in the context of schools included principals, teachers, and students. Other variants of this type of approach, though, would include the recipients themselves as partners, since as argued in this chapter they are crucial stakeholders in any such partnership initiative, and provide valuable insights and experience. The final stage in Cassidy's model is the actual achievement of the results.

These two types of model have many similar elements, and the differences between them are primarily ones of emphasis, depending on whether the concern is more with the delivery of development outcomes or the maintenance of the partnership. Both aspects are clearly important, and there are many possible combinations of partnership delivery. The crucial point that nevertheless needs to be emphasized again is that anyone embarking on

ICT4D partnerships must be aware of their complexity, and the amount of time and effort that needs to be devoted to delivering them if they are to be effective. The main reason that such partnerships have often failed in the past, is that frequently they have been put together haphazardly and with insufficient thought and planning. They are partnerships in rhetoric, but not effectively in reality.

Finally, though, it should also be emphasized that it is very important to have a clear, open, and transparent process for engaging partners in any such ICT4D initiative. The precise framework adopted for this does not necessarily matter, but it is crucial that the interests underlying such an engagement are fully understood by all involved. One such approach, for example, was the ICT roundtable process adopted by the International Institute for Communication and Development (IICD, 2004). Once again, though, all such processes take time, and it is not always easy to build the trust required. Failure to be absolutely clear about the benefits that each partner seeks to gain from being involved in the partnership, and what they are willing to contribute in terms of resources and time in exchange, will nevertheless usually lead to problems downstream in delivering the intended outcomes (Unwin, 2005). The lack of trust and mutual respect between governments, the private sector, and civil society that often exists in the context of ICT4D, makes brokering such partnerships a particularly interesting challenge. Nevertheless, it is a challenge that must be overcome if sustainable partnerships to deliver real benefits for poor and marginalized communities at scale are to be implemented. These partnerships must also involve such communities as fundamental stakeholders; ICT4D must be *with* them rather than for them, if they are to be truly empowered through their use of ICTs.

125

5

From Regulation to Facilitation

The Role of ICT and Telecommunication Regulators in a Converging World

My earlier book on ICT4D (Unwin, 2009) briefly discussed the regulation of the ICT and telecommunication sector, but it did so very much from the perspective that regulation was part of the context within which ICT4D initiatives had to operate, rather than as an integral element of such initiatives that determined whether or not ICTs could indeed be used to make a positive difference to the lives of poor people and marginalized communities. Discussions with many regulators and their staff over the last five years have transformed my views, and have made me acutely aware of the central role that regulatory policies, as well as the styles and approaches of individual regulators, can have on the likelihood of success of ICT4D programmes. All too often poorer countries have been encouraged by donors and international organizations to adopt standardized models of regulatory practice that may not actually be in the interests of their poorest citizens. This chapter seeks to place regulation at the heart of ICT4D, and to argue that new models of regulation need to be introduced if the poorest are indeed to be empowered through the use of ICTs.

* * *

The task of being a telecommunications regulator is one of the very toughest jobs in the sector. Regulators come in all sorts of different shapes and sizes, but most are men. Some are charismatic, some are extroverts, some are quiet. Some are former academics with a strong technical background; others are political appointees, being rewarded for past services to the party or the president. They all have the extremely tricky job of balancing the interests of the voiceless majority against those of the rich and powerful, be they senior executives of global corporations or influential politicians. It is scarcely surprising that so many regulators are at best disliked, and at worst arraigned before *the courts, either during or after their tenure, on charges of favouring one company or political group over another. Good regulators have to have tough skins, sound technical knowledge, creative imaginations, strong convictions, an ability wisely to weigh up complex arguments, and above all a commitment to being fair in reaching sound decisions. Perhaps they also need good lawyers as friends.*

* * *

Much has already been written on telecommunication regulation, with the ITU-*info*Dev (regularly updated) toolkit providing a particularly useful introduction to the practicalities of telecommunication regulation, and Walden's (2009a) authoritative text being an essential guide to telecommunications law and regulation (see also Blackman and Srivastava, 2011; Rodine-Hardy, 2013; Hill, 2014). This chapter draws on these, but focuses particularly on key aspects of regulation that have implications for reducing poverty and inequality. At the heart of regulation lies the idea that the largest possible number of people should be able to access telecommunication and ICT services at affordable prices. The chapter begins with a brief overview of the interests underlying regulation in general, and ICT-telecommunications regulation in particular, before focusing in more detail on the technical complexities surrounding the role of telecommunications regulators in generating revenue for governments, and the hotly debated arguments surrounding Universal Service or Access Funds. It concludes with reflections on the importance of regulators acting as facilitators, and ways through which new models of such facilitation need to be introduced that focus more explicitly on poverty reduction rather than market competitiveness. This again implies a shift in the balance of power towards an increased role of the state, and away from the interests of the private sector.

5.1 A Balance of Interests

In the middle of the twentieth century, most public utilities, such as water, gas, and electricity, were delivered by publicly owned companies, responding directly to the control of government ministries. The telecommunications sector was no different, with nationally owned monopoly operators being overwhelmingly dominant. However, with the rise of the neoliberal agenda of privatization, driven in large part by the belief that the private sector can deliver such services more cost effectively and efficiently, most governments have introduced regulatory mechanisms to balance the interests of the private sector, citizen-consumers, and the governments themselves in the delivery of utilities (Crew and Parker, 2006). This section provides a broad overview of some of the core arguments around regulation in general, and then concentrates on particular issues of relevance for the ICT and telecommunications sector. It does so, above all, focusing on the importance of regulation in serving the poorest and the most marginalized, recognizing that governments have the ultimate responsibility to serve all of their 'citizens', those people whom private sector companies see primarily as 'consumers' or 'customers'. Furthermore, it highlights the parallels between the structure of the different interests involved in regulation and the threefold framework of governments, the private sector, and civil society that was explored in detail in the previous two chapters. The regulatory context of privatization, and the shift to multi-sector partnerships, are both central features of the impact of neoliberal ideology in the ICT sector.

5.1.1 *The Regulation of Privatized Utility Companies*

Much has been written about why regulation is necessary to manage competition between private companies delivering public services (Crew, 1991; Walden, 2009a), and how best regulators should undertake their roles (Crew and Parker, 2006a). Likewise, there have been many different approaches to regulation theory, including principal-agent models and mechanism design theory, price-cap and incentive regulation, access pricing and regulated competition, and default service provision (Crew and Parker, 2006b). It is, though, particularly important to understand the rationale behind regulation if it is to be used as a mechanism to serve the interests of the poorest and most marginalized alongside those of the shareholders of private sector companies that now generally deliver these services.

   Four broad reasons underlay the privatization of publicly owned companies from the early 1980s onwards, initially in the richer capitalist countries of the world, and then successively in the recently independent states of Africa and Asia. Above all, this was an ideological decision, through which the values of profit-making and competition that lie at the heart of neo-liberalism, replaced those of universal service that had previously been prominent. Instead of taxes being levied by governments from all citizens to pay for utility services, private sector companies were now able to charge customers for such provision, and the shareholders of these companies were able to accrue profits from their investments therein. Regulators were necessary to ensure that competition operated effectively thereby keeping prices low; market forces instead of government policy were to be the arbiter of price. This was seen especially vividly in the dramatic transformation of the former Soviet states in the 1990s, when capitalist free-market principles rapidly overturned the previous ideology of state-run provision of services and utilities.

Second, one of the key drivers of privatization was the need to attract investment into utilities and other state-run companies so as to replace ageing infrastructure, much of which dated back to the nineteenth century, as for example with Europe's railways and sewerage systems. Governments could not afford to invest sufficiently in these creaking infrastructures, especially at a time when the ideological agenda was towards ever lower levels of taxation. Such arguments, though, are much less relevant in poor countries that did not have much infrastructure that required replacing. Third, it was argued that the private sector was much more efficient at delivering these services than were the old state-run monopoly enterprises. Whilst this seems almost always to be the case in practice, there are few sound arguments why this should *necessarily* always be the case. Fourth, as with the arguments for governments to engage in PPPs (Chapter 4), divesting themselves of utility companies meant that governments could reduce the risks of political fallout should problems emerge in the delivery of a service or utility.

Walden (2009b) has usefully highlighted two important dimensions of regulation: first, regulators need to manage competition issues so as to ensure that markets operate efficiently and effectively; but second, there are also non-competitive public policy issues, relating to such things as universal access, that need to be addressed. Moreover, he also highlights that regulation operates at various levels, from the national to the regional and the global. Thus countries in the European Union not only have their own telecommunication regulatory authorities, but these are subject to the EU's regulatory framework for electronic communications (2009), and above these also to the ITU's regional and global standards regulation and the WTO trade agreements. This multiple layering adds to the complexity of regulation, and the importance of ensuing effective international dialogue and processes for reaching global agreements (see also Chapter 3).

The neoliberal hegemony of the past twenty years has meant globally that it has become almost unthinkable for governments not to liberalize their utility markets and privatize their former government-controlled monopoly providers, especially in the telecommunications sector. The efficacy of this is rarely questioned. Countries such as Ethiopia that retains a monopoly telecommunications sector under the control of Ethio Telecom are thus frequently castigated on the grounds that this keeps costs artificially high, and has delayed the roll-out of the latest technologies. Likewise, Tunisie Telecom's monopoly over Internet infrastructure in Tunisia in the early 2010s was widely blamed for the high bandwidth costs that then prevailed. In this context, multilateral donors such as the World Bank frequently make liberalization of markets a core requirement for any loan agreements. Whilst there is undoubtedly evidence that opening up these markets and increasing competition has indeed lowered costs and encouraged widespread beneficial dissemination of technology, the underlying logics of privatization and regulation do need to be revisited in the interests of the poorest.

As noted earlier, privatization and competition are based in large part on the efficiency savings that are usually gained in practice when private sector companies take over state-run monopolies. However, there have been few attempts to model in detail the balance between these efficiency savings and the profits accrued by the shareholders of privatized companies. In essence, privatization makes sense for the poor in purely monetary terms only if such profits are less than the relative losses involved in continuing to deliver a given level of services through state-run monopolies. If the profits gained by the private sector are substantially greater than the efficiency savings, then the shareholders of private sector companies are benefiting unfairly at the expense of the poor who do not hold such shares. These considerations, though, are rarely addressed in the headlong rush towards privatization and deregulation, which tends to be dominated by technical discussions and political-economic ideology, rather than an understanding of the interests that underlie them, which may well disadvantage the poor.

Regulators have the unenviable task of balancing the differing interests of governments, the private sector, and citizens. To do so, it is usually argued that it is essential for them to be, and to act, largely independently. However, the reality is often very different, and the meanings of independence vary considerably in practice in different countries. The debate over the independence of regulators has a long history, and Smith's (1997, p. 1) comments in the late 1990s remain as true today as they were when they were originally written: 'many issues remain contentious, particularly the notion of agency independence. Some governments are reluctant to surrender political control over regulatory decisions. And even those who agree on the desirability of independent agencies may question whether they are feasible or appropriate in all country settings.' In general, independence is seen as comprising a *distinctive identity*, with both arm's length relationships with governments, companies, and citizen-consumers, and also *organizational autonomy*, particularly with respect to legal mandate and financial independence. Smith (1997, pp. 2–3) goes on to emphasize that in practical terms, 'The two main elements of independence— insulation from improper influences and measures to foster the development and application of technical expertise—are mutually supporting: technical expertise can be a source of resistance to improper influences, and organizational autonomy helps in fostering (and applying) technical expertise.'

5.1.2 *Regulating the Dynamic ICT and Telecommunication Sector*

Many of the arguments in the previous subsection apply specifically to the privatization of public utilities. There has, though, been some debate as to whether the telecommunication sector should be included in such a defin-ition. Telecommunications and ICTs were not considered to be a public utility before they came to be seen as an essential part of human life. However, as broadband Internet access is increasingly now considered to be a human right in itself (UNGA, 2011; African Declaration, 2014), the grounds for seeing telecommunications infrastructure as being a public utility are much stronger. Crawford (2013, p. 3) has vividly raised these issues in the context of the USA, where she comments that 'Truly high-speed wired Internet access is as basic to innovation, economic growth, social communication, and the country's competitiveness as electricity was a century ago, but a limited number of Americans have access to it, many can't afford it, and the country has handed control of to it over to Comcast and a few other companies.' For her, the creation of monopolies, as a result of government decisions, has led to citizens of the USA paying much more for Internet access than those of many other countries, not least some of those where the regulatory environment is much stronger. The free market in the USA has thus paradoxically not led to the lower cost and faster connectivity that some had predicted.

Regardless of whether telecommunications are seen as a public utility or not, the sector has seen very rapid and fundamental restructuring over the last thirty years that has required regulation. In the early 1980s most countries had state-owned monopoly providers, but as Rodine-Hardy (2013, p. 10) has noted, 'By 2002, more than 129 counties had created separate regulators for telecoms, and 106 countries had at least partially privatized their monopoly incumbent telecommunications operators.' Telecommunications are thus archetypical of the issues and challenges that surround the privatization of a major industrial sector, and the need for regulation not only to ensure the competition deemed necessary to reduce prices, but also to resolve the chal-lenge of enabling universal access. Whilst many regulators have achieved the former of these, very few have achieved the latter. Hence, to date, regulation seems primarily to have served the interests of the competitive marketplace and the private sector, rather than those of the poorest and most marginal-ized. Yet, regulation does have the potential to achieve a shift in the balance of power which is so important in ensuring a more equitable and fairer distribu-tion of the benefits of ICTs.

In this context, Walden (2009b) has noted that the World Trade Organiza-tion's Basic Agreement on Telecommunications in 1997 marked the inter-national community's recognition that the sector had shifted from a mainly monopolistic context to a competitive marketplace. Importantly, though, he goes on to comment that 'Such acceptance has been driven by a recognition that telecommunications is a strategic economic sector, in terms of it being both a tradable service in its own right as well as the infrastructure over which other goods and services are traded, and in an age of electronic commerce, delivered' (Walden, 2009b, p. 4). Although many of the principles of good utility regulation still apply, it is therefore very different from most utilities, because of its acceleratory effect (Castells, 2000) that greatly magnifies the impact of any regulatory decisions. Hence, it is even more critical to get telecommunications regulation right than is the case in many other sectors.

Against this background, it should be recognized that there is considerable variation in the level of autonomy and independence amongst telecommunication regulators, from countries where the regulator is very much subservient to ministers, to those where they operate more or less independently. Indeed, the ITU-*info*Dev regulatory toolkit (regularly updated) emphasizes that regulators cannot be entirely independent, because they must implement government policies, and can only work within the framework of their legal authority. In general, the balance of interest in most poor countries is for the regulator to be heavily influenced by government, and this has often been seen as being detrimental to their success not only from the perspective of the private sector, but also in the interest of citizens, especially the poorest and most marginalized. Regulators are usually appointed by governments, and can readily be replaced when a new government comes into power, or if they are not deemed to be acting in the government's interest. The key point about independence, though, is that regulators should be able to undertake their designated activities impartially and without transitory political interference.

Moreover, there are often tensions between the boards of regulatory authorities, and their executive management teams, as illustrated by the court battles between the board of Directors and the Executive of the Communications Authority of Kenya between 2014 and 2016. Members of boards are often political appointees, and frequently do not have a sufficient understanding of the technical aspects of regulation, especially of the ways through which regulation can play a key role in delivering services in the interests of the poor. It is therefore crucial not only that telecommunication regulatory authorities should be as independent as possible, but also that there is a clear distinction between the roles of boards and executives. It is generally accepted good practice that boards should be drawn from all stakeholder groups, and should provide a strategic and oversight role, ensuring that the executive acts independently within the legal framework in place. The role of the executive, in contrast, is to develop and implement strategies that independently balance the interests of governments, the private sector, and citizens, to ensure the efficient and safe delivery of ICTs and telecommunications in the interests of all.

Much of the guidance on telecommunications regulation has a very technological focus, as exemplified in the *info*Dev and ITU's regulatory toolkit and handbook (Blackman and Srivastava, 2011). Likewise, Crew and Parker

(2006b, p. 2) suggest that 'The changes in telecommunications have been dramatic because of the changes in the underlying technology. Technologies that existed only in rudimentary form in 1982 are now ubiquitous—personal computers, optical fibre, the Internet and Wireless Technologies.' This rapid technological change has had two important ramifications for regulation: first, the challenges associated with legacy technologies; and second, the implications of convergence (see Section 2.1). The former of these applies most significantly in those countries where there was already an extensive copper cable based telephone network, for which new operators were invited to bid and revitalize. The costs of redeveloping this legacy infrastructure were substantial, and have often acted as a break on the efficiency and innovative abilities of those companies that won the initial tenders. In practice, many of these have found difficulties in competing with the newer mobile operators who from the mid-2000s onwards entered this very competitive field without having to maintain the expensive fixed technologies, whilst also being able to operate in entirely new ways. One of the significant implications of this for regulators is the need to ensure that their decisions are as far as possible technologically neutral, so that they do not benefit one particular technology over another.

The challenges of convergence are an equally significant implication of the rapidity of technological change in the sector. As highlighted in Chapter 2, the separate and distinct technologies such as radio, television, computers, and telephony that existed in the 1980s have now largely merged, and yet the regulators for each of them often remain distinct. Thus many countries still have separate regulators and censors for television, telephony, and print media, which gives rise to considerable complexities not only in deciding what falls under each domain, but also in how best to deal with the regulation of new technologies such as social media that do not fit within the traditional regulatory framework. There is therefore an increasing tendency towards merged regulation in the ICT and telecommunication sector, but in poor and especially small countries with little expertise in regulation, such transformations place a considerable additional burden on government resources. As ICTs pervade other sectors of the economy there also needs to be close cooperation between the ICT/telecommunication regulators and the relevant regulators in these allied fields. This has particularly been the case, for example, with the development of the mobile money sector, which requires close collaboration between banking regulators and ICT/telecommunication regulators, and which has often been the cause of delays in implementing effective policies and practices. This in turn suggests that there is likely to be much further simplification of the structure of national regulatory authorities in the future so that they become more generic rather than being specifically sector-based.

5.2 Technical Aspects of ICT and Telecommunication Regulation

Telecommunication and ICT regulatory authorities are generally seen as delivering some or all of seven main types of activity (Box 5.1). Each of these requires careful judgement, and standardized guidance such as that provided by international agencies including the ITU and the World Bank has tended to lead to considerable uniformity across the sector, regardless of whether it is necessarily in the best interests of poor people. In part this reflects the powerful and skilful lobbying by the private sector and especially mobile operators (GSMA, 2016a). Particularly challenging decisions need to be made around the revenue generation potential of regulation, and whether or not to create Universal Service or Access Funds. These issues are addressed in more detail in Sections 5.4 and 5.3 respectively. The remainder of this section focuses on some of the other more technical aspects of regulation.

One of the most important technical aspects of regulation is to enable management and monitoring of usage of the radio spectrum for ICTs to be used effectively. As noted in Chapter 2, international agreements brokered by the ITU provide the context for managing the global radio spectrum, and for dealing with the problems of interference, particularly at international borders. However, national authorities have some degree of flexibility in determining how the spectrum is managed within their territories, and have a critical role to play in monitoring its usage. As with most aspects of regulation, the decisions made by regulators need to balance carefully the interests of the private sector with those of citizen-consumers, and reflect the overall policy agendas set by governments.

Box 5.1 SEVEN ROLES OF TELECOMMUNICATION AND ICT REGULATORS

1. Implementing the authorization framework that provides opportunities for new companies and investors to establish ICT businesses.
2. Regulating competition (including tariffs) involving the effective enforcement of fair and equitable competitive market principles, restraining the power of dominant suppliers and leveling the playing field for new entrants.
3. Interconnecting networks and facilities.
4. Implementing universal service/access mechanisms to ensure the widespread and affordable diffusion of ICT.
5. Managing the radio spectrum effectively to facilitate new entrants and new technologies.
6. Establishing sufficient safeguards to ensure that consumers, particularly children, are protected against bad business practices, cyber crimes and violations of data privacy.
7. Minimizing the burden and costs of regulation and contract enforcement.

Source: ITU-*info*Dev, regularly updated, Section 1.2.4.

The Radio Regulations ratified by member states of the ITU provide the international framework for spectrum management and allocation, and seek to provide as much uniformity as possible (Section 3.3.2). This functions not only to prevent interference and create large harmonized markets for which standardized equipment and services can be produced, but also to create considerable efficiency savings from which consumers can theoretically benefit, providing the markets operate to reduce costs in their interests. National governments have some flexibility within these internationally agreed frameworks, particularly with respect to policy, planning, standards, and spectrum allocation. The policies adopted by governments and implemented by regulators are of critical importance for determining who benefits most from ICTs and telecommunications. It is thus widely argued that there should be considerable stakeholder engagement in the decision-making around these policies, but all too often such discussions are dominated by dialogues between governments and the private sector, and fail sufficiently to take into consideration civil society representation and especially the views and interests of the poor. In the second decade of the twenty-first century, four aspects are of particular significance in determining the likely effects of regulation policy: allocation, licensing and auctions, the so-called digital dividend, and the potential use of white spaces.

One of the key roles of the regulator is to set out the frequency allocations dedicated to particular uses. Whilst the division of the world into three regions within the ITU's Radio Regulations provides the overall allocation framework, national regulators have some flexibility to assign spectrum for different uses and users, which has important implications for access and efficiency. Most countries allocate frequency bands consistent with the overall ITU Frequency Allocation Tables, with some minor differences between allocations for the different ITU regions. As described in Chapter 2, different bands of spectrum are technically suited to varying uses, but regulators do have some freedom through allocating less favourable frequencies to particular new uses and encouraging the development of techniques that can enable the spectrum to be used more productively. Moreover, this is not just a one-off exercise, because regulators need to consider future potential spectrum needs, and how these may vary as technologies change. Increasing mobile broadband demand, for example, has placed pressure on the spectrum over the last decade, and the dramatic expansion of demand that will result from the implementation of the Internet of Things is going to place very much heavier requirements on the spectrum than have previously been encountered. The critical lesson of spectrum allocation for poverty reduction, though, is that regulators need to ensure that sufficient spectrum is available for the uses from which poor and marginalized communities will benefit most, and that they do not simply focus on what is best for dense affluent urban populations with high demand for uses such as video streaming.

The next key stage for regulators is to determine how best to authorize both usage of the spectrum and the operation of a telecommunication service. As Blackman and Srivastava (2011, p. 64) note, 'The development and implementation of authorization policies is one of the most important steps in reforming the ICT sector. Authorization policies determine the structure and level of competition and, ultimately, the efficiency of the supply of ICT services to the public.' Whilst some assignments of frequencies, such as those for military or emergency use, can be allocated effectively by default, various different market-based methods have been adopted for licensing commercial usage, primarily in poorer countries through the use of spectrum auctions, but also including lotteries, first-come-first-served methods, and comparative evaluation processes based on merit (*info*Dev and ITU, regularly updated; Blackman and Srivastava, 2011). Whichever method is used, great clarity is required in terms of the authorized duration of the licence, its geographical coverage, and the types of technology authorized. As with all aspects of regulation, regulators perform a very difficult balancing act to ensure that the spectrum offerings are sufficiently attractive to operators, whilst also ensuring the quality of service and the spatial coverage to serve as many people as effectively as possible. To this end, spectrum auctions have often been the preferred method of choice for regulators, because a well-designed auction has the potential to enable spectrum resources to be allocated to those who can use them most efficiently, whilst at the same time achieving optimal economic rent for the use of the spectrum. Moreover, auctions are generally relatively transparent, and if there is sufficient competition they can generate substantial revenue for the government (although, see Section 5.4).

The financial implications of spectrum allocation and the options available to regulators are considered in more depth in Section 5.3. At a technical level, though, it is of fundamental importance that interference is avoided, and this can be difficult to ensure, especially when licences are flexible and traded, often for new purposes. Whereas in the past, most authorizations were based on the issuance of individual licences—and this is still by far the dominant practice in poorer countries of the world—the increased convergence and complexity of the technologies has meant that in richer countries with a longer tradition of regulation, there is an increasing trend towards general authorization regimes, in which few specific conditions are imposed on a service provider and instead rules are applied equally to all providers of the same class, or across the ICT sector as a whole (Blackman and Srivastava, 2011). This evolution of regulation places particular burdens on poorer countries with limited and overstretched administrations, which now need to decide whether and when to evolve towards such general regimes having already invested heavily in developing their existing regulatory strategies and frameworks.

Two particularly important recent technical developments associated with regulation have sought to provide different solutions to the increased pressure on the spectrum: a shift from analogue to more spectrum-efficient digital technologies; and the use of parts of the spectrum that are not used in a particular location and at a particular time, known as white spaces. Recognizing the global pressure on the spectrum, governments from Europe, Africa, and the Middle East attending the ITU Regional Radiocommunication Conference in 2006 agreed to switch over radio and TV broadcasting, which was being provided in the VHF and UHF bands, from analogue to digital by June 2015 (see also Section 2.4). Whilst this was often advocated to citizens on the grounds that it would lead to improved quality and quantity of broadcasting services, there were three underlying reasons for the change: that it would lead to more efficient use of the bands, thereby releasing more spectrum for other uses; that governments could therefore generate additional revenues from the allocation of the spectrum released; and that the private sector would also be able to reap financial benefits from this new allocation of spectrum resources. This gave rise to the term 'digital dividend' in terms of the benefits, primarily financial, that could be accrued from technological switchover.

In practice, many countries, especially in Africa and Eastern Europe, failed to achieve switchover by this deadline, although the ITU has claimed that 119 countries overall did indeed deliver on it.[1] A year after transition was supposed to be complete, the ITU portal noted that transition had been completed in only fifty-four countries, was ongoing in seventy-one countries, and had not yet started in fourteen countries.[2] There were three main reasons for this delay: the switchover was technologically challenging and financially expensive; governments had other priorities and failed to embark on preparation for the transition early enough; and insufficient support and training were given to countries with limited administrative expertise. In practice, many countries have continued to run analogue services alongside digital ones for a transition period, there have been numerous problems with the distribution of set-top boxes, and switchover has focused primarily on urban centres, leaving rural areas much less well served. The long-term benefits of switchover, though, are significant in that it will release considerable amounts of spectrum for regulators to allocate. As ever, though, the challenge is over what the released spectrum will be allocated for, and it is important that regulators do not just

---

[1] <http://www.itu.int/net/pressoffice/press_releases/2015/25.aspx#.V499ao6M8ik>.
[2] <http://www.itu.int/en/ITU-D/Spectrum-Broadcasting/Pages/DSO/default.aspx>, accessed 20 July 2016.

consider the optimal market choice, but give serious attention to the ways through which these allocation processes could benefit all of their citizens, and not just the urban rich.

As noted in Section 2.4, the use of TV white spaces also offers regulators considerable potential to make use of spectrum in the interests of the poor. In essence, unused spectrum in the television broadcasting bands at particular times and places can be used to provide wireless connectivity for a range of different digital services. The technical challenges around interference and the use of authentication databases to identify which spectrum is in use where and when, are increasingly being resolved, and trials in various parts of Africa, as well as in Europe, have shown the potential that this technology has to offer. However, little substantive progress has yet been made in rolling out such services, in large part because of the complexities of regulation, the fear of interference to licensed users, and also because of opposition from existing service providers. Given that the spectrum has already been allocated for television use, it is often argued that the services provided through white spaces should be licence exempt, and could therefore be offered to unconnected people in rural areas at low prices (Song, 2013a). Advocates of this approach tend to be companies such as Google and Microsoft, which are eager to find new ways of providing their services, but they have been opposed by mobile operators who see this as unfair competition. As the GSMA (2016a, p. 165) has argued on behalf of existing mobile operators, 'The use of TV white spaces must not distort the market through inappropriate regulation. Eliminating the cost of acquiring licensed spectrum to provide cellular-type mobile services could create an unfair advantage.' This conflict has been typified in India, where Microsoft's initiative to use white spaces to provide low-cost broadband Internet to villages in Andhra Pradesh has been strongly opposed by the Cellular Operators Association of India (Microsoft, 2015). So far, most regulators have been reluctant to disrupt the market by permitting licence-free use of TV white spaces, but this does provide an excellent example of the ways in which regulators need to consider innovative changes in technology, and how they might be used to support the poorest and most marginalized (see Section 5.5).

As the list of activities with which this section began emphasizes (*info*Dev-ITU, regularly updated), most guidance to date on good practices in regulation has focused primarily on economic agendas concerned with ensuring competition and enabling the market to function as effectively as possible in determining the price of services. However, regulators do have other functions, and it is important to emphasize the important role that they play in ensuring that consumers, especially children, are protected against bad business practices, that abuses relating to data privacy are reduced, and that there is cyber-security vigilance (see Chapter 6 for further discussion). This requires regulators to ensure the security of networks and infrastructure, to maintain an appropriate balance between security and privacy, to reduce the prevalence of malware, and to protect users from what is deemed to be inappropriate content.

5.3 Universal Service and Access Funds

One of the central challenges of regulation is to identify the best way to ensure that as many people as possible can access telecommunication and ICT services at prices that they can afford. Put simply, it is much easier for private sector operators to generate profits in areas of high demand and where it is easy to provide connectivity, than it is in remote, isolated, and inaccessible locations. Whilst licences from regulators usually do include clauses related to coverage, these are often quite flexible with respect to the timing of roll-out to distant and isolated areas. As newer, faster, and greater capacity networks are provided for urban areas, people living in isolated rural areas usually become increasingly marginalized as they have to cope with unreliable and ageing technologies.

Since the late 1990s, one of the most widely advocated mechanisms for trying to redress this inequality has been the creation of Universal Service or Access Funds, which are intended to enhance connectivity for those people without affordable connectivity, be they living with disabilities, in isolated areas, or otherwise disadvantaged (ITU, 2013). Such funds were often initially managed by regulators, but more recently many have been established as, or converted to, independent funds with their own management team and boards. Where such funds exist, licensed operators are usually required to pay a proportion of their taxable income into them, with the amount varying substantially. In Malaysia, for example, fixed and mobile operators are required to contribute 6 per cent of their weighted revenues to the fund, whereas in Pakistan there is a 1.5 per cent levy on all operators (GSMA, 2013). Usually, the levy is between 1 per cent and 2 per cent of revenue, and in some instances additional contributions from other sources are also used to support the funds. The funds are then used to support a variety of initiatives designed to enhance access and/or service delivery. The idea behind and impetus for such funds, as with so many other ICT initiatives, came primarily from the USA, where a Universal Service Fund was created in 1997 in compliance with the 1996 Telecommunications Act. Since then, many donors, and particularly USAID and the World Bank, have strongly supported the creation of such funds in many of the world's poorest countries as one of the main mechanisms for ensuring availability, affordability, and accessibility of telecommunication services.

* * *

Universal Service and Access Funds, though, have become increasingly controversial. I recall vehement arguments at a conference on Connecting Rural Communities in Africa, convened by the CTO in Sierra Leone in 2012, where representatives from operators argued strongly that they were much better than governments in providing connectivity in rural areas of the continent, and would do so more rapidly if they did not have to pay levies into such funds. Against such views, it was pointed out that the levies were actually relatively small, were doing some good, and there was negligible evidence that the profit motives of the operators would lead them to prioritize rural connectivity without some incentives to do so. Indeed, from a regulatory perspective, it was noted that few operators would tender for licences if universal connectivity was an essential short-term require-ment. I left the meeting, though, feeling that the operators had a strong case, and that many Universal Service and Access Funds were not actually delivering what they were meant to. Interestingly, two years later, the CTO's Broadband Africa Forum held in Nairobi reflected a rather different set of views, with many of the regulators and representatives of such funds present being highly critical of recent reports, particularly by the GSMA (2013, 2014), that had highlighted problems with the implementation of their funds.

* * *

Views are therefore polarized about the effectiveness and efficiency of such funds. On balance, whilst they have the *potential* to deliver valuable support for enhancing access and affordability for some people and communities, the reality to date in many poor countries has been that they have not usually delivered systematically on this potential. In particular, the revenues gener-ated have often not been spent because of complexities in determining how they can best be used, as well as concerns about the probity of the decision-making process when funds are disbursed. In practice, much of what has been spent has been allocated to specific small-scale projects which do not enable the structural changes to take place that are necessary for achieving universal access. Although they predominantly represent the perspective of mobile operators, the GSMA's (2013, 2014) recent reports provide sound empirical evidence of many of these challenges. Their study of sixty-four Universal Service Funds showed that US$11 billion was waiting to be disbursed, and 36 per cent of funds had not yet disbursed any funding at all (GSMA, 2013). Furthermore, they suggest that in some countries, such as Brazil and India, there is neither the need nor the capacity to develop sufficient projects to utilize the substantial funds that have already been raised. They highlight strong evidence of political intervention in the allocation of funding, even in circumstances where the funds are meant to be independent. Many projects supported by such funds have also not been sustainable because they have failed to take into sufficient consideration the wider contexts within which

---

Box 5.2 SUCCESS FACTORS IN IMPLEMENTING UNIVERSAL SERVICE FUNDS

- An appropriate well-defined legal and regulatory framework.
- Well-articulated policies on universal service provision, with the responsibilities of the fund being clearly articulated and defined.
- The fund should be separate, independent, and autonomous.
- Measurable objectives should be defined and regularly monitored.
- Administration of the fund should be highly transparent, visible, and accountable to all stakeholders.
- Relevant stakeholder groups should be involved in defining the objectives of the fund and in its administration.
- There should be clear guidelines on working with other sources of funding.
- Sustainability issues and complementary services should be considered in policy formulation and project delivery, with mechanisms established for effective collaboration in delivering projects.
- The processes for allocation of funding should be fair and unbiased.
- There should be incentives for project participants.
- There should be clarity in what is meant by digital inclusion, and the groups intended to benefit from such funds.

Source: Derived in part from ITU (2013) and GSMA (2013).

ICTs can be used to enhance education, health, or rural development initiatives (see also Trucano, 2015, for evidence on education). Furthermore, few funds set clear targets, and of those that do, only eight are actually achieving most of them (GSMA, 2013).

This catalogue of failure is all the more surprising since the basic requirements for delivering effective funds are well known (Box 5.2). If these good practices were incorporated effectively into such funds, they would deliver their remits more efficiently and appropriately. However, doing so requires the political will for the funds to be used in the interests of the poorest and most marginalized. There is also a need for sufficiently well-trained personnel to administer and implement them, sufficiently integrated government systems in place to ensure a joined-up approach to delivery, and clear partnership mechanisms in place for the appropriate stakeholders to be effectively engaged. The need for training and the availability of appropriate resources for such funds to be successful has been particularly stressed by Townsend (2015), who highlights the shortage of skills with respect to finance, market analysis, procurement, project management, and monitoring and evaluation that are required for them to be successful. Even then, most Universal Service and Access Funds are used to support projects that are often relatively small-scale and designed to enable particular groups of disadvantaged people to gain enhanced access to ICTs, rather than making a systemic intervention that will fundamentally change the inequalities associated with the roll-out of ICTs. In a sense, they are like sticking plasters, covering up wounds that continue to fester, because their root cause is insufficiently addressed.

5.4 The Challenge of Revenue Generation

Most ICTs are tangible. Mobile phones and computers are physical objects that can be bought and sold, and the amounts people spend on mobile connectivity are readily measurable and accountable. Hence, ICTs can provide governments with an easily taxable source of revenue. However, as noted in Section 3.1.1, ICT and telecommunications ministries are usually not amongst the most important government departments in most countries, and ministers and regulators are often relatively junior appointments in the government hierarchy. Hence, even if ICT and telecommunication ministers and regulators want to make technically wise decisions in the wider interests of their countries, they are frequently constrained by the revenue-generating aspirations of presidents, prime ministers, and finance ministers.

This is starkly highlighted in the widely variable taxation and licensing regimes pertaining in different countries. Both operators and consumers are liable to a range of fees and taxation. Costs to consumers include taxation on calls and services, as well as on the hardware and software that they might have installed on their phones. In 2014, consumer taxation as a proportion of total cost of mobile ownership in the fifty highest taxed countries varied from 41.2 per cent in Turkey to 20.5 per cent in Kenya (GSMA, 2015b). It is significant also that these costs have been increasing over the last decade, rising from a global average of around 17.4 per cent in 2007 to 20.1 per cent in 2014 (GSMA, 2015b, p. 12). For operators, there are significant initial licensing and spectrum fees, Universal Service Fund charges, recurring corporation and revenue taxation costs, ongoing spectrum and licence fees, as well as customs duties on imported equipment, and other charges which make up these costs. The GSMA (2015b) thus notes in a survey of twenty-six countries that the total tax and fee payments as a proportion of mobile revenues in 2013 varied from 10.6 per cent in Nigeria to 58.3 per cent in Turkey, with the average being 31.9 per cent. In Ghana, for example, mobile operators contributed 9.1 per cent to the government's total tax revenues, whilst their turnover represented only about 3.2 per cent of Ghanaian GDP. From these figures, it can be seen not only that the amounts charged by regulators and the particular licensing regimes that they adopt vary significantly in different countries, but also that the level of these charges can be very high, serving as a serious disincentive for investment by the private sector in further connectivity and upgrading of existing networks.

Governments have adopted very different strategies with respect to taxing the ICT and telecommunications sectors in their countries. Moreover, there is some evidence that the higher the regulatory payments and taxation, particularly sector-specific taxation, the slower the roll-out of connectivity and the more unequal the impacts of any ICT-based development initiatives. Although arguing very much from the perspective of mobile operators, the GSMA (2016a, p. 109) has a case in suggesting that 'Discriminatory, sector-specific taxes deter the take-up of mobile services and can slow the adoption of information and communication technologies (ICT). Lowering such taxes benefits consumers, businesses and socio-economic development.' Regulators, if permitted, can therefore play a very significant role in shaping the impact not only of the ICT sector itself, but also the wider impact that ICTs can have in contributing to the wider development of their countries.

In broad terms, two main strategies can be adopted by governments with sufficient strategic foresight to achieve this. First, lowering the entry costs to participation in the digital economy, be it as a mobile operator, a software developer, or a company importing networking equipment, can reduce the overall cost to consumers, thereby enabling larger numbers of poor people to participate. Moreover, it can also encourage increased innovation and competition as new participants enter the market, and challenge long-established businesses that can be resistant to change in their working practices. Qiang and Rossotto (2009, p. 45), in a highly influential World Bank report, suggested that 'the growth benefit that broadband provides for developing countries' is 'about a 1.38 percentage point increase for each 10 percent increase in penetration'. Although this is contested, not least on the basis that it is an average that is not achievable everywhere, because local context is crucially important for translating any increase in broadband connectivity into economic growth, it does imply that governments can explore a range of alternative strategies for generating income through novel regulatory mechanisms that can take advantage of this anticipated greater economic growth. In particular, if regulators were willing to lower their revenue expectations from the initial licensing of spectrum, this could enable operators to invest more in the expansion of their networks and charge less for the resultant services offered, thereby making them more affordable to poorer consumers. Theoretically, the resultant expansion in economic activity could generate even greater sums for their country's treasuries than would be derived from higher initial licensing fees. The difficulty here is that it may not always be easy to realize such increased general taxation, particularly in countries without robust and mature taxation regimes, because much of the economic activity that would result from increased Internet connectivity may be in parts of the economy that are not easily taxed. In countries with weak taxation regimes, it is much more efficient to tax the measurable ICT and telecommunications sector, quite simply because it is relatively easy to do so. Prime ministers and finance ministers, eager to try to balance the national finances, therefore remain very committed to maximizing the revenue from the telecommunication sector.

Second, as the figures above indicate, consumers are often taxed heavily in their usage of ICTs, especially on using mobile broadband. Taxation as a percentage of total costs of mobile ownership varies considerably around a global average of about 20 per cent, and there is some evidence that where these taxes are lower there is more rapid expansion of mobile telephony, which has knock-on effects for wider economic growth. Decisions made by governments and regulators to reduce taxation on mobile use by consumers can indeed lead to much greater access to networks, although the very poorest people may still not be able to afford them. Indeed, careful modelling of usage and taxation can enable greater revenues to be generated from lower rates of taxation, if these encourage proportionally greater usage. The GSMA (2015b) is particularly critical of governments that levy taxes disproportionally on mobile services, and argues strongly that these taxes present significant barriers to the economic and social development that mobile networks and devices can provide. Regulators and governments are often criticized, for example, for charging high tariffs on imported mobile devices, with organizations such as the Alliance for the Affordable Internet (A4AI, 2014) claiming proudly that they persuaded the Ghanaian government to drop the 20 per cent import duties on smartphones in 2104. This is overly simplistic, though, because the poorest people generally cannot afford smartphones regardless of the taxation on them. If such policies are really going to assist the poorest, much more sophisticated taxation regimes are required that, for example, encourage the development and import of low cost smartphones with little or no import duties, whilst still ensuring that richer people who want to buy high end phones are taxed at an appropriate rate they can afford.

5.5 New Models of Facilitation in the Interests of the Poor

This chapter has explored some of the many ways that regulation fundamentally influences the vitality of the ICT sector, and how decisions made by regulators can play a very significant role in determining the extent to which poor people can benefit from ICTs. At its heart has been an argument that to date the balance of power in regulatory decisions has generally been in favour of the private sector and not enough in favour of the poorest and most marginalized citizens. This is typified in most of the handbooks and texts on good practices in regulation. The influential *Telecommunications Regulation Handbook* produced by the ITU and World Bank agencies (Blackman and

Srivastava, 2011), for example, begins with chapters on effective competition and growing the market, before moving on to technical aspects of spectrum management and network access; universal access is left to the sixth chapter. Although broader issues around the need for regulation to serve the interests of everyone are indeed touched on in the introductory chapter, as would be expected from a World Bank publication these are still largely treated from an economic and financial perspective. For poor people and marginalized communities to benefit from ICTs there needs to be a fundamental reappraisal of regulatory frameworks, reflected in a clear commitment from governments, the international community, and the private sector to use regulation more effectively to reduce inequality and support the interests of the poor and marginalized, rather than simply to increase economic growth.

*   *   *

A discussion on regulation at the ITU's Telecom World event in Doha in 2014 generated many new ideas about how some of these challenges can be addressed. In particular, as so often happens when people are brought together to discuss issues rather than simply to regurgitate received wisdom to an audience from a high platform, the session took on a life of its own. One particular idea that emerged was that we should start by reconceptualizing the role of a regulator as being that of a facilitator. I have often thought about this since, although few people seem ready yet to adopt the notion. Language, however, matters. The notion of regulation generally implies some form of control, whereas facilitation implies assistance and support. Regulation almost inevitably generates conflict, as evidenced by many in the private sector who rail against the actions of regulators. In contrast, facilitation is much more in line with concepts associated with partnerships that were discussed in Chapter 4. It may take time, but if there is a shift in attitudes away from the controlling aspects of regulation and towards collaborative facilitation, then it may be that new kinds of framework that can truly benefit the poor and the marginalized might be developed. This concluding section of the chapter therefore seeks to summarize some of the ways through which facilitation could deliver this.

*   *   *

It is clear that the neoliberal hegemony that currently dominates much of the world is not going to be replaced overnight, and it would be naïve in the extreme to expect existing frameworks swiftly to be changed fundamentally in the interests of the poor and away from the rich and powerful. However, if development is indeed about reducing inequality as argued earlier in this book, then there needs to be a change in balance in the benefits of the growth of the ICT sector, and regulators are exceptionally well placed to help deliver this. Following the launch of the SDGs in 2015 (see Section 3.2) there has been an increasing coalition of interests in finding ways to provide Internet access to all of the world's people, with the majority of practitioners, especially in the private sector, focusing on ways through which the 'next billion' can be reached. A much smaller group of often lone voices, are focusing instead on connecting the 'bottom billion' (Collier, 2008), or what I prefer to call the 'first billion' because they are of most importance from a pro-poor perspective. If ICT policies and strategies do not place sufficient importance on delivering solutions for the first billion, then inequality will undoubtedly increase yet further. This distinction is of crucial importance in developing the notion of regulation as facilitation.

Given existing structures and interests, it is important that regulators facilitate the roll-out of networks and services as swiftly as possible in the interests of those who do not already have connectivity. Based on the arguments in this chapter, there is much that they can do to facilitate the private sector in extending their networks using existing technologies and practices. Of most importance is that there needs to be a constructive dialogue between regulators and the private sector, and that good practices that have been shown to work in similar contexts elsewhere are adopted more widely. Where the burden of taxation and fees is punitive, for example, there is a strong case for lowering the costs of spectrum licensing, ongoing fees, and taxation on both imports of equipment and network usage. However, this must be done alongside strict agreements on infrastructure expansion. A few countries have chosen to forgo the likely revenues from an auction and opted instead to assign spectrum via a process of comparative evaluation of bids using specific criteria for evaluation. This was done, for example, in Trinidad and Tobago in 2012 where the selection criteria were: speed of roll-out of network; coverage to be achieved in specific periods; indicative pricing for specific speeds (2MB, 5MB, and 10MB); and speeds that would be offered to consumers. The focus was therefore not on revenue, per se, but on providing services at affordable rates to the majority of consumers.

Furthermore, there are numerous technical things that can be done relatively easily to reduce costs still further, especially around infrastructure sharing. Providing issues of incompatibility and interference are addressed, regulators, for example, can require operators to share radio base stations and masts, especially in rural areas where access is limited (see Figure 5.1). Indeed, the launch of companies specializing in the construction and maintenance of towers, such as Helios Towers which has integrated and built 6,500 towers in Africa in six years, indicates the potential for much greater integration and coordination in this area.

Another important issue is the need for an integrated government approach to infrastructure projects, so that, for example, when roads are being planned they should be constructed with service conduits that can be used for laying fibre. Likewise, some regulators have been exploring how existing infrastructure,

Figure 5.1 Proliferation of radio masts near Aburi, Ghana, 2016
Source: Author.

such as household drains, might be used for supplying fibre to the home, thereby reducing the cost and inconvenience of laying cable. Furthermore, one of the highest costs and causes of delay in laying cable in some countries is the amount that landowners seek to claim for permission to lay cable across their land; landowners also often seek to impose high leases for land for masts. The telecommunications sector is widely seen as being prosperous, and therefore everyone wants a share in its profits. To counter this, regulators, and governments more generally, can seek to impose standardized rates for such access rights.

All such initiatives are likely to lower the costs of extending networks and ICT infrastructure into rural and more marginal areas. However, it is axiomatic that it is usually most expensive to provide connectivity in the least accessible and most marginalized areas, especially where there is also a low level of demand. Here, the advantages of satellite connectivity come into their own, and technological advancements in satellite design and management have undoubtedly also reduced costs, thereby making them more affordable for such uses (see Section 2.3). Whilst geostationary satellites are not ideally suited for interactive communications, because of high latency, the Yazmi initiative[3] for example is designed to provide educational content to rural Africa and Asia. Low earth orbit satellites possess much lower latency and are being actively pursued, as with the O3b initiative and the OneWeb project.[4]

An important facilitating role that regulators can play in such circumstances is also to encourage innovation and the development of new business models that can help to provide solutions. In small island states with low populations, for example, the standard mantra of encouraging competition between operators to reduce costs may not actually deliver the best level of service, and the maintenance of a monopoly provider, possibly with government investment, may well offer the optimal solution. More research needs to be undertaken to identify the precise circumstances, as well as the population and demand levels that can effectively sustain more than one operator.

If connectivity is to be made available for the poorest and most marginalized people, the 'first billion', then new business models and approaches are going to be needed, alongside further technological innovation. This requires a high level of governmental commitment to connectivity for all, and a willingness to provide government resources to support such initiatives. In such circumstances, independent regulators can help to facilitate the creation of multi-sector partnerships to deliver connectivity across the country. In some contexts, Universal Service Funds could be used to support such partnerships, but closure of such funds and direct support from the general government budget and international loans is often a more efficient means of supporting them.

Nevertheless, digital marginalization is not just spatial, and as Section 3.1 highlighted, people with disabilities, the elderly, and women in patriarchal societies, often live in areas that are relatively well connected, but they cannot easily access these technologies, or use them to their advantage. Again, integrated policies across government departments, and a true commitment to universal accessibility are required if these people are to be able to use ICTs effectively to empower themselves. Where there would otherwise be insufficient central government funding, a case can be made that well-managed Universal Service Funds could be used to support clearly identified and specific marginalized groups of people.

In concluding this chapter, three key points about regulation need to be reiterated. First, it is essential for regulators to act, and to be seen to be acting, as independently as possible in resolving the competing interests between the private sector, governments, and citizen-consumers. To date, the balance of power in many poor countries has largely been shared between the private sector and government officials. If regulation is going to be used as an integral

---

[3] <http://www.yazmi.com>.
[4] <http://www.o3bnetworks.com>; <http://oneweb.world>.

part of development policy, and this is to be designed to reduce inequalities, then it is important that regulators ensure that they facilitate dialogues and mechanisms that consciously benefit the poor and the marginalized. Second, as emphasized at the beginning of the chapter, regulation is extremely difficult, and many poor countries with small bureaucracies have insufficient numbers of appropriately trained personnel working in their regulatory authorities. There is therefore a considerable ongoing need for training and support for both board members and executive staff in ICT and telecommunication regulatory authorities, particularly with respect to identifying new ways through which they can exert their authority to support universal connectivity, especially in the interests of poor and marginalized communities. Finally, independent regulators can play an important role in helping to ensure an integrated approach is adopted across government departments to deliver effective ICT for development. As many of the examples cited in this chapter indicate, it is crucial to have a whole government approach to delivering ICT4D in the interests of all citizens, not only across all entities responsible for infrastructure and electricity, but also in terms of health, education, and rural development departments. In the absence of such integration and shared commitments, interventions designed with good intent to support the least advantaged all too often fail.

6

Reflections on the Dark Side of ICT4D

ICTs are a remarkable and powerful accelerator of human interaction (see Sections 2.9 and 5.1.2). Where there are inequalities, they will therefore enhance those inequalities unless specific actions are taken to prevent this. Consequently, as is increasingly being recognized (UNDP, 2015; World Bank, 2016a), in an unequal world, ICTs are likely to serve the interests of the rich and powerful more than they do those of the poor. The huge wealth of industry visionaries and leaders such as Bill Gates and Mark Zuckerberg, at one level, for example, needs to be weighed up against the increasing global inequalities that the technologies that they have shaped have generated. This may be one reason why many such leaders of ICT corporations have turned to philanthropy as a palliative. I use the word palliative here deliberately, because such philanthropy tends to deal with the symptoms rather than the underlying causes of increased relative poverty. This is by no means to suggest that such individuals, and indeed corporations, have necessarily intended to do harm, but the unintended consequence of their contributions over the last two decades and more has indeed been to enhance the better off whilst leaving the poorest and most marginalized relatively disadvantaged.

As this entire book has argued, such increased inequality as a result of the interests underlying the original design of many ICTs, together with the ways that they have been exploited and utilized, raises fundamental moral challenges, and requires a consideration of the darker side to ICTs. The global impact of ICTs, for example, highlights important questions around the balance between development interventions that focus primarily on the economic growth agenda as against those that place emphasis on reducing inequalities. The irony here is that many people in the early 2000s, including me, saw ICTs as offering entirely new forms of beneficially disruptive, and indeed anarchic, forms of human interaction (Unwin, 2009), and yet it is the economic agendas, the ways that ICTs can contribute to economic growth and entrepreneurship, that have largely come to dominate ICT-related development discourse a decade later. Increased inequality can itself be seen as one of the darker sides to ICTs, but it is an insidious, deeply embedded, and all-pervasive characteristic. For the many who believe that economic growth is the solution to reducing poverty (Sachs, 2005), this is an inevitable consequence, and the fact that many poor people are able to benefit from ICTs is justification enough for continuing to expand the roll-out of ICTs across the world, even if the very poorest are increasingly becoming even more marginalized as a result. However, there is also a more overt dark dimension to ICTs that even advocates of the technology-led economic growth agenda see as being hazardous, because it undermines the very essence of such growth. It is with this specifically dark side to ICTs that this chapter is particularly concerned, because it also fundamentally disrupts the potential use of ICTs to empower the poorest and the most marginalized. It begins with a discussion of the impact of ICTs on both privacy and security, before exploring some of the more deeply worrying corridors of the darker side of the Internet. This is followed by a discussion of key aspects of what has become known, somewhat problematically, as cyber-security (see Section 2.1), before the chapter concludes by returning to the more visible darker aspects of the use of Big Data, the Internet of Things, and an increasingly cyborg-dominated world. As argued earlier in this book, ICTs are often seen as being inherently good. This chapter serve as a reminder that this is by no means always the case.

6.1 Privacy and Security

A decade ago, I argued strongly against the introduction of biometric identity cards, and drawing on the seventeenth-century works of Locke (1987) I adopted a very libertarian approach towards new forms of digital surveillance, arguing that the values of individual judgement, political freedom, and the maximization of autonomy are all too often undermined by such technologies, but are nevertheless important and worth preserving (Freedom House, 2009). I pointed to the use of radio in the genocide in Rwanda (Thompson, 2007), and reflected on what governments that had detailed biometric data on all of their citizens might be able to do in the future. I railed against the widespread use of closed circuit television (CCTV) that increasingly meant I could not travel anywhere in my own country without being watched. I tried to avoid going to countries where I had to give my fingerprints on entry, because I did not want other states to possess this aspect of my identity. And then something changed. It was not the increasing use of digital technologies by those planning attacks that would murder hundreds of people, or the increasing amount of hacking of individual data that altered my views. It was not even that it had become impossible to do my job without giving my fingerprints to the security services of numerous states across the world. Rather, it was an increasing understanding that the very freedoms I valued were being undermined by many of those who were using new digital technologies, and that something had to be done to address this. It was a realization that across the world, the lives of thousands of poor people, especially women and girls in patriarchal societies, were being devastated through online exploitation and abuse. It was recognition that there are many people using ICTs to try to destroy the very fabric of what I consider to be a civilized society, and that something needs to be done to stop them. This made me return to the work of Locke (1987) and indeed Hobbes (1996), to reflect further on the origins of social contract theory, and the crucial role that European societies have traditionally allocated to the state in balancing human self-interest and the desire for peace (Rawls, 1971; Hampton, 1986).

* * *

At the heart of much discussion on the ways in which ICTs have changed the relationships between citizens and states have been debates over privacy and security (Dutton et al., 2005; Vaccaro, 2006). However, in grappling with the implications of new technologies for these debates, it must be recognized that as long as there has been communication, agents of the state have always sought to intercept the means through which that communication has taken place (see for example, Malcolm, 2016). A benign view of such surveillance is that it has been used to ensure the stability of states in the interests of their citizens; a harsher view is that it has often been used to impose control by minority regimes eager to maintain power through violence and oppression. Much existing legislation can, though, be used to ensure that there are appropriate checks and balances in place to manage this situation. The fundamental changes that new ICTs have introduced in the context of surveillance are the ability to create, store, and access vast amounts of data about individuals, their movements, and their communications. Moreover, whilst governments have in the past largely been the entities that have sought to maintain such information about their citizens, this role has now been surpassed many times over by the enormous amounts of individual information that global private sector corporations now possess about millions of people across the world. It is ironic that the opprobrium resulting from the Snowden revelations (Greenwald, 2014), and the flow of information from WikiLeaks (2015), for example, has so far been directed primarily at states, whereas private sector companies, be they mobile operators or social media corporations, often know far much more about individuals than do the governments of the states in which they operate. Indeed, governments in democratic societies have to face elections, and can be replaced if they act unjustly in such matters, whereas companies acting within the law are only responsible to their shareholders. Hence, again, as noted in Chapter 5, the regulation of corporate behaviour in the ICT sector particularly in terms of the ways through which individual data are stored, accessed, and managed is of paramount importance. These concerns are also of particular relevance in the roll-out of e-government projects in poor countries, most of which create large databases about their citizens. All too often, the ethical dimensions of such programmes are ignored in the face of the economic interests that usually propel them forward, although Estonia provides a rare example of a small country that has addressed the complexity of these issues to generate a system where the interests of individuals and the state seem to be approximately balanced (Kalvet, 2007; Unwin, 2010).[1]

One difficulty of grappling with these moral issues is that notions of trust and privacy are not only contested, but are also culturally bound. Interestingly, anecdotal evidence from Africa in the context of ICTs, for example, suggests that where governments are not trusted, people are much more willing to share their personal information with companies, whereas where governments are trusted, citizens prefer to trust them rather than companies. Although trust in the corporate sector globally declined considerably following the US-led financial crisis of 2008 (Kramer, 2009), it is remarkable that in the ICT sector companies have generally managed to retain a trustworthy identity, despite the huge amounts of information about their customers that they make use of (Connolly, 2013; see also Gerck, 2004). It is, though, important to emphasize that people need to enter trust relationships distinct from those involved in their actual use of ICTs before such things as effective e-government processes can be used effectively. No amount of technology, for example, will make governments change their attitudes towards citizens, unless those governments have already decided to adopt new ethical standards on concepts such as transparency, equity, and fairness (Unwin, 2010).

As with notions of trust, there has been considerable debate over the meanings of privacy, and whether these have been changed through the use of ICTs (Unwin, 2010; Bennett and Parsons, 2013). The most commonly accepted argument in this context is the largely economic perspective that privacy is merely a good that people weigh up against others in reaching a decision. As Etzioni (2005) has commented, idealist questions about privacy are often false because they are posed as being cost free, whereas actually people weigh up different costs and consider actions in the light of their various benefits. This economic argument, that people make rational decisions about their choices based upon full information is, though, highly problematic in the context of privacy considerations relating to ICTs. Most people, let alone the poor and the illiterate, for example, never read the privacy related licensing agreements when they use computer software and apps, and although companies can legally claim that users have indeed read these, because they can only be used

---

[1] See also <http://www.ega.ee>.

when the agreed box has been ticked, most people have very little idea of their content, and how their own personal information will be used.

As Etzioni (2005, p. 260) notes, privacy is but one good among many other often incompatible ones, and 'we must constantly weight how much import-ance we ought to accord privacy, and how much importance we ought to accord other values, above all, the protection of our families, communities, and homeland'. This has important implications for the digital relationships between citizens and states, because if governments can persuade citizens that there is an increasing threat to their personal security as a result of the use of digital technologies by some people, then it is likely that citizens will agree to relinquish some of their individual privacy in the interests of the wider common good. However, all too often, governments fail to engage sufficiently with citizens in an open and transparent dialogue before seeking to impose legislation to enable them to access digital communications and information. An irony here is that they also usually have to access this from the private sector, who are already using such information for their own profitable benefit.

There are, though, important alternative approaches to privacy. Friedman (2005, p. 264) adopts a more idealist stance, suggesting that 'privacy gives each of us more control over our own life—which on average, if not in every case, is likely to lead to a freer world'. Accordingly, privacy is not an economic good that can simply be weighed up against other such goods, but is rather something that is inherent to individual identity, and indeed part of what makes us human. From this perspective, the ways that governments wield power are particularly significant. Governments always have more coercive power than individual citizens do, and so the more governments know about each citizen, the easier it is for them to implement such power. Thus, as Friedman (2005, p. 265) again comments, 'Reducing government's ability to do bad things to us, at the cost of limiting its ability to protect us from bad things done to us by ourselves or by other people, may not be such a bad deal.' ICTs have greatly facilitated the ways through which governments can gain information about both other governments and their own citizens. This may not matter if governments can be trusted to be good, but it becomes deeply worrying when that is not the case. Not all governments serve the interests of all their citizens, and there is no guarantee that a future government would not use information previously gathered by its predecessor for harmful pur-poses that were not originally intended.

* * *

The arguments in the previous paragraphs are grounded in a largely European conceptu-alization of privacy, derived from Enlightenment traditions, social contract theory, and a distinctive set of ideas around the autonomy of the individual. This conceptualization, however, is far removed from the reality of the lives of many poor people living in Asia,

Africa, and Latin America. As a friend from Pakistan recently said to me, the poor rarely know privacy. Many poor people spend most of their lives sharing a one- or two-room home with numerous siblings, parents, and grandparents. Others live on the streets where all their actions are visible to anyone who cares to look. Privacy is not of concern. Yet privacy is now globally seen as being a fundamental human right, and in Pakistan the constitution reaffirms the inviolability of this right (Bytes for All, 2014). This has very significant implications for the ways through which poor people conceptualize privacy in the context of their use of ICTs. On the one hand, they may well have few qualms about posting material on social media sites, whilst, on the other, possessing a mobile phone can enable poor people to be more private by storing images and information hidden from the view of others. Which of these is the more empowering depends very much on the perspective from which it is seen.

* * *

Generally speaking, though, and in line with international agreements around human rights and privacy, most governments and regulators have been encouraged to adopt strict data privacy rules (see also Section 5.2), often based on those prevailing in OECD countries (Freshfields Bruckhaus Deringer, 2014). Thus, for example, since 2005, when the Asia-Pacific Economic Cooperation (APEC) member countries agreed a privacy framework, many countries in the region have now created explicit data privacy regimes. Yet again, however, these are fundamentally driven by economic interests, rather than the important moral and social concerns noted previously in this section. As law firm Hogan Lovells notes, 'It is now clear that data privacy compliance is a critical business issue across the Asia-Pacific region. Failure to comply can have consequences far beyond simply monetary fines and other regulatory sanctions: very often reputational issues are also in play' (2014, p. 1).

6.2 The Dark Side

ICTs are imbued with considerable positive symbolic value. Indeed, the whole notion of ICT for development is one of positive hope, or a belief that ICTs can make the world a better place. However, there is nothing inherently 'good' about ICTs. They are merely technologies designed with particular interests in mind, most of which are fundamentally driven by the profit-seeking motives of the private sector. As with all technologies, they can be used for positive or negative purposes, depending on the motives and moralities of their designers and users. Even when the original intention is positive there can be unintended consequences that are negative. It is not surprising that the vast majority of publicity and research has concentrated on the positive aspects of ICTs, given the overwhelming underlying interests of those seeking to promote expansion of the sector for their own gain. There are indeed undoubtedly many positive benefits in the use of ICTs for and by poor people (Unwin, 2009). However, there is also a darker side to their use that is too often ignored or suppressed, and this section therefore seeks to redress the balance, by highlighting some of the more disturbing aspects of the use of ICTs. It does so by focusing especially on the Internet, the most powerful of all ICTs, in its potential to connect people and things at great speeds anywhere in the world.

In exploring the darker side of the Internet, it is important to distinguish between the relatively small fraction of material that is accessible openly, and the much greater amount that is hidden. As outlined in Chapter 2, the Internet is a network of networks, with information sharing and communication being feasible through the use of various protocols and languages. The Web, for example uses HTML for the formatting of pages that are accessible through the use of HTTP. This 'Surface Web' can be indexed through search engines such as Google, Bing, or Yahoo, which enable users to find the information that the engines' algorithms think they want. Not all of the Web, though, is accessible to such search engines, and these unsearchable parts have become known as the Deep Web. Given its hidden nature, it is impossible to know how large the Deep Web is, but early estimates suggested it was between 400 and 550 times larger than the Surface Web (Bergman, 2001), and given the exponential growth of the Web since then it is now likely to be very much larger. This term is often, but erroneously, used synonymously with the terms Dark Web or Dark Net. The Dark Web is properly the term used to refer to that part of the Deep Web that requires specific software and authorization to access it, with the best known examples being The Onion Router (Tor) network and hidden services,[2] the I2P network and its eepSites,[3] and the Retro-Share network[4] (see also BrightPlanet, 2014; Owen and Savage, 2015). The Dark Net (or Darknet) refers to the overlay networks on which the Dark Web content exists, and likewise requires particular configurations, software, and authorizations to access it.

A real challenge in discussing the morality of Internet use is that whether something is considered good or bad very much depends on the perspective of the viewer. By bouncing communications around a distributed network of servers run by volunteers across the world, Tor provides added security for those who want more privacy and are concerned about traffic analysis and network surveillance. However, such networks can also be used for a wide range of hidden activities that many people would consider to be inappropriate or criminal in intent.

---

[2] <https://www.torproject.org/about/overview.html.en>.
[3] <http://www.eepsite.com>.
[4] <https://trac.torproject.org/projects/tor/wiki/doc/HowBigIsTheDarkWeb>.

6.2.1 *The Dark Side of the Surface Web*

The Surface Web itself, through websites and social media, has long been used for activities that many people decry, such as sharing pornographic images and planning so-called terrorist attacks. Other relatively accessible parts of the Internet, such as newsgroups, are also widely used for criminal activity (Mann and Sutton, 1998), and the increasing prevalence of online commerce and banking has opened up huge opportunities for fraud, with criminals able to benefit considerably from obtaining sensitive personal information through phishing attacks, or by hacking into personal or corporate systems. The rapid expansion in the extent of malware, such as computer viruses and worms (Ligh et al., 2011), often accidentally downloaded by unsuspecting individuals, also gives rise to serious concern, both for the economic impact it causes, and also the potential psychological and financial damage to individuals that can ensue.

A fundamental challenge in grappling with these activities is that there are few areas in which there is more or less global agreement on the actions that should be taken with respect to such activity, not least because of different cultural views and because security agencies can often benefit more from monitoring such activities than from closing them down. The one area where there is most widespread agreement has been with respect to child online abuse and pornography, much of which exploits children living in poor and marginalized communities (Special Representative of the Secretary-General on Violence against Children, 2014). The ITU's Child Online Protection initiative[5] has thus brought together a coalition of partners to develop guidelines on child online protection, and to support countries willing to tackle the issue. One particularly successful example of organizations working in this area is the UK based Internet Watch Foundation (2015), which seeks to minimize child sexual abuse content hosted anywhere in the world, as well as other obscene or sexual content hosted in the UK.[6] In its 2015 report, for example, it confirmed 68,092 reports of child sexual abuse URLs, with 69 per cent of victims being assessed as aged 10 or under (Internet Watch Foundation, 2015). Perhaps more worryingly, it also recorded a 417 per cent increase in reports of such images and videos since 2013, although it is not easy to ascertain whether this is because more people are reporting such material to them, or there has been a real increase in the amount produced. What this does show, though, is that there is an unacceptable amount of child abuse taking place across the world, and that this is distributed widely across the Internet. Poor countries without the resources to tackle this issue need considerable support and encouragement to do so. Hence, global initiatives

---

[5] <http://www.itu.int/en/cop>.   [6] <http://www.iwf.org.uk>.

that seek to provide examples of good practices and coordination, such as the Global Resource and Information Directory (GRID, 2016), supported by UNICEF, can play an important role in helping counter the damage caused by online child abuse. Knowing about something, though, is not enough; action needs to be taken to reduce the extent.

Other worrying aspects of the Surface Web are the ways through which social media can be used for harmful actions such as advocating and planning terrorist attacks (Weimann, 2006; Dienel et al., 2010; UNODC, 2012), trolling (Phillips, 2015; Fichman and Sanfilippo, 2016), or sexual harassment. Having been trolled myself, albeit in a limited way, I am only too aware of the psychological and reputational damage that it can cause.[7] Moreover, much greater global attention needs to be paid to online sexual harassment which is one of the most worryingly damaging aspects of the contemporary use of the Web. This varies in extent from revenge pornography, with which the legal systems of several countries are now beginning to come to grips, to the far more threatening and destructive harassment of women online in patriarchal societies. Although the precise extent of this is difficult to determine, it is very clear, for example, in Pakistan that many women, and indeed some men, are regularly blackmailed about images, often quite innocent ones, that are posted on social media (Hassan and Unwin, 2017). Likewise, many suicides and honour killings have been blamed on the use of mobile phones and the Internet, and the extent of these incidents is probably very much greater than has been reported (Human Rights Commission Pakistan, 2016). There are three aspects of the use of social media and the Internet that have helped to promote gender-based violence: first, it is easy to upload images and once they are published they are very difficult to remove; second, once uploaded, the information and images spread very rapidly and can become widely seen; and third, such imagery can then be used as visible, firm evidence to incite traditional cultural norms of behaviour related to family honour, even in circumstances when the imagery might, to other cultures, appear quite innocent. It is not only violence against women, though, that can be promulgated through social media, and the killings that took place in Bangladesh in 2015 and 2016 represent contrasting recent examples of anti-secular and gender-based violence being directed against bloggers and gay activists who use social media.

It is possible in some instances to respond to such activities through existing legislation in countries that have robust and well-established legal systems, although going through the courts is costly and often painful. Almost always

[7] <https://unwin.wordpress.com/2015/11/16/citizen-journalism-trolls-and-international-terrorism>.

it is beyond the means of the poor. However, the legal systems in many countries are insufficiently robust or insufficiently flexible to be able to adapt to the advent of new technologies, and even where judgements are reached it can be difficult to enforce the courts' decisions. Hence, there is an urgent need for support to be given to the police and judiciary in poor countries, not only to assist them in developing systems through which such behaviour can be appropriately brought to trial, but also so that such actions can be used to change abusive online behaviours. Moreover, a very real challenge facing the implementation of such change is that legal systems generally move very much more slowly than does the evolution of technology. It is therefore essential that, as far as possible, legislation should be technology-neutral and based on core principles around what people in a particularly country see as being right and wrong.

6.2.2 *The Darker Side of the Dark Web*

Those who seek to undertake activities that contravene the existing normal acceptable standards of behaviour in any society, as reflected in its legal system, have always sought to do so hidden from view. Whilst the Internet has the ability to make many aspects of behaviour far more visible than was previously the case, it has also enabled the Dark Web to flourish as a medium for those who want to undertake activities hidden from the purview of enforcers of the existing criminal justice system based upon the norms of behaviour in any particular society. There are many aspects of the Dark Web that most people would see as being largely positive, such as enabling greater individual privacy, protecting dissidents in oppressive regimes, and enabling whistleblowers to share information more widely. Even here, though, there are problems of interpretation, because some might see China as being oppressive, whereas others would describe the USA in such terms.

However, there are also many less obviously positive aspects to the Dark Web, including its use for the sale of illegal goods such as drugs, its use to promulgate computer crimes, and its use for sharing files, particularly pornography. Given its overtly hidden nature, it is extremely difficult to estimate the extent and character of usage of the Dark Web. Owen and Savage (2015) have explored the popularity of the content accessed through Tor by the two million people on average who used it in June 2015. As they comment 'Perhaps unsurprisingly, the majority of sites were criminally oriented, with drug marketplaces featuring prominently. Notably, however, it was found that sites hosting child abuse imagery were the most frequently requested' (Owen and Savage, 2015, p. 1). They highlight that the most common hidden service sites were those for drugs, following by generic marketplaces, fraud, and bitcoin currency exchanges, but that in terms of usage, requests to access abuse sites accounted for more than 80 per cent of the total, although these represented only 2 per cent of the hidden services available.

One important characteristic of the Dark Web is that those involved in creating and managing its services are not only highly capable technically, but also very resilient and flexible. The Silk Road, for example, was created in 2011 as a platform for selling illegal drugs using bitcoins, and it is estimated that some US$15 million of transactions were conducted on it in 2012 alone (Cristin, 2013). By March 2013, at least 10,000 products were on sale on the Silk Road, more than two-thirds of which were drugs. Although this was seen by many as being a risk-free way of obtaining drugs that were illegal in many jurisdictions, the US government closed its operations, arresting its founder in 2013. Soon, though, Silk Road 2.0 was launched, being closed in its turn in November 2014. However, other marketplaces have continued to evolve, seeking to fill the gap that has been left. As long as there is an Internet, this evidence suggests that activities that many governments and citizens see as being illegal will continue to thrive on it.

Not all such activities on the Dark Web are as relatively benign as markets in illegal substances. Bartlett (2014) has identified many distinct subcultures, not only the drug markets such as the Silk Road, but also self-harm communities, cam-girls, those sharing pornographic and abusive materials, and those who use social media to propagate racist and other extreme positions, many of whom engage in highly destructive behaviours. In particular, he draws attention to the contrasting activities of 'transhumanists' (see also Livingstone, 2015), those who seek to use technology to speed up the evolution of humans, and extreme 'crypto-anarchists' who use cryptography to evade and thereby try to subvert the entire global social and economic system based on capitalism. Significantly, he concludes that in this dark world there is little moral certainty; instead there is much ambiguity. It is with this ambiguity that governments and citizens across the world need to engage so that both the positive and the negative ways through which ICTs are used become more fully appreciated and discussed. ICTs, as emphasized elsewhere in this book, are powerful accelerators, either for good or for evil. In the pursuit of all the positive things that these technologies can contribute, their negative potential must also be recognized and contained. All too often, governments and people living in poorer countries are encouraged to focus on the former, with insufficient attention being paid to the latter. The next section therefore turns to ways of enhancing a more robust and resilient global digital infrastructure in the interests of everyone, and especially the poor.

6.3 From 'Cyber-Security' to Resilience

The issues discussed in the previous section are just some of those that face people and governments across the world as they seek to grapple with the complexities of the rapid expansion and evolution of digital technologies. Most of them relate to criminal activity (Kshetri, 2010), but as Glenny (2011) has highlighted there are many other types of threat, particularly overt warfare through the use of ICTs (Kaplan, 2016), as well as industrial espionage (see also Singer and Friedman, 2014). As Glenny (2011, p. 1) emphasizes, 'In humanity's relentless drive for convenience and economic growth, we have developed a dangerous level of dependency on networked systems in a very short space of time.' This global interconnectedness lies at the heart of many of the challenges that face the international community in enabling digital networks to function securely. At the simplest level, it is not always easy to determine exactly where a criminal activity has taken place, and thus under what jurisdiction the perpetrator can be tried. Most importantly, as the tentacles of the Internet spread ever more widely, those seeking to use it for illegal activities in one jurisdiction, can readily undertake them physically in one place but enable access to them elsewhere through the Internet. Hence, it can be expected that illegal activity will spread rapidly to those most-connected, least-protected countries that also have the weakest legal frameworks. These are most often the poorest countries, and there is considerable need not only to train officials in these countries about effective security measures, but also to ensure that they have appropriate technologies in place to detect and deter. At present, most cyber threats are directed at some of the largest, and most digitally active countries in the world, with Kaspersky's real time map of threats indicating that the top five most infected countries in descending order on 2 August 2016 were the USA, Russia, Vietnam, Brazil, and India.[8] Poor countries, though, are equally vulnerable, and interestingly the top three countries in terms of local infections were Ethiopia, Yemen, and Bangladesh, indicating the significant burden that these poor countries have to face.

Given the global emphasis on the contribution of economic growth to development and the reduction of poverty, much attention has been placed on the economic impact of digital crimes, with a report by McAfee (2014) suggesting that its total annual cost to the global economy is more than US $400 billion, with some 800 million individuals in 2013 having their personal information stolen. There is therefore considerable global emphasis on reaching agreements on how such activity can be reduced (Singer and Friedman, 2014). However, it must be recognized that all digital systems are at least theoretically

---

[8] <https://cybermap.kaspersky.com/stats>, accessed 2 August 2016.

hackable, and there is a constant ongoing battle between those seeking to penetrate systems, and those seeking to protect them. The challenge for companies and governments in poor countries is that such protection is costly, and there is therefore a substantial need for international collaboration and support for the development and implementation of cyber-security strategies in such countries, because the world is only as secure as its weakest link. Moreover, breaches of digital security are invariably caused by human error, and it is therefore crucial for an integrated approach to be adopted that includes much greater public awareness. No one, for example, who used the commercial Ashley Madison website to facilitate their extra-marital affairs, should have been surprised about the release of twenty-five gigabytes of data, including user details, by those who hacked into the site in 2015.[9]

Governments have adopted very different strategies to deal with the cyber-security threat, many of which relate to their varying approaches towards the balance between privacy, freedom, and security (Section 6.1) as well as their attitudes towards international espionage. These differences have meant that it has been extremely difficult to reach international agreement and consensus, particularly between China, the European Union, Russia, and the USA (Sofaer et al., 2010; Touré et al., 2014) (see also Chapter 3). Likewise, ICT companies have also adopted very different approaches to the threat, which have often been polarized between those, such as Kaspersky, McAfee (now part of Intel Security), and Symantec that sell software and services to detect and eliminate known threats, and others that seek to ensure that their hardware and software is as robust as possible against those threats. In practice, a combination of both approaches is undoubtedly wise. If the darker aspects of the Internet outlined in this chapter are to be addressed effectively it is crucial not only that there is much greater collaboration across all sectors involved in the industry and beyond, but also that there is transparent dialogue between companies, governments, and citizens to reach culturally appropriate approaches in different countries within a broad global framework. This will not be easy to achieve, but unless such dialogues lead to constructive outcomes, the threats to global security will undoubtedly increase.

One of the most pressing of these is the threat to critical infrastructure, especially the electricity grid, but also other key sectors such as banking. A well-known example of the potential of such threats was the Stuxnet worm, thought to have been developed by the USA and Israel to sabotage Iran's nuclear programme (Zetter, 2014), but such attacks pose very real threats to national security, particularly in poor countries with insufficient defences in place. Indeed, given that all computer systems require electricity

---

[9] <https://www.oaic.gov.au/privacy-law/commissioner-initiated-investigation-reports/ashley-madison>.

to function, and most do so based on supplies from national grids, aggressive hacking into a country's electricity supply infrastructure could have potentially catastrophic impacts on the entire economy and way of life of its people, because most people and organizations are now so reliant on digital connectivity. The first known example of this was the hacking of Ukraine's power grid at the end of 2015 (Zetter, 2016), and it seems likely that this will become an increasingly common phenomenon elsewhere.

Given the potential vulnerability of all infrastructure to hacking, there has been increasing recognition that attention should focus as much on the resilience of systems as on preventive security (Christou, 2016). Systems will always be hacked, and whilst it is clearly important to defend against such attacks, it is even more important to ensure that infrastructures are resilient and able to be restored as quickly and cost-efficiently as possible. This has been recognized in the support that international organizations such as the ITU and CTO have given to the development of national Computer Emergency Response Teams (CERTs), also known as Computer Incident Response Teams (CIRTs) and Computer Security Incident Response Teams (CSIRTs) (Bada et al., 2014). In 2016, the ITU listed 103 national CIRTs,[10] and although this list appears to be incomplete (the Software Engineering Institute at Carnegie Mellon University lists 108 CSIRTs),[11] it is clear that many of the poorest countries, especially in Africa and the island states of the Pacific and Caribbean, still require support in putting these in place. Moreover, the progress from assessment, through implementation actually to running drills to test their response effectiveness has been slow, and many CERTs exist largely on paper.

As these examples show, cyber-security is of the utmost importance to all countries, but it is the poorest countries that are most at risk because of a lack of expertise and resources to be able to implement effective processes. The interconnected world is only as secure as its least secure country, and it is therefore incumbent on richer countries to work in partnership with those elsewhere to increase the resilience of national infrastructures and digital systems more broadly. Moreover, within poor countries it is often the poorest people who are most vulnerable to any perturbations in the economy or political volatility. Even if they do not have access themselves to computers or mobile phones, the costs to the wider economy of cybercrime disadvantage them, and when they do use such devices, the impact of crime can be greater for them than for richer people. The loss of the same amount of money through online banking fraud, for example, has much greater impact on a

---

[10] <http://www.itu.int/en/ITU-D/Cybersecurity/Pages/Organizational-Structures.aspx>, accessed 29 July 2016.
[11] <http://www.cert.org/incident-management/national-csirts/national-csirts.cfm>, accessed 29 July 2016.

poorer than a richer person. In Kenya, where many poor people have been encouraged in recent years to adopt mobile banking services, there has been a 'sharp rise in financial fraud within banks through mobile money, system tampering and mobile network exploitation' (Serianu, 2015, p. 16). Whilst there are undoubted benefits of mobile money systems, especially for poor people, they also have the most to lose when such systems are hacked.

6.4 The Big Con: Social Media, Google, and Big Data

One of the most remarkable transformations brought about by global ICT corporations, and epitomized by companies such as Google (Vise, 2005; Stross, 2008) and Facebook (Kirkpatrick, 2011), has been their ability to make very large profits by giving people something that they think they want 'for free'. Everyone who does not directly pay to use commercial social media, search engines, mapping software, and even sometimes cloud services provides the companies hosting them with vast amounts of information and data, from which these companies are then able to generate substantial profit, both through advertising revenues and also by selling the data to third parties. Facebook, for example, noted in 2016 that it gathers ninety-eight pieces of data about each person who uses its site, and it then uses this information to provide a more tailored service to paying advertisers.[12] Those who generate financial profit from such services are not the users, but rather the employees and shareholders of these global corporations. To be sure, such services do indeed have value for users, who previously had to buy maps, or send letters and photographs by post to each other, but the value to the companies is far greater financially than to the individuals who use the services. This is the source of corporate surplus value, in a Marxist sense of the term. Most users are insufficiently aware of how much of their private identities they are revealing when they use such services, let alone the risks they face from hacking and malware. Individuals generally underestimate the financial value of their information, and are willing to give it away for nothing for the limited perceived benefit that they gain. The rich can thus be seen, yet again, as performing a very effective con in exploiting the poor.

A second fundamental way through which many ICT companies maximize their profits is by exploiting global differences in taxation regimes. Rubin (2015) notes that one means by which they do this is by stockpiling their offshore profits, with Microsoft, Apple, Google, and five other major ICT companies accounting for more than a fifth of the $2.1 trillion in profits that

---

[12] <https://www.facebook.com/ads/about/?entry_product=ad_preferences>.

US companies hold overseas, thereby reducing the taxes that they pay to the US government. More worryingly, though, many of these companies pay little or no taxation in the countries in which they operate, or in which their users live. Companies such as Google, Facebook, and Amazon are well known for paying little or no tax in many of the countries where their users live, and it is only recently that some governments, particularly in Europe, have begun to take action over this. To date, few poorer countries have dared challenge the power of these global corporations, but India, following the example of OECD countries, introduced a new equalization levy in 2016, known locally as the 'Google tax', which imposes a levy of 6 per cent on the payments that advertisers make for international digital services.[13] This has been seen as one way through which governments of poorer countries can begin to share in the profits of US corporations, and if used wisely could be a means to enable the poor to gain some benefit from their activities.

The vast amount of information that such companies have about the people who use their services is similar in character, albeit at a much larger scale, to that which telecommunication operators also possess about their customers, and use not only to improve their services, but also to generate revenue. Telefónica, for example, launched a new global business unit in 2012 to monetize the information that they have about their customers, by using anonymized and aggregated network data to offer retailers and local councils information about the numbers of people visiting particular locations at different times.[14] Such activities are good examples of the increasing use of 'Big Data' in helping to understand the complexities of a rapidly changing world. As Hilbert (2016) has noted, dramatic expansion in bandwidth, data storage, and computational capacity has led to rapid increases in velocity, volume, and variety of data, giving rise to the use of the term 'Big Data' to describe the phenomenon. Usually, the analysis of such data is seen as offering huge potential, not only for companies to generate additional profit, but also to improve the lives of the poor. As with all technologies, though, there are both positive and negative implications of such usage. As the World Economic Forum (2012, p. 1) notes, 'Concerted action is needed by governments, development organisations, and companies to ensure that this data helps the individuals and communities who create it' (see also Privacy International, 2013). All too often, though, this has not happened, and it is the large global corporations with the ability to manage and analyse such data effectively that have benefited the most from Big Data. To be sure, there have

---

[13] <http://economictimes.indiatimes.com/news/economy/policy/modi-governments-new-way-to-tax-google-facebook-kicks-in-from-tomorrow/articleshow/52512712.cms>.

[14] <https://www.research-live.com/article/news/telefnica-taps-mobile-data-for-location-insights/id/4008420>.

been many initiatives, particularly in the analysis of health data, that have used Big Data to offer new understandings and insights from which poor people can theoretically benefit, but too often these have not resulted in real practical action to benefit them.

Spratt and Baker (2015) have usefully explored the potential impact of Big Data for developing countries across economic, human development, rights, and environmental axes, and conclude that the direct impacts are likely to be mainly negative, although the indirect impacts in terms of production and services, marketing and organizational structure, are more evenly balanced. In the context of the discussion earlier in this chapter (Section 6.1) most concerns are around issues of privacy and security, as well as the rights that companies might have to use such data, and also the rights that individuals should have to data about themselves (see also Song, 2013b). Hilbert (2016, p. 172) likewise emphasizes that Big Data offers both opportunities and threats for development. On the one hand, it can help decision-making in areas such as health-care, disaster management, and economic productivity, but on the other hand structural characteristics mean that there is an unequal diffusion process that leads to a divide in data-driven knowledge. As Spratt and Baker (2015, p. 33) conclude, it is clear that the costs and benefits of Big Data will be unevenly shared 'between and within countries, but also that these outcomes can be influenced by policy if we choose to act'. Hence, if Big Data is to be used to empower poor and marginalized people, it is essential that effective policies are rapidly put in place that will address their needs on an equal basis to those of the commercial benefits of Big Data to powerful companies. Even here, though, there is a challenge, because most discussion about Big Data and development today focuses on how Big Data can be used *for* the poor, rather than *by* the poor. For poor and marginalized people truly to be empowered by Big Data, they need to be able to use it to influence their own lives, and yet almost by definition poor people have neither the wherewithal to afford the technology to use Big Data effectively, nor the expertise to analyse it.

An equally disturbing trend has been the blending together of arguments concerning Big Data and Open Data (Gurstein, 2011; Janssen et al., 2012; Song, 2013b). Governments are increasingly being encouraged, largely by the private sector, to open up the data that they collect in many areas, so that it can be used to generate profit and thus drive economic growth. In a development context, this is generally seen as being positive, since economic growth is widely considered to be essential for the elimination of poverty (Chapter 1) (World Bank, 2016b). There are undoubtedly benefits in being able to use such data for making better-informed decisions, for creating opportunities to develop new business opportunities, and to develop innovative solutions for healthcare provision and urban management. Nevertheless, alongside the ethical issues involved, it represents a fundamental transfer of resources from the poor to the rich. Typical of ethical concerns are the ways through which government health services sell patient data to the private sector, an issue which was the subject of considerable debate in the UK in 2014.[15] However, the biggest con is in the way that the private sector, represented both by companies and by academic researchers, benefits at virtually no cost from a resource that all taxpayers, and thus ultimately the poor, have paid for. Once again, even if they receive some benefits from the analysis of Open Data, which remains an open question, the voiceless poor are being exploited by the rich who have the technology and expertise to gain most from its analysis and exploitation. There is certainly a cost to the private sector in analysing Open Data, which is why governments have often not used it effectively in the past, but the potential financial benefits to companies and universities from its exploitation remain considerable. If such research is undertaken explicitly in the interests of the poor, and they are involved in its design and analysis, then there is reason to hope that Open Data might indeed be empowering, but as yet there is insufficient evidence to suggest that they will benefit more than global corporations from its use.

This section of the chapter has challenged assumptions that are all too often taken for granted about the value that the analysis of large amounts of data can contribute to reducing poverty. It has suggested that there are important ethical issues that need to be addressed and also that the economic benefits of such analysis are unequally distributed. It seems likely, at least in the short term, that the explosion of interest in data analytics will continue rapidly to expand, driven above all by the commercial interests involved therein. It is therefore crucial that governments, especially in poor countries, recognize the critical significance of the privacy and identity of individuals and information about them, and put in place and implement effective policies and strategies to ensure that the poorest and most marginalized do indeed also benefit from such data and their analysis.

6.5 Dehumanization: Cyborgs and the Internet of Things

I remember once walking along Queen Victoria Street in London one evening, and looking down through a window beneath street level to see row upon row of computers, each with their human attached, working away at delivering some unknown products. It so reminded me of my early readings of Marx's (1976) *Capital* about the dehumanization of labour through the factory system that was designed to extract yet greater surplus value for the capitalists. Although people like to think that they are in control of their ICTs, this is

---

[15] <https://www.theguardian.com/society/2014/jan/19/nhs-patient-data-available-companies-buy>; <https://www.england.nhs.uk/2014/01/guardian-story/>.

Figure 6.1 Young people communicating at the Hotel International and Terminus, Geneva, 2013

Source: Author, 19 May 2013 (taken with permission of all five people shown in the photograph).

increasingly not the case. Office workers come into their open-plan work spaces, and 'their' computers force them to log in so as to access the information and communication tools necessary to do their work.

Often, people communicate together by mobile devices even when they are in the same room (Figure 6.1). The art and skill of face-to-face conversation is swiftly being eroded, mediated instead through technology. Internet addiction is now widely recognized as a compulsive-impulsive spectrum disorder (Block, 2008) involving excessive use, withdrawal, tolerance, and negative repercussions (see also Cash et al., 2012), with rehabilitation centres being created across the world, from China to the USA, in order to try to help addicted people.

One particularly prescient early image of the relationship between humans and technology is Villemard's depiction in 1910 of how he thought a school might look in 2000, showing books being dropped into a machine that transforms the information, which then passes through electric cables into each pupil's headsets (Figure 6.2). Conceptually, this is not that different from the online learning systems that now increasingly dominate classrooms in both rich and poor countries alike.

At the GSMA's Mobile World Congress held in Barcelona in February 2014 smartwear was all the rage, and I remember thinking as I walked past Sony's advertisement for Xperia on the metro platform wall (Figure 6.3) that there were things about my life that I would

Figure 6.2 Villemard's 1910 image *À l'École*, depicting how he thought a school might look in 2000
Source: http://expositions.bnf.fr/utopie/grand/3_95b1.htm.

Figure 6.3 Sony's poster 'Log your life with SmartWear' on the wall of a metro station in Barcelona during Mobile World Congress, 2014
Source: Author, 28 February 2014.

169

definitely not want to log, and would certainly not want others to have access to by hacking either my devices or the cloud servers where they might be stored. Yet countless people have purchased such devices, and regularly have their health data automatically uploaded so that companies can analyse it and generate profits without paying them anything in return. This is an extreme example of Big Data surplus extraction, because not only do people have to buy the devices in the first place, and sometimes the software, but they also then give the data to the companies for no pecuniary return, and generally receive little back individually that might actually enhance their lives.

* * *

The organic relationships between peoples and machines have long formed a topic of heated debate, especially since the emergence of the notion of cyborgs (cybernetic organisms) in the 1960s (see Clynes and Kline, 1960; Harraway, 1985, 1991). Likewise, the increasing presence of the Internet of Things (Greengard, 2015) raises questions of critical ethical importance for the empowerment of poor and marginalized peoples. As the examples at the start of this section highlight, humans and machines are becoming ever more interwoven. In essence, a cyborg is an organism that has enhanced abilities through the integration of components that rely on a feedback system. Usually, it refers to humans or other animals with an added technological component, but it is equally possible to conceive of machines with human components. Assistive Technologies linked to their biological systems have transformed the lives of many people with disabilities, and technological innovations in the future will further empower them to have ever-greater control over their lives. It also does not require much imagination to think how the technology associated with smartwear could readily be implanted into humans, so that they did not have to bother with strapping it on when they want to use it. Likewise, the rapid expansion of virtual reality, although largely initially through headsets for gaming and for military use, offers interesting potential for immersive experiences that could enhance the understanding of workers in international development, as well as sensitizing people in richer countries to the reality of poverty.[16] These are but small steps in the transhumanists' evolving vision of technology enhanced humans (Section 6.2.2; Livingstone, 2015).

There are undoubted benefits to be gained from the increasingly interwoven physical engagement of humans with technology, and it is important that their benefits are explored in the context of empowering the poor. Nevertheless, they raise significant ethical questions, not least over the meaning of being human, and about privacy and control. At the simplest and most

---

[16] <https://matterport.com/haiti-communitere-uses-virtual-reality-international-development>.

practical level, such technologies are currently expensive, far beyond the reach of poor people, and so will further increase inequality and the marginalization of the poor. However, if appropriate policies are to be put in place now to guide the development of chipped-humans or other types of cyborg, it is crucial that people look into the future and imagine the various divergent scenarios that could emerge. For example, the rich and powerful might, on the one hand, seek to keep digital implants to themselves so that they can benefit exclusively from the advantages of enhanced life experiences. Or, on the other hand, they might seek to live lives unenhanced by implanted technology, and use ICTs instead to enslave the minds and bodies of those who labour to keep them in power. As the previous examples cited in this chapter imply, the increasing interweaving of humans and ICTs also raises fundamental questions about privacy and control. The point here, though, is not so much that the rich and powerful are either in control of or can afford to guard their privacy, thereby leading to greater inequalities in the world, but rather that new technological developments are enhancing this trend, and therefore increasing inequality at an ever more rapid rate.

Similar arguments apply to the headlong pursuit towards the Internet of Things (IoT) (see also Section 2.7), which has too often been seen as yet another technological boon for development, without its ethical and practical implications being sufficiently considered. The coalition of interests between international agencies and the private sector driving this agenda forward is particularly well illustrated in the ITU and Cisco's recent report for the Broadband Commission, which asserts that 'The IoT and connected sensors are driving improvements to human wellbeing in healthcare, water, agriculture, natural resource management, resiliency to climate change and energy (as reflected in the UN's post-2015 sustainable development goals)' (ITU and Cisco, 2016, p. 7). The overwhelming emphasis of this report is about the positive benefits of the IoT, primarily in the context of ensuring that the private sector can use it efficiently to contribute to economic growth, without referring to any of the ethical concerns alluded to so far in this chapter. In contrast to the discussion earlier (Section 6.2), for example, it suggests only that 'Privacy (related to confidentiality) is the ability to define the intended target audience for data' (ITU and Cisco, 2016, p. 44). The challenges it identifies likewise focus mainly on those at the technical and policy level that might limit the rapid expansion of the IoT, rather than explicitly those that might prevent it from empowering poor and marginalized people and communities.

The scale of the IoT will be vast, and will require connectivity far beyond anything currently in place (see also Section 2.7). It will involve a world of complete connectivity between humans and machines, and one where the amount of machine to machine (M2M) communication will soon vastly outreach communication from person to person (P2P). Machines may soon be more important than poor people; indeed some would say that they already are. A small example of the way that this is insidiously affecting the entire way that those in the ICT sector think about this issue is in the language used in the ITU and Cisco (2016) report just mentioned. Typical of others in the sector, alongside M2M and P2P, the report refers only to M2P (machine to person) communication. This largely reflected the views of those involved in the case studies that shaped the report, but it is still indicative of the dominant language used in the sector. Many may not see this use of language as being strange at all, but it is hugely important in suggesting the interests underlying the roll-out of the IoT, and indeed ICTs more widely. Quite simply, M2P gives prominence to the machines doing the communicating. It is no coincidence that this is the terminology that is being used, rather than P2M, or person to machine communication. It shows where the power lies.

Howard (2015) has very usefully highlighted some of the tensions and complexities that underlie the roll-out of the IoT. He notes that it has great potential for increasing global stability by making government more transparent, widening access to information, and empowering citizens. However, he also emphasizes that the use of ICTs to date has not necessarily achieved this, commenting that 'Having more information and communication technologies hasn't made international affairs more transparent, honest, or democratic. If anything, global politics seems more convoluted and complex with the arrival of the internet' (Howard, 2015, p. 44). In particular, he argues that the IoT substantially threatens privacy, and raises the potential for political manipulation and even greater social control. All too often these complex tensions are ignored in the hype of how the IoT can contribute to development, and it is crucial that governments and people throughout the world, but especially in poor countries, are fully aware of, and appreciate, these tensions when considering the development of relevant policies, regulatory matters, and legislation. The lure of the private sector to contribute to a country's economic growth, and the potential individual benefits that can be gained from lucrative contracts with foreign companies, nevertheless frequently mean that such concerns are ignored in the rush to adopt the latest modern technologies.

6.6 In the Interests of the Poor and Marginalized

This chapter has focused explicitly on some of the more complex and challenging moral issues surrounding the rapid evolution of ICTs. To be sure, as noted in Section 2.7 the IoT has very considerable potential to improve the lives of the poor (Zennaro and Bagula, 2015), but whether that potential is realized or not is another matter. Likewise, the Internet has hugely positive potential to provide enhanced education, health, and governance that are of benefit to poor people, but it is also used for much darker purposes that most people would see as threatening their lives, as with the use of the Internet for violent terrorist activities (UNODC, 2012).

It is therefore fundamentally important that there is extensive consultation across all sectors about the dark issues raised in this chapter, so that wise decisions are made not only by governments, but also by private sector companies and individuals. Fundamentally, privacy issues relate to individuals, and individuals can make choices. No one *has* to be on social media; no one *has* to store large amounts of personal data on external servers or the Cloud. However, increasingly it is becoming impossible to engage socially, politically, and economically without so doing. This insidious all-pervasive domination of human life by machines is what is perhaps most worrying. As governments increasingly move to a digital-by-default approach, partly in their drive to reduce costs, they increasingly marginalize those who cannot, or do not want to, use ICTs. For the private sector, who are very much leading such processes, it is important for everyone to be connected, so that they can have as large, and as uniform, a market as possible for their products and services. From such connectivity, they gain access to a large amount of information about individuals, from which they seek to generate yet further profit. Yet, as emphasized throughout this chapter, this poses a considerable threat to the individual, because no data is ever totally secure.

7

...In the Interests of the Poorest and Most Marginalized

There are faces that I will never forget. They haunt me. The young girl in a market in Bangaon (India). The elderly blind beggars on a street corner in Beijing (China). The children in danger of living and working on the streets in Nazret (Ethiopia) (Figure 7.1). The Maasai boys and girls in a boma near Arusha (Tanzania). When I think about ICTs for development, these are the faces that come into my mind. These are some of the poorest and most marginalized people I have met. This book has fundamentally been about exploring ways through which their lives could have been improved through the appropriate use of ICTs, and trying to understand why, despite all of the rhetoric about the power of ICT4D, very poor people are becoming even more marginalized as a result of the interests that underlie the transformative spread of these new technologies. But I still hold on to the hope that this need not be so, and that it remains possible for them to be empowered through the use of ICTs.

*   *   *

This concluding chapter seeks both to spell out the reasons for such optimism, and also to outline some of what needs to be done for it to be realized. I remain a descendant of the European Enlightenment, and retain a belief that we can make the world a better place. There is no one solution, no silver bullet, that will transform ICT4D. However, there are many things that can be done to shift the balance, so that ICTs can be used to create a fairer and less unequal world. These are context-specific, and geography matters (Unwin, 1992). As I have argued elsewhere, ICT4D is a moral agenda (Unwin, 2009). There is no best practice, but instead good practices that people can reflect on and shape for their own contexts. The evolving structure of this book reflects these tentative conclusions; it is another way through which the intertwining self-reflection of theory and practice in Critical Theory can indeed empower people. Some answers thus lie in crafting relevant technical solutions, some in reshaping the role of government and regulation, others in building effective partnerships, yet others in ensuring that digital systems are resilient, and

Figure 7.1 Children at risk of living and working on the street in Ethiopia, 2002
Source: Author.

all need to be underlain by effective learning and understanding. Above all, everyone involved in ICT4D needs to begin by focusing their attention on the needs and interests of the poorest and most marginalized of our brothers and sisters, those on very low incomes, those with disabilities, and those excluded because of their race, colour, or gender.

7.1 ICTs and Empowerment

Empowerment is a term fraught with difficulties (Chapter 1), but at its heart it implies people gaining increasing power over their own lives. By outlining the challenges associated with effective ICT4D, this book will therefore hopefully enable everyone who reads it, be they government officials, academics, those working in civil society organizations, or managers in the private sector, to become empowered by reflecting on their own practices, and thereby shaping better ICT initiatives in the future in the interests of the poor. One fundamental message of this book is that *we should not be working for the poor, but rather with the poor* if they are truly to be empowered. Far too many ICT4D initiatives have been designed *for* the poor, often with good intentions, but they fail because they have insufficiently involved the poor in their design and implementation.

The instrumental belief that technologies have some kind of power of their own to make a difference to the lives of poor people is fundamentally misguided. Technologies are designed and developed with particular interests in mind, and unless poor people are prioritized in such design they will not be the net beneficiaries. This book has therefore concentrated especially on revealing ways through which these different interests work constantly to disadvantage the poor. In effect, ICTs are transformative accelerators, and it is hardly surprising that those in power have sought to use them to retain their power. Hence, in unequal societies, ICTs have primarily been used to reinforce and extend inequality. As increasing numbers of reports by the UNDP (2015) and World Bank (2016a) are now recognizing, the poorest and most marginalized have been excluded from the benefits of ICTs, and are thus becoming increasingly disadvantaged. For those who define poverty in a relative sense, the poor are therefore becoming increasingly impoverished.

It is unrealistic to expect there to be a fundamental shift in the short term in the hegemonic view that economic growth will eliminate poverty. However, if this is not at the very least balanced by an emphasis on reducing inequality then relative poverty will continue to increase apace, with serious detrimental effects, not least increasing social tensions and politically inspired violence (OECD, 2015a). This has, to some extent, been recognized in the tenth Sustainable Development Goal (SDG), which aims to reduce inequality within and among countries. ICTs are widely seen as being important promoters of economic growth, but far less attention has to date been placed on their role in reducing inequality. Indeed, none of the ten targets for SDG 10 makes specific reference to the potential role that ICTs can play in the reduction of inequalities.[1] Given the significant role that ICTs have in increasing existing social and economic trends, there must be a fundamental refocusing of attention on the ways through which ICTs can indeed reduce inequality, especially by governments and civil society, if this target is to be achieved. *The fundamental focus for anyone still believing in ICT4D rather than D4ICT needs to be on the poorest and most marginalized,* as well as on enhancing processes that increase equality. This implies, for example, that policies to extend mobile broadband

---

[1] <http://www.un.org/sustainabledevelopment/inequality>.

and Internet access to the 'next billion' should be replaced by those focusing explicitly on the poorest, those I prefer to call the 'first billion' because they are of most importance (see Section 5.5). The private sector is already connecting the next billion, aided ably by international organizations (see for example IGF, 2016; World Economic Forum, 2016), but companies not unsurprisingly remain reluctant to address the needs of those who cannot afford the tariffs required by existing business models. It is therefore up to governments, at national and international levels, to put in place mechanisms and incentives whereby the poor and marginalized can be enabled to gain access.

However, it is not just access to technology that matters. As recent OECD (2016) research indicates, even when people from very different socio-economic backgrounds do have access to the Internet, they use it in different ways, with the already advantaged using it for more productive purposes that contribute to their further benefit, whereas the less advantaged tend to use it simply for chatting or playing games. ICT initiatives focused on the poorest therefore need to be holistic, bringing together relevant stakeholders in their design and implementation, not only to provide access to connectivity, but also to develop appropriate content that will explicitly empower the poor, and to integrate this with comprehensive programmes to help them to use it in their own interests.

Finally in this section, the warnings of Chapter 6 that ICTs are increasingly being used to control, rather than empower, people also need to be heeded. This applies most obviously to the power that global corporations and governments now have to monitor and influence everyone, both rich and poor, through their use of the Internet. However, it is also pertinent to the opportunities that new ICTs, particularly associated with the Internet of Things and cyborgs, provide for all human life itself to be controlled (Figure 7.2). Undoubtedly, ICTs can be used to benefit the lives of marginalized people, as for example with the dramatic changes that assistive technologies and digital prosthetics can make to empowering people with disabilities. Nevertheless, empowerment implies autonomy and freedom, and as ICTs become ever more pervasive and integrated with human life, the potential for this to constrain and limit human creativity and freedom needs to be recognized. ICTs themselves are neither good nor bad; it is how they are designed and used that determines this. Hence, there needs to be much more open and transparent discussion and debate globally about the moral dimensions of such technologies. To date, the private sector, driven by its rapacious desire for profit, has worked actively to limit widespread discussion of the negative ramifications of ICTs. The time has come for governments and international organizations to initiate much more active debate of these, both in their own countries and also in the international arena.

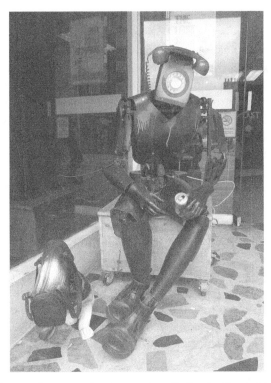

Figure 7.2 The future of communication: art installation in Cambridge, 2013, entitled 'Communication Breakdown' by Giles Walker
Source: Author, 20 July 2013.

7.2 Technical Options for Empowering the Poor and Marginalized

There is increasing recognition that technical innovation as well as changes in policy, the development of innovative business models, and the creation of relevant content are all necessary for the poor and marginalized to benefit from expansion in the use of ICTs (World Bank, 2016a). Most recent global attention, though, has tended to focus primarily on maximizing access to the Internet (Broadband Commission, 2015). This is clearly illustrated by Target 9c of the SDGs, which states that adherents will 'Significantly increase access to information and communications technology and strive to provide universal and affordable access to the Internet in least developed countries by 2020'. Access is undoubtedly of crucial importance, because without it none of the benefits that might accrue to poor and marginalized people can be achieved. However, improving access alone is not enough. As Table 7.1 suggests, even where there is access many people do not use the Internet, and also when it is

Table 7.1 Framework for considering priorities in enhancing the use of the Internet by poor and marginalized people

	Those without access	Those with access but not using	Those with access and using
Extending infrastructure	**Providing infrastructure**	Enhancing quantity and quality of existing infrastructure	Enhancing quality of existing infrastructure
Affordability	Lowering costs, technical innovation and new business models	**Lowering costs, technical innovation and new business models**	Lowering costs, technical innovation and new business models
Skills and critical awareness	Improving digital literacy and understanding	**Improving digital literacy and understanding of appropriate use**	**Improving digital literacy and understanding of appropriate use**
Local adoption, adaptation, and use	Ensuring context-relevant content	**Ensuring production and use of context-relevant content**	**Ensuring production and use of context-relevant content**

Note: Items in bold indicate highest priorities.
Source: Based in part on World Economic Forum (2016).

available it may not be used to alleviate poverty (OECD, 2016). Indeed, the amounts spent by poor people on connectivity, often for social media and games, can represent a serious drain on their resources, thus making it even harder for them to escape from poverty.

The World Economic Forum (2016) has summarized much accepted wisdom around ways of accelerating Internet access and adoption, suggesting that there are four main areas where action is required: extending infrastructure, making access more affordable, increasing the skills and awareness necessary for people to use the Internet effectively, and developing locally relevant content so that people can clearly see a benefit from its use. Table 7.1, though, shows that the prioritization of these actions needs to vary according to the circumstances pertaining. Thus, where there is no connectivity, the highest priority should be on extending the infrastructure, but where access is present then affordability, training, and relevant content become of most importance. This emphasizes once again that there are no best practices, but rather that a range of good practices should be drawn upon to reach locally relevant contextual solutions. All too often, such frameworks have been driven largely by private sector companies, eager to get as many people connected as possible so as to maximize profits from their networks, content, and services (GSMA, 2016b; World Economic Forum, 2016). While private sector involvement is indeed important in expanding networks, governments and civil society also have key roles to play if the poor and marginalized are to benefit.

Universal access, affordable mobile devices, affordable connectivity, and relevant content are all essential for poor people to take advantage of the potential of ICTs to transform their lives. Great strides are already being made in delivering connectivity, and it is now theoretically possible for access to the Internet to be provided anywhere in the world through a combination of satellites, fibre, and wireless networks. Costs of delivering connectivity in rural areas are also falling, particularly as new satellite technologies are introduced. Moreover, innovative solutions, such as Google's Project Loon[2] and Facebook's Aquila solar-powered plane,[3] are showing what can be achieved if sufficient investment is made in supporting creative solutions for rural connectivity. Likewise, 4G mobile devices are becoming much more affordable, and can now for example be purchased in India for between Rs 4000 and 5000 (£45 and £60). Free wireless zones are enabling everyone to connect to the Internet in some urban areas, which undoubtedly benefits the poor. Other initiatives provide access to limited Internet services for free in many parts of the world through zero-rating of some services, although Facebook's Free Basics[4] initiative has proved highly controversial, especially in India, where it is has been banned for infringing the fundamental principle of Net Neutrality (Song, 2016).

Two important related areas where further research and implementation are necessary, though, are in electricity solutions and the sustainability of ICTs. ICTs are useless without electricity, and the development of new solutions, both grid and off-grid, is essential for the widespread dissemination of access. Many small-scale local initiatives have indeed been developed, including the use of bicycles for recharging mobile devices (Collings, 2011), and micro-hydro installations powering telecentres, as in Sarawak (Yeo, 2015), but such good practices need to be spread much more widely so as to benefit poorer people elsewhere in the world. Likewise, much further research needs to be undertaken on reducing the energy requirements of ICTs, and extending the battery life of mobile devices. Furthermore, as noted in Chapter 2, the ICT sector is fundamentally built on a model of unsustainability, with companies designing mobile devices and tablets with limited durability expectancies so that they usually need to be replaced within a couple of years. This places an unacceptable burden on poor people, as well as on governments of poor countries committed, for example, to providing schoolchildren with such devices. The continual upgrading of software and hardware, which over time become incompatible thereby requiring additional purchases, likewise

---

[2] <https://www.solveforx.com/loon>.
[3] <https://www.facebook.com/notes/mark-zuckerberg/the-technology-behind-aquila/10153916136506634>.
[4] <https://info.internet.org/en/story/free-basics-from-internet-org>.

presents poor people with an additional burden. Poor people need to have robust devices that last and can be used for a considerable length of time so as to reduce the overall costs of mobile use. More also needs to be done to reduce the exploitation of poor children in mobile device production, as highlighted by Amnesty International (2016) in its research on cobalt mining in the Democratic Republic of the Congo.

Most such new technological initiatives have, however, been initiated and developed *for* poor people rather than *by* or *with* poor people, and the countless failings of innovative ICT projects designed with good intent by people from Europe and North America for use in Africa and Asia should serve as a salutary warning about the balance of interests involved in implementing ICT4D initiatives. Much more multidisciplinary research therefore still needs to be done so that the needs and interests of poor people can be better understood, and relevant hardware and software designed in the light of this understanding so as to serve their interests.

7.3 The Roles of Governments and International Organizations

The private sector is the engine of economic growth, and undoubtedly has a key role to play in models of absolute poverty reduction by increasing the overall productivity of the global economy. However, its primary interests are concerned with generating profit for shareholders and employees; it is much less interested in the poorest and most marginalized, other than as potential new customers from whom further profit can be extracted, or as cheap labour. It cannot be expected to lose money enabling people to access services that otherwise they would not be able to afford. While CSR initiatives do indeed offer some palliative support to ICT4D projects around the world (Sections 2.1.1 and 4.1) most of these are not sustainable; it is essential that the business end of companies is centrally involved if sustainability is to be achieved. It is therefore primarily up to states to put in place mechanisms whereby *all citizens* have the potential to benefit from new technologies such as ICTs. However, governments are frequently seen as being inefficient, self-seeking, and lacking the knowledge and expertise to design and roll out effective ICT4D policies. Indeed, frustration with so-called corruption and political ineptitude, not only within individual countries but also in international organizations, has led many to argue that the private sector should take a much more prominent role in global governance (Martens, 2007). Moreover, where people do not trust their governments they are frequently much more willing to trust companies, not least with digital information about themselves.

Despite such issues, governments retain a fundamentally important role in shaping the legislative and policy environment within which ICTs can be used to empower poor people. It is easy to argue in principle that governments should therefore seek to enable the private sector to deliver effective and relevant ICTs to as many people as possible, whilst also putting in place mechanisms whereby the poorest and most marginalized can also benefit. The challenge is in deciding how best to implement this in specific contexts. Referring back to the first column of Table 7.1, for example, governments need to encourage companies to deliver connectivity to as many people as possible, but then develop innovative solutions to ensure that those that are still left without connectivity are provided for. The precise ways that this can be achieved will vary from country to country, but there are three key principles and issues that need to be considered by governments in most circumstances.

First, ICT and telecommunications *regulators* have a central role to play, and it is important that they are independent, transparent, and effective. As argued in Chapter 5, there needs to be a shift in thinking away from a controlling view of regulation to one that is focused primarily on *facilitation*. Regulators have the unenviable task of trying to balance the very differing interests of the private sector, governments, and citizens. However, they only act within the context of legislation promulgated by governments, and it is therefore essential that governments implement wise overall laws and policies within which regulators can facilitate the development of the ICT sector, particularly in the interests of the poor.

Second, governments and regulators should be *innovative and open to new approaches and ideas*. Existing structures and accepted wisdom over the last twenty years have failed to deliver ICT policies and practices that have sufficiently empowered the poor and marginalized, and it is time to think anew creatively. In particular, there needs to be a reassessment of the efficacy of Universal Service Funds, and the potential that reducing levies from spectrum auctions and licences might have for encouraging increased access and use of ICTs. In contexts where there are effective taxation mechanisms in place, it may well be possible for governments to raise greater revenue by taxing the increased economic vitality enabled by the wider use of ICTs than they have done previously from the higher levies imposed on operators that have restricted their potential to roll out networks more extensively. Likewise, for small island states, the mantra of introducing competition to reduce prices for consumers may not always be effective. Much more thought needs to be given to whether or not competition really works in the interests of the poor in the context of very small populations.

Third, governments need to adopt *holistic approaches*, not least involving many different government departments, if ICTs are to be used effectively to support poor and marginalized people. There are many existing good practices that could easily be adopted if there was the will to do so. These include, for example, policies to require infrastructure sharing, and to limit the amounts payable to landowners for laying cable or raising radio masts. It is likewise essential for there to be close collaboration between ICT ministries, finance ministries and those ministries, such as health, education, and rural development, which have remits to oversee the delivery of services that can directly benefit poor people. All too often ICT4D initiatives tend to be less effective than they might be because they are driven by a single ministry, with insufficient collaboration and understanding across government departments that are essential for their success (ITU, 2015a). The importance of a holistic approach also applies to the development of innovative partnerships with civil society and the private sector that have the potential to be most effective in reaching the poorest and most marginalized (see Section 4.3).

Similarly, considerable attention needs to be paid to the practices of international organizations with interests in the use of ICTs for development, especially those related to issues such as Internet governance. Two issues are of special concern. First, there is far too much wasteful overlap and duplication of effort across the many different international organizations convening forums to discuss these issues. As highlighted in Chapter 3, companies, governments, and civil society all seek to use the plethora of global conferences and summits to ensure that their own interests are represented as effectively as possible. There needs to be much greater focus and rationalization of such events and activities if the poor are really to benefit. The thrust of this chapter so far has been that governments need to play a stronger role if their poorest citizens are to benefit appropriately from ICTs. It is, after all, governments that determine legislation in their own countries, and sign international treaties that shape the overall framework within which the ICT sector, and particularly telecommunications, can flourish. This implies that all countries should commit to working much more closely through the ITU, as the UN agency with responsibility for the telecommunications sector, to help ensure the promulgation of effective global standards, and the sharing of good practices that would benefit the poorest and most marginalized. Some governments, however, retain concerns about the efficacy of, and the balance of power within, the ITU. In particular, those countries advocating a neoliberal stance towards global development remain eager to limit the power of the ITU, and to ensure that enabling rather than constraining legislation is put in place that will permit the private sector to have the freedom to shape the future of the sector. It therefore seems likely that for the foreseeable future the existing balance of interests between the private sector, governments, and civil society will lead to continued stasis in international discourse on these issues.

Second, it also seems highly likely that this stasis will not lead to policies and practices that truly represent the interests of the world's poorest people. This goes far beyond merely the absence of poor people themselves at such gatherings. Indeed, the difficulties that poor countries and small states have in participating in such international forums is but one of the many challenges that they face. It is impossible for countries with limited budgets and insufficient numbers of appropriately qualified officials to be represented at all of the relevant global forums that they need to be for their voices to be sufficiently heard. This is not simply a question of international organizations providing financial support to enable such participation, but more importantly the scarcity of suitably experienced personnel from poor countries is something that is very much more difficult to overcome. There are only so many meetings a year that a minister, regulator, CEO, or head of a civil society organization can possibly attend. As yet, virtual participation through video links has not proved to be a particularly effective means of convening such international forums, in part because of connectivity issues, but also because of the need for informal negotiations to take place between different interested parties during such events. One solution that requires further thought in trying to ensure that the voices of the poor are heard at such gatherings is to place greater emphasis on the role of regional or collective organizations in representing such interests. This raises considerable challenges, not least in matters of voting and in taking into consideration the interests of these intermediate organizations themselves, but the work of the CTU for Caribbean countries and the CTO for Commonwealth countries in building consensus and representing their member countries at international forums are models that could well be developed further.

7.4 The Power of Multi-Sector Partnerships

Many people advocate partnerships as a solution for delivering effective ICT4D initiatives at a wide range of scales, but few actually deliver effective partnerships in practice (see Chapter 4). This is not only because the skills required to convene and deliver partnership initiatives are often absent, but it also reflects the powerful interests at play in continuing to promote PPPs that fail to include civil society or which do not focus on actually delivering effective development interventions.

* * *

In 2016 I was involved in trying to help very well-intentioned colleagues in a large international organization develop an exciting new partnership initiative on an aspect of ICT4D about which I care passionately. However, it has been a truly frustrating experience, in large part because most participating organizations and individuals have little interest in really working together in partnership to deliver practical outcomes, despite liking to claim that they want to work in partnership. This encapsulates so much that is wrong with ICT4D partnerships, and it seems to reflect a systemic unwillingness to recognize or take into consideration all of the existing advice and good practices that exist. In this particular initiative, private sector and civil society representatives alike merely seem so far to want to use the aura of the international organization to profile their own specific interventions in the field in question, rather than to work practically together to deliver real solutions for the very complex and difficult issues with which the initiative is concerned. Hopefully this self-interest will decline as the initiative moves forward, so that the intended beneficiaries do indeed gain.

* * *

Despite such challenges, well-managed multi-sector ICT4D partnerships that include as many relevant stakeholders as possible can provide a very effective mechanism for delivering outcomes that will benefit the poorest and most marginalized. This is not only because of the pooling of resources and expertise that such partnerships can offer, but also because they provide a forum through which the interests of the various stakeholders can be openly discussed and understood (see Chapter 4). In particular, when combined with government regulatory policies that seek to maximize the opportunities for private sector companies to extend networks as widely as possible, appropriately designed partnerships, combined with the innovative use of technologies, can indeed enable the least connected and most marginalized people and communities to gain access to the Internet when the market alone would not enable companies to roll out such networks. Much hope has been placed in Universal Service Funds to achieve this outcome, but given their frequent failure to deliver, not least as a result of a lack of trust from many operators, partnerships offer a more likely and sustainable means of connecting the unconnected. This is primarily because well-crafted partnerships enable outcome-oriented negotiations to take place in the design of such initiatives, which ensure the buy-in of the relevant partners from different sectors in their delivery.

In engaging in such partnerships, governments must, though, recognize that there are costs involved, and that taxation revenue, or support from bilateral and multilateral donors, will need to be allocated to such initiatives. All too often, governments have tended to engage in such partnerships primarily in the hope that companies will contribute to the financial burden of delivering public services and share in the risk of such initiatives, whereas it is actually the private sector's technical knowledge and expertise in managing such activities efficiently and cost-effectively that are of most value to ICT4D partnerships. Engaging the private sector from the beginning of such partnerships, and designing them at scale, are key factors in helping to ensure their ultimate sustainability.

Much attention has rightly focused on providing connectivity to physically marginal rural areas of the world where the low population density has not made commercial sense for companies by themselves to invest in providing infrastructure. However, it is important that such ICT4D partnerships also address the needs and interests of other marginalized communities, such as women and girls in patriarchal societies and people with disabilities. These people often live in areas where there is connectivity, but frequently they cannot afford the technologies, do not see any relevance in them, or are sometimes explicitly excluded from using them. Here too multi-sector partnerships that bring together the very different strengths of the private sector, governments, and civil society, can play a significant part in delivering beneficial outcomes that can empower such groups of people. It nevertheless remains of central importance that these partnerships are designed and implemented carefully, always focusing on a clear development outcome that focuses explicitly on the needs of poor and marginalized people.

7.5 The Dark Side: Managing Security and Resilience

The use of ICTs is dramatically changing human interaction, both for better and for worse (Wittel, 2016). As emphasized throughout this book, the instrumental view of technology that so dominates thinking about its use for development fails to address critical issues around the interests underlying its design and use. ICTs can undoubtedly bring enormous benefits to poor people, not least in the enhanced access to information that they provide with respect to education, health, and agriculture. However, as discussed in Chapter 6, their darker side presents fundamental challenges at all levels from countries to individuals, and can have particularly negative impacts on the poorest and most marginalized, who are most vulnerable to exploitation. Five issues are particularly significant with respect to the ways in which the dark side of the digital world impacts the poor.

First, there is no doubt that ICTs, particularly through the Internet, are being used for deeply concerning purposes, but as with all moral issues it is difficult to reach widely agreed positions about most of them. The use of social media to incite violent political change and undermine governments, for example, is seen by some people as being good, but by others as being bad. Everything depends on context and culture. There is, however, reasonably wide international agreement that stability is generally preferable to instability, and therefore that reducing the potential for ICTs to be used in too disruptive a manner is desirable. Hence, much attention has been devoted to digital security issues and to creating resilient systems. Even here, though, there are tensions, because one of the key features of ICTs that is indeed often applauded is their disruptive potential, particularly in the context of enabling new business models and political processes to emerge. In the economic context, crowdfunding thus provides a fundamentally different model of raising capital for new businesses, and in the political arena innovative apps, such as Appgree,[5] enable communities of any size to determine what issues are of importance to them and then to vote on them, thus potentially enabling completely new models of democracy to emerge. Given the difficulties of resolving these moral dimensions, it is of fundamental importance that there is *widespread, open and transparent dialogue within countries about the role of ICTs*, and particularly the balance between security and privacy. Many governments, though, are cautious to engage actively with the citizens they serve over these issues, and it is therefore incumbent on international organizations to support and facilitate such dialogues. In so doing, it may be that international agreement on some of the most difficult issues around the security of digital systems may be resolved more swiftly.

Second, poor countries, and particularly poor small island states, often *lack the human and physical infrastructures to be able effectively to implement basic digital security measures*. As the world becomes ever more digitally connected, it still only remains as safe and secure as its weakest country. The potential for well-connected but poorly protected states to become havens for illegal activity becomes ever greater. There is therefore a real need for the sharing of expertise and technical capacity by richer countries and international organizations, so that there is enhanced global digital security. Whilst this raises concerns about privacy, and as argued above these need to be debated openly and transparently within countries, the global threat is such that coordinated and holistic approaches do need to be developed that involve poor countries on an equal footing in decision-making. In particular, initiatives to provide training for relevant stakeholders in digital security need to be expanded considerably, and further attention needs to be paid to the opportunities for more collective regional solutions to be developed, for example in the Caribbean and Pacific island states.

Third, much *more attention needs to be paid to the balance of interests between the rich and the poor in the ways through which data are used*. As argued in Section 6.4, our increasingly networked world is one where those with the power and expertise to use large amounts of data are able to reap significant benefits, most often at the expense of the poor. Everyone who uses a mobile phone, or links to social media sites, or uses a search engine to explore the Internet, is providing valuable information to the companies that provide such services, which is then monetized to generate profits. At the very least, increased attention needs to be paid to where these companies pay tax, so that some of these revenues are indeed returned through taxation to the places

---

[5] <http://www.appgree.com/appgree/en>.

where they are generated. However, it must also be recognized that until poor people themselves are able to analyse and use Big Data for their own purposes, they will not truly be empowered by it. As a starting point, it is important that the voices of the poor are listened to much more by those who are shaping such initiatives, and that they are not simply mediated by self-seeking civil society groups who have their own set of interests to maintain. To be sure, the analysis of large amounts of data can indeed help researchers and corporations understand the emergence and spread of diseases, and can ensure that urban systems run more efficiently, but this is completely different from suggesting that such knowledge will necessarily benefit the poorest and most marginalized.

Fourth, there are complex issues surrounding the *relationships between poverty and privacy*. European notions of privacy that have emerged over many centuries, and which are closely linked with the emergence of individualism, capitalism, and human rights, have largely come to dominate global understanding, particularly with respect to ongoing debates about privacy and security in the digital world. However, for most of the world's poorest people privacy is something that is almost unknown in the European sense of the word. There is little that can be considered to be truly private for those who live their lives on the street, or who share a room with many family members. As noted in Section 6.1, this has very significant implications for debates about the privacy implications of social media, and indeed more generally for the use by 'others' of data about poor people. The danger here is that it is very easy for poor people to be yet further exploited by those, even those with good intent, who wish to use in their own interests the data generated by the lives of poor people.

Closely linked to this issue of privacy is the *abuse of ICTs deliberately to exploit and harass poor and marginalized people*. One of the few areas of exploitation where there is more or less unanimous agreement that global action needs to be taken is child pornography, and it is generally poor people who suffer most from this (EC-Council, 2017). Worryingly, despite initiatives to deal with this (see Section 6.2) the scale of online child pornography seems to be increasing. However, this is just the tip of the iceberg, and much further attention needs to be paid by governments, civil society, and the private sector alike to limiting the extent to which ICTs are used to harass and exploit all those poor and marginalized people who are suffering from such abuse. Although all people can be subject to online bullying, it is frequently women who suffer most, especially in patriarchal societies. A recent report about New Zealand, for example, has highlighted that 72 per cent of women under 30 have experienced online harassment, and 70 per cent of women likewise saw this as a serious problem in 2016 (Norton, 2016). From anecdotal evidence, the situation is very much worse in some societies, as in parts of South Asia where women are frequently harassed and even killed for their online behaviour which can be seen as threatening family honour. In this context it is good to see that the ITU and UN Women developed the EQUALS initiative in 2016 as a major new partnership to address gender equality in the digital age (see also UNESCO, 2015).

These are but a few of the more important, but all too often neglected, issues around the darker aspects of ICTs, particularly in the context of poor people and countries. If ICTs are indeed to contribute to development in the broadest sense of the word, it is absolutely crucial that this darker side is widely and publicly discussed, not least so that poor and marginalized people are aware of the more negative aspects of the use of ICTs, as well as their undoubted benefits. It is also incumbent on international organizations and the private sector to engage much more actively in promoting such discussion and implementing strategies that will not only shed light on such darkness, but also initiate action to make the use of digital technologies both safer and fairer.

7.6 Enhancing Learning, Understanding, and Action

A recurring theme in this concluding chapter has been the importance of developing greater awareness and understanding in the use of ICTs to empower poor and marginalized people and communities. Self-reflection lies at the heart of Critical Theory, and encouraging all stakeholders to engage in appropriate reflection and learning is thus of central importance to reclaiming ICT4D. This requires considerable investment at all levels in raising awareness about the good, the bad, and the unexpected that can happen when ICT4D initiatives are conceived and implemented. Despite there being many such initiatives and opportunities, lessons are all too often not learned, and mistakes continue to be made. This implies not only that there needs to be more and better training provision, but also that there are some people whose interests are in limiting such openness and transparency because they benefit directly from existing inequalities in knowledge.

* * *

My own experiences have shown all too clearly the potential that such training can bring for mutual understandings and better policy practice. While at the CTO, I had long been interested in using space in our building to develop a high quality training facility that we could use to support our members. This was my interest. Coincidentally, our Chair, then from Kenya, had also identified a real need to provide new members of regulatory boards with an opportunity to learn more about the potential of their role in shaping the effective use of ICTs in development. Together, and with the support of one of the CTO's members,

Promethean,[6] who provided hardware and resources to renovate the facility, we were able to bring together an amazing partnership of people from governments, the private sector, and civil society to shape a series of week-long courses that started in 2014. The support from these contributors highlighted the value that they saw in contributing to such an initiative, and the participants undoubtedly had an opportunity to reflect productively on their roles. Whether this leads to better regulation in the countries from which they came remains to be seen, but it does show what can be achieved when multi-sector partnerships are crafted effectively to deliver real intended development outcomes.

* * *

Many similar training initiatives have been developed by organizations to support their members, not least by the ITU, bilateral donors, regional bodies, and also industry associations such as the GSMA, but there remains a pressing need for enhancement in both the quantity and quality of such provision, especially for politicians and officials in those governments that do not have the financial resources or time to afford sufficient training. Much of the discussion in the previous chapters has hinged on the argument that governments have a central role to play if ICTs are to be used effectively to support poor and marginalized people. This implies not only that civil servants are well trained and versed in the ways through which this can be achieved, but also that governments are indeed well-intentioned towards all of their citizens. All too often, it has been a fear of poor or inefficient government that has led those in the private sector to advocate a downsizing of government, and the increasing privatization of the functions of government. However, unlike the private sector, most governments are in some form or another elected, and are thus beholden to serve the needs of their electorates if they are to remain in power. Hence, promoting better understanding in government about how to deliver effective ICT4D initiatives has to remain of central importance, even if not all governments are necessarily benign.

It is not only governments, though, that require effective training in delivering appropriate ICT4D initiatives. If staff in private sector companies understood more about the challenges of delivering appropriate development interventions, and civil society organizations likewise better understood how technology can contribute both positively and negatively to development, then much greater progress could be achieved in helping to deliver appropriate initiatives in the interests of the poor. Above all, though, it is important that everyone has greater understanding of the role of ICTs, and the interests underlying their use in our lives. Digital security, for example, begins with the

---

[6] <https://www.prometheanworld.com>.

individual, although changes in technology are increasingly making it harder for users not to engage more widely in networks that can make them vulnerable. Everything is hackable, and so individuals need to make knowledge-based judgements about the risks involved, particularly with respect to the private information that they make available to others. There therefore need to be many more effective programmes directed in support of poor and marginalized people, so that they better understand how to use ICTs appropriately in their own interests while also avoiding the negative aspects associated with such use.

A final aspect of the links between understanding and action that is crucial for effective ICT4D implementation is the importance of rigorous, impartial monitoring and evaluation. Despite the emphasis often placed on these in theory (Wagner et al., 2005), it is remarkable how few ICT4D initiatives have incorporated high quality monitoring and evaluation as an integral part of their activities. This means that it remains difficult to understand the real success factors behind effective ICT4D interventions, and even when such studies are undertaken, many of them reflect the particular interests of their authors, and therefore do not necessarily provide valid evidence of good practices that can be replicated elsewhere. There are indeed some examples of good studies (Geldof et al., 2011; Jigsaw Consult, 2014), but insufficient funding for them, poor research design, the lack of baseline surveys, deliberate attempts to bias the portrayal of prestigious projects, and the low priority attributed to monitoring and evaluation all mean that there remains much uncertainty about how best to use ICTs to empower the poor in many particular contexts. Without good evidence, donors and practitioners alike are often unwilling to provide the resources necessary for effective intervention programmes that will really benefit the poor.

7.7 Reclaiming ICTs for Development

The design of ICTs and their rapid deployment have been one of the main causes of increasing inequality in the world. One of the underlying themes of this book is that this inequality is exacerbated by the linkage between ICTs and development defined as economic growth. Indeed, advocacy that ICTs can contribute positively to economic growth, and that this will reduce or eliminate poverty, has actually served to increase inequality and thus further marginalize the poor. The idea of 'development' itself has become a vehicle through which the technological interests of the private sector in particular, but also those of governments and civil society, can be further promoted. Expansion in the use of ICTs has thus become the primary focus of attention (D4ICT), rather than the development outcomes that might be facilitated by

ICTs in the interests of the poor and marginalized (ICT4D). This is scarcely surprising, given the long history of the use of technologies to serve and maintain the interests of the rich and powerful.

Many factors have influenced this state of affairs. In particular, the increasing power of the private sector in global governance, the dominance of an instrumental view of ICTs that sees them as necessarily a force for good, the diminution in the role of governments in serving the interests of all their citizens, the symbolic power of modernity embodied in ICTs, and an emphasis on enhancing economic growth rather than reducing inequality, have all been very significant in shaping the current intersection between ICTs and development. To be sure, there are many instances where ICTs have been used to enhance the lives of groups of poor and marginalized people, but the overwhelming balance of evidence is that most such initiatives fail to go to scale or be sustainable. Moreover, there is also a growing body of evidence that the dark side of ICTs is seriously harming many poor people, and especially women and girls.

Paradoxically, the main ways through which the use of ICTs can be reclaimed for development that might empower poor and marginalized people have rather little to do with the technologies, but much more to do with attitudes and approaches adopted by all those engaged in serving the interests of the poor. First, the idea that ICTs in general, or the roll-out of mobile broadband in particular, is some kind of panacea, or silver bullet, that can reduce poverty must be abandoned. This should be combined with a realization that policies designed purely to increase economic growth through the use of ICTs will necessarily continue to increase inequality. There needs to be a fundamental shift in thinking by governments, civil society, and those who fund development interventions away from the economic growth agenda and instead towards the explicit use of ICTs to support the poor and the marginalized. The private sector will continue to serve as the engine of growth, and thereby drive the use of ICTs by the majority of people, but its profit-taking voracity needs to be tempered by a realization that the technological Jinn that it releases may well eventually do more harm than good. This requires a fundamental reorientation of much research to focus primarily on the development of ICTs through which the very poorest might be empowered. This needs to begin with a humble realization that academics interested in ICT4D should become the servants of the poor and marginalized, learning from them, and using their skills and expertise to serve the interests of the poor rather than their own careers, or the interests of global ICT corporations. Research and practice should be with the poor rather than merely for the poor. Governments and regulators have a central role in facilitating such a shift, but it would be naïve to suggest that all governments are benign and without self-interest. Politicians of all hues therefore need to be convinced that increasing inequality is ultimately a greater threat to stability and their own political futures than would be any reduction in economic growth. Likewise, private sector companies have much to contribute to this renewed vision of ICT4D. Those that can develop innovative new technologies and business models to deliver affordable services to the poorest 'first billion', for example, will necessarily be able to undercut companies still focusing on the 'next billion', and thereby make considerable gains in market share.

*   *   *

Above all, those who share my passion for technology, and the ways through which it can be used to help empower the poorest and the most marginalized, the limbless beggars in Sierra Leone, the blind musicians playing on street corners in China, or the young women in Pakistan at threat of being murdered because of the images they post on social media, must begin by reflecting on their own practices. We need to change from being part of the problem to being part of the solution. Once we have begun to be enlightened ourselves about the role of technology in development, we may in turn be able to help empower others through crafting new ICTs and the strategies through which they can be implemented in the interests of the poorest and most marginalized.

*   *   *

References

A4AI (2014) 'Ghana Drops Import Tax on Smartphones Following Advocacy by A4AI-Ghana Coalition'. <http://a4ai.org/ghana-drops-import-tax-on-smartphones-following-advocacy-by-a4ai-ghana-coalition>.

Adomi, E. E. (ed.) (2011) *Handbook of Research on Information Communication Technology Policy: Trends, Issues and Advancements*. New York: Information Science Reference.

African Declaration (2014) 'The African Declaration on Internet Rights and Freedom'. <http://africaninternetrights.org/articles>.

Alchele, C., Flickenger, R., Fonda, C., Forster, J., Howard, I., Krag, T., and Zennaro, M. (2006) *Wireless Networking in the Developing World: A Practical Guide to Planning and Buildng Low-Cost Telecommunications Infrastructure*. Seattle: Hacker Friendly LLC. <http://wndw.net>.

Alkire, S. (2010) 'Human Development: Definitions, Critiques, and Related Concepts'. Background paper for the 2010 Human Development Report. Oxford: Oxford Poverty and Human Development Initiative, Working Paper No. 36. <http://www.ophi.org.uk/wp-content/uploads/OPHI_WP36.pdf>.

Amnesty International (2016) *This is What We Die For: Human Rights Abuses in the Democratic Republic of The Congo Power the Global Trade in Cobalt*. London: Amnesty International. <https://www.amnesty.org/download/Documents/AFR6231832016 ENGLISH.PDF>.

Anon. (2014) 'Jürgen Habermas'. *Stanford Encyclopedia of Philosophy*. <http://plato.stanford.edu/entries/habermas/>.

APC (2003) Association for Progressive Communications (APC) comments on WSIS documents dated 21 March. WSIS/PC-3/CONTR/56E.

A. T. Kearney (2012) 'Winning the OTT War: Strategies for Sustainable Growth'. <http://www.atkearney.co.uk/communications-media-technology/ideas-insights/article/-/asset_publisher/LCcgOeS4t85g/content/winning-the-ott-war-strategies-for-sustainable-growth/10192>.

Avgerou, C. (2010) 'Discourses on ICT and Development'. *Information Technologies and International Development*, 693, pp. 1–18.

Bada, M., Creese, S., Goldsmith, M., Mitchell, C., and Phillips, E. (2014) *Computer Security Incident Response Teams (CSIRTS): An Overview*. Oxford: Global Cyber Security Capacity Centre. <http://www.elizabethphillips.co.uk/Research/CSIRTs.pdf>.

Banks, K. (2013) *The Rise of the Reluctant Innovator*. London: London Publishing Partnership.

Bartlett, J. (2014) *The Dark Net: Inside the Digital Underworld*. London: William Heinemann.

References

Beardon, H., Munyampeta, F., Rout, S., and Williams, G. M. (2008) *ICT for Development: Empowerment or Exploitation? Learning from the* Reflect *ICTs Project*. London: ActionAid.

Beddoes, Z. M. (2012) 'For Richer, For Poorer'. *The Economist*, 11 October. <http://www.economist.com/node/21564414>.

Beehler, R. and Drengson, A. (1978) *The Philosophy of Society*. London: Routledge.

Behague, D., Morrison, J., Rosato, M., Some, T., and Tawiah, C. (2009) 'Evidence-Based Policy Making: The Implications for Globally-Applicable Research for Context-Specific Problem-Solving in Developing Countries'. *Social Science and Medicine*, 69(10), pp. 1539–46.

Bekkers, R. (2001) *Mobile Telecommunications Standards: GSM, UMTS, TETRA and ERMES*. Norwood: Artech House.

Bennett, C. J. and Parsons, C. (2013) 'Privacy and Surveillance: The Multidisciplinary Literature on the Capture, Use, and Disclosure of Personal Information in Cyberspace'. In W. Dutton (ed.), *The Oxford Handbook of Internet Studies*. Oxford: Oxford University Press, pp. 486–508.

Bergman, M. K. (2001) 'The Deep Web: Surfacing Hidden Value'. *Journal of Electronic Publishing*, 7(1), unpaginated. <http://quod.lib.umich.edu/j/jep/3336451.0007.104?view=text;rgn=main>.

Bergold, J. and Thomas, S. (2012) 'Participatory Research Methods: A Methodological Approach in Motion'. *FQS Forum: Qualitative Social Research*, 13(1), Art. 30. <http://www.qualitative-research.net/index.php/fqs/article/view/1801/3334>.

Bettig, R. V. (1996) *Copyrighting Culture: The Political Economy of Intellectual Property*. Boulder, CO: Westview Press.

Bevir, M. (2012) *Governance: A Very Short Introduction*. Oxford: Oxford University Press.

Blackman, C. and Srivastava, L. (eds.) (2011) *Telecommunications Regulation Handbook: Tenth Anniversary Edition*. Washington, DC: World Bank, *info*Dev, and ITU.

Block, J. J. (2008) 'Issues for DSM-V: Internet Addiction'. *American Journal of Psychiatry*, 165(3), pp. 306–7.

Boni, H., Schluep, M., and Widmer, R. (2015) 'Recycling of ICT Equipment in Industrialized and Developing Countries'. In L. M. Hilty and B. Aebischer (eds.), *ICT Innovations for Sustainability*. Cham: Springer International, pp. 223–41.

Bonnah Nkansah, G. and Unwin, T. (2010) 'The Contribution of ICTs to the Delivery of Special Educational Needs in Ghana: Practices and Potential'. *Journal of Information Technology for Development*, 16(3), pp. 191–211.

Bottomore, T. (2002) *The Frankfurt School and its Critics*. London: Routledge.

BrightPlanet (2014) 'Clearing Up Confusion—Deep Web vs. Dark Web'. <https://brightplanet.com/2014/03/clearing-confusion-deep-web-vs-dark-web>.

Broadband Commission (2015) *The State of Broadband 2015*. Geneva: ITU and UNESCO.

Bronner, S. E. (2004) *Reclaiming the Enlightenment: Toward a Politics of Radical Engagement*. New York: Columbia University Press.

Business Partners for Development (2002) *Business Partners for Development 1998–2001: Tri-Sector Partnership Results and Recommendations*. London: Business Partners for Development. <http://www.oecd.org/unitedkingdom/2082379.pdf>.

Buskens, I. (2015) 'ICT and Gender'. In R. Mansell and P. H. Ang (eds.), *The International Encyclopedia of Digital Communication and Society*. Chichester: Wiley-Blackwell, pp. 451–61.

Buskens, I. and Webb, A. (eds.) (2009) *African Women and ICTs: Investigating Technology, Gender and Empowerment*. London: Zed Books.

Buskens, I. and Webb, A. (eds.) (2014) *Women and ICT in Africa and the Middle East: Changing Selves, Changing Societies*. London: Zed Books.

Butcher, N. (author), Kanwar, A., and Uvalić-Trumbić, S. (eds.) (2015) *A Basic Guide to Open Educational Resources (OER)*. Paris and Vancouver: UNESCO and COL.

Bytes for All (2014) *Conflicting with the Constitution: Privacy Rights & Laws in Pakistan*. Islamabad: Bytes for All. <https://content.bytesforall.pk/sites/default/files/PrivacyLaws.pdf>.

Cade, M. (2015) 'Inter Regional Dialogue Session—Report of the Session held at the 2015 IGF'. <http://www.intgovforum.org/cms/documents/igf-meeting/igf-2015-joao-pessoa/igf2015-reports/641-igf2015inter-dialogue-session/file>.

Camfield, L. (ed.) (2014) *Methodological Challenges and New Approaches to Research in International Development*. Basingstoke: Palgrave Macmillan.

Campbell, B. (2012) 'Corporate Social Responsibility and Development in Africa: Redefining the Roles and Responsibilities of Public and Private Actors in the Mining Sector'. *Resources Policy*, 37(2), pp. 138–43.

Cantoni, L. and Danowski, J. A. (eds.) (2015) *Communication and Technology*. Handbooks of Communication Science, Volume 5. Berlin: De Gruyter.

Carpentier, N. and Staes, J. (2006) *Towards a Sustainable Information Society: Deconstructing WSIS*. Bristol: Intellect.

Carr, W. and Kemmis, S. (1986) *Becoming Critical: Education, Knowledge and Action Research*. Melbourne: Deakin University Press.

Cash, H., Rae, C. D., Steel, A. H., and Winkler, A. (2012) 'Internet Addiction: A Brief Summary of Research and Practice'. *Current Psychiatry Reviews*, 8(4), pp. 292–8.

Caspersz, D. and Olaru, D. (2014) 'Developing "Emancipatory Interest": Learning to Create Social Change'. *Higher Education Research & Development*, 33(2), pp. 226–41.

Cassidy, T. (2007) *The Global Education Initiative (GEI) Model of Effective Partnership Initiatives for Education*. Cologny: World Economic Forum.

Castells, M. (2000) *The Rise of the Network Society*. Oxford: Blackwell.

Castells, M. (2012) *Networks of Outrage and Hope: Social Movements in the Internet Age*. Cambridge: Polity Press.

Cave, M., Doyle, C., and Webb, W. (2012) *Essentials of Modern Spectrum Management*. Cambridge: Cambridge University Press.

Cerf, V. G. (2016) 'The IANA Transition'. *Communications of the ACM*, 59(5), p. 7.

Chaduc, J.-M. and Pogorel, G. (eds.) (2008) *The Radio Spectrum: Managing a Strategic Resource*. London: ISTE and John Wiley.

Chambers, R. (1992) 'Rural Appraisal: Rapid, Relaxed and Participatory'. Brighton: Institute of Development Studies, IDS Discussion Paper 311. <https://www.ids.ac.uk/files/Dp311.pdf>.

Chambers, R. (2007) *From PRA to PLA and Pluralism: Practice and Theory*. Brighton: Institute of Development Studies, IDS Working Paper 286.

References

Chambers, R. (2014) *Into the Unknown: Explorations in Development Practice*. Rugby: Practical Action Publishing.

Chandhoke, N. (2002) 'The Limits of Global Civil Society'. In M. Glasius, M. Kaldor, and H. Anheier (eds.), *Global Civil Society 2002*. Oxford: Oxford University Press, pp. 35–53.

Charlton, J. I. (1998) *Nothing About Us Without Us: Disability Oppression and Empowerment*. Berkeley: University of California Press.

Chevalier, J. M. and Buckles, D. J. (2013) *Participatory Action Research: Theory and Methods for Engaged Inquiry*. London: Routledge.

Chomsky, N. (1998) *Profit over People: Neoliberalism and the Global Order*. New York: Seven Stories Press.

Christou, G. (2016) *Cybersecurity in the European Union: Resilience and Adaptability in Governance* Policy. Basingstoke: Palgrave Macmillan.

CIS (2016) 'CIS' Statement on Sexual Harassment at ICANN55'. <http://cis-india. org/internet-governance/blog/cis-statement-on-sexual-harrasment-at-icann55>.

Clynes, M. E. and Kline, N. S. (1960) 'Cyborgs and Space'. *Astronautics*, September, pp. 26–7 and 74–6.

Coe, N. M. and Yeung, H. W.-C. (2015) *Global Production Networks: Theorizing Economic Development in an Interconnected World*. Oxford: Oxford University Press.

Colina, A. L., Vives, A., Bagula, A., Zennaro, M., and Pietrosemoli, E. (2015) *IoT in 5 Days*. Trieste: The Abdul Salam International Centre for Theoretical Physics. <http://wireless.ictp.it/school_2015/book/book.pdf>.

Collier, P. (2008) *The Bottom Billion: Why the Poorest Countries Are Failing and What Can Be Done About It*. Oxford: Oxford University Press.

Collings, S. (2011) *Phone Charging Micro-Businesses in Tanzania and Uganda*. London: GVEP International. <http://www.energy4impact.org/sites/default/files/phone_char ging_businesses_report_with_gsma_final_for_web_0.pdf>.

Collins, D. (2004) *Spying: The Secret History of History*. New York: Black Dog and Leventhal.

Connolly, R. (2013) 'Trust in Commercial and Personal Transactions in the Digital Age'. In W. Dutton (ed.), *The Oxford Handbook of Internet Studies*. Oxford: Oxford University Press, pp. 262–82.

Cooke, P., Searle, G., and O'Connor, K. (2013) *The Economic Geography of the IT Industry in the Asia Pacific Region*. Abingdon: Routledge.

Cord, D. J. (2014) *The Decline and Fall of Nokia*. Helsinki: Schildts & Söderströms.

Cowen, M. P. and Shenton, R. W. (1996) *Doctrines of Development*. London: Routledge.

Crawford, S. (2013) *Captive Audience: The Telecom Industry and Monopoly Power in the New Gilded Age*. New Haven, CT: Yale University Press.

Crew, M. (ed.) (1991) *Competition and the Regulation of Utilities*. New York: Springer.

Crew, M. and Parker, D. (eds.) (2006a) *International Handbook on Economic Regulation*. Cheltenham: Edward Elgar.

Crew, M. and Parker, D. (2006b) 'Development in the Theory and Practice of Regulatory Economics'. In M. Crew and D. Parker (eds.), *International Handbook on Economic Regulation*. Cheltenham: Edward Elgar, pp. 1–33.

Crewe, E. and Harrison, E. (1998) *Whose Development? An Ethnography of Aid*. London: Zed Books.

Cristin, N. (2013) 'Travelling the Silk Road: A Measurement Analysis of a Large Anonymous Online Marketplace'. In *Proceedings of the 22nd International Conferences on World Wide Web*. New York: ACM, pp. 213–24.

Crooks, D. and Altamirano, P. (2013) 'The ITU's Quest for Relevance'. *International Policy Digest*, 22 May. <http://intpolicydigest.org/2013/05/22/the-itu-s-quest-for-relevance>.

CTO (2015) 'Statement on the Role of ICTs in the Post-2015 Development Goals'. <http://www.cto.int/media/pr-re/Post-2015developmentgoals.pdf>.

Cullen, A. E., Coryn, C. L. S., and Rugh, J. (2011) 'The Politics and Consequence of Including Stakeholders in International Development Evaluation'. *American Journal of Evaluation*, 32(3), pp. 345–61.

Dahlman, E., Parkvall, S., and Sköld, J. (2014) *4G: LTE/LTE-Advanced for Mobile Broadband*, 2nd edn. Amsterdam: Elsevier.

David, K. (ed.) (2008) *Technologies for the Wireless Future: Wireless World Research Forum, Volume 3*. Chichester: Wiley.

Davis, E. P. and Sanchez-Martinez, M. (2014) 'A Review of the Economic Theories of Poverty'. London: National Institute of Economic and Social Research, Discussion Paper No. 435. <http://www.niesr.ac.uk/sites/default/files/publications/dp435_0.pdf>.

De Bastion, G. (2013) 'Technology Hubs in Africa: A New Culture of Community Driven Innovation?' *Digital Development Debates #09: Prejudice*. <http://www.digital-development-debates.org/issue-09-prejudice–african-innovation–technology-hubs-in-africa.html>.

DeNardis, L. (2014) *The Global War for Internet Governance*. New Haven, CT: Yale University Press.

Desai, V. and Potter, R. B. (eds.) (2014) *The Companion to Development Studies*, 3rd edn. London: Routledge.

DFID (2001) *Imfundo: Partnership for IT in Education. Inception Report*. London: DFID.

DFID (2006) *Eliminating World Poverty: Making Governance Work for the Poor. A White Paper on International Development*. London: HMSO.

Dhaliwal, I. and Tulloch, C. (2012) 'From Research to Policy: Using Evidence from Impact Evaluations to Inform Development Policy'. J-PAL, Department of Economics, MIT. <https://www.povertyactionlab.org/sites/default/files/publications/With%20JDE%20Revisions%20and%20Footnotes%202012.09.03.pdf>.

Dickinson, S. (2016) 'Drafting the WSIS Resolution for ECOSOC at the CSTD 19th Session'. <http://linguasynaptica.com/2016/05/>.

Dienel, H.-L., Sharan, Y., Rapp, C., and Ahituv, N. (eds.) (2010) *Terrorism and the Internet: Threats—Target Groups—Deradicalisation Strategies*. Amsterdam: IOS Press.

Du Boucher, V. (2016) 'A Few Things We Learned about Tech Hubs in Africa and Asia'. GSMA Mobile for Development. <http://www.gsma.com/mobilefordevelopment/programme/ecosystem-accelerator/things-learned-tech-hubs-africa-asia#.V6SrKRY2Bj8.twitter>.

Dutton, W. H. (ed.) (2013) *The Oxford Handbook of Internet Studies*. Oxford: Oxford University Press.

Dutton, W., Guerra, G. A., Zizzo, D. J., and Paltu, M. (2005) 'The Cyber Trust Tension in e-Government: Balancing Identity, Privacy, Security'. *Information Polity*, 10(1–2), pp. 13–23.

Easterly, W. (2002) *The Elusive Quest for Growth: Economists' Adventures and Misadventures in the Tropics*. Cambridge, MA: MIT Press.

Easterly, W. (2006) *The White Man's Burden: Why the West's Efforts to Aid the Rest Have Done so Much Ill and so Little Good*. New York: Penguin.

EC-Council (2017) *Investigating Network Intrusions and Cybercrime*, 2nd edn. Boston: Cengage Learning.

Epstein, D. and Nonnecke, B. M. (2016) 'Multistakeholderism in Praxis: The Case of the Regional and National Internet Governance Forum (IGF) Initiatives'. *Policy & Internet*, 8(2), pp. 148–73.

Ericsson (2014) *Carbon and Energy Report: National Assessment of the Environmental Impact of ICT*. Stockholm: Ericsson. <http://www.ericsson.com/res/docs/2014/ericsson-energy-and-carbon-report.pdf>.

Ericsson (2015) *Ericsson Mobility Report June 2015*. Stockholm: Ericsson. <http://www.ericsson.com/res/docs/2014/ericsson-energy-and-carbon-report.pdf>.

Escobar, A. (1995) *Encountering Development: The Making and Unmaking of the Third World*. Princeton, NJ: Princeton University Press.

Esterhuysen, A. (2005) *APC's Reflections—Multi-Stakeholder Participation and ICT Policy Processes*. Geneva: APC.

Etzioni, A. (1973) 'The Third Sector and Domestic Missions'. *Public Administration Review*, 33(4), pp. 314–23.

Etzioni, A. (2005) 'The Limits of Privacy'. In A. Cohen and C. H. Wellman (eds.), *Contemporary Debates in Applied Ethics*. Oxford: Blackwell, pp. 253–62.

Farrell, G., Isaacs, S., and Trucano, M. (2007) *The NEPAD e-Schools Demonstration Project: A Work in Progress*. Washington: *info*Dev/The World Bank. <http://www.infodev.org/infodev-files/resource/InfodevDocuments_355.pdf>.

Feenberg, A. (1991) *Critical Theory of Technology*. Cambridge: Cambridge University Press.

Feenberg, A. (1996) 'Marcuse or Habermas: Two Critiques of Technology'. *Inquiry*, 39(1), pp. 45–70.

Fichman, P. and Sanfilippo, M. R. (2016) *Online Trolling and its Perpetrators: Under the Cyberbridge*. Lanham, MD: Rowman & Littlefield.

Fitzgerald, B. (2006) 'The Transformation of Open Source Software'. *MIS Quarterly*, 30(3), pp. 587–98.

Forsyth, T. (ed.) (2004) *Encyclopedia of International Development*. London: Routledge.

Frau-Meigs, D., Nicey, J., Palmer, M., Pohle, J., and Tupper, P. (eds.) (2012) *From NWICO to WSIS: 30 Years of Communication Geopolitics—Actors and Flows, Structures and Divides*. Bristol: Intellect.

Freedom House (2009) *Freedom on the Net: A Global Assessment of Internet and Digital Media*. Washington, DC: Freedom House.

Freedom House (2015) *Freedom on the Net 2015: Privatising Censorship, Eroding Privacy*. Washington: Freedom House. <https://freedomhouse.org/sites/default/files/FOTN%202015%20Full%20Report.pdf>.

Freeman, R. E., Harrison, J. S., Wicks, A. C., Parmar, B. L., and de Colle, S. (2010) *Stakeholder Theory: The State of the Art*. Cambridge: Cambridge University Press.

Freshfields Bruckhaus Deringer (2014) *Asia Data Privacy Guide*. Hong Kong: Freshfields Bruckhaus Deringer. <http://www.freshfields.com/uploadedFiles/Locations/Global/Digital/content/Asia%20data%20privacy%20guide.pdf>.

Friedman, D. D. (2005) 'The Case for Freedom'. In A. Cohen and C. H. Wellman (eds.), *Contemporary Debates in Applied Ethics*. Oxford: Blackwell, pp. 262–75.

Fukuyama, F. (2001) 'Social Capital, Civil Society and Development'. *Third World Quarterly*, 22(1), pp. 7–20.

Geldof, M., Grimshaw, D., Kleine, D., and Unwin, T. (2011) 'What are the Key Lessons for ICT4D Partnerships for Poverty Reduction? Systematic Review Report'. London: Department for International Development. <http://r4d.dfid.gov.uk/PDF/Outputs/SystematicReviews/DFID_ICT_SR_Final_Report_r5.pdf>.

Gerck, E. (2004) 'Toward Real-World Models of Trust: Reliance on Received Information'. <http://safevote.com/papers/trustdef.htm>.

Geuss, R. (1981) *The Idea of a Critical Theory: Habermas and the Frankfurt School*. Cambridge: Cambridge University Press.

Giddens, A. (1998) *The Third Way: The Renewal of Social Democracy*. Cambridge: Polity Press.

Gillet, J. (2014) 'Measuring Mobile Penetration: Untangling "Subscribers", "Mobile Phone Owners" and "Users"'. GSMA Intelligence. <https://gsmaintelligence.com/research/2014/05/measuring-mobile-penetration/430>.

GIP Digital Watch (2015) *WSIS+10 Summary Report from the UN GA WSIS Review Meeting*. <http://digitalwatch.giplatform.org/sites/default/files/WSIS10SummaryReport.pdf>.

Glasius, M., Kaldor, M., and Anheier, H. (eds.) (2002) *Global Civil Society 2002*. Oxford: Oxford University Press.

Glenny, M. (2011) *Dark Market: Cyberthieves, Cybercops and You*. Toronto: House of Anansi.

Global e-Sustainability Initiative (2008) *The Contribution the ICT Industry Can Make to Sustainable Development*. Brussels: Global e-Sustainability Initiative. <http://gesi.org/files/Reports/The%20Contribution%20the%20ICT%20Industry%20Can%20Make%20to%20Sustainable%20Development.pdf>.

Government of the Netherlands (2016) 'Public–Private Partnerships'. <https://www.government.nl/topics/development-cooperation/contents/development-cooperation-partners-and-partnerships/public-private-partnerships>.

Graham, M. (2013) 'Geography/Internet Ethereal Alternate Dimensions of Cyberspace or Grounded Augmented Realities?' *The Geographical Journal*, 179(2), pp. 177–82.

Graham, M. and De Sabatta, S. (2013) 'Geography of Top-Level Domain Names'. <http://geography.oii.ox.ac.uk/?page=geography-of-top-level-domain-names>.

Graham, M. and Foster, C. (2016) 'Geographies of Information Inequality in Sub-Saharan Africa'. *The African Technopolitan*, 5, pp. 78–85.

Green, L. (2001) *Technoculture: From Alphabet to Cybersex*. London: Allen & Unwin.

Greengard, S. (2015) *The Internet of Things*. Cambridge, MA: MIT Press.

Greenwald, G. (2014) *No Place to Hide: Edward Snowden, the NSA, and the US Surveillance State*. New York: Metropolitan Books.

GRID (2016) 'Making the Internet a Better and Safer Place'. <http://fosigrid.org/about>.

Grimsey, D. and Lewis, M. K. (2004) *Public and Private Partnerships: The Worldwide Revolution in Infrastructure Provision and Project Finance*. Cheltenham: Edward Elgar.

Gross, A. G. (2010) 'Systematically Distorted Communication: An Impediment to Social and Political Change'. *Informal Logic*, 30(4), pp. 335–60.

Gross National Happiness Commission, Royal Government of Bhutan (n.d.) 'About Us'. <http://www.gnhc.gov.bt/about-us>.

GSMA (2013) *Universal Service Fund Study*. London: GSMA (prepared by Ladcomm Corporation).

GSMA (2014) *Sub-Saharan Africa—Universal Service Fund Study*. London: GSMA (prepared by Ladcomm Corporation).

GSMA (2015a) *The Mobile Economy 2015*. London: GSMA.

GSMA (2015b) *Digital Inclusion and Mobile Sector Taxation*. London: GSMA (prepared by Deloitte).

GSMA (2016a) *Mobile Policy Handbook*. London: GSMA.

GSMA (2016b) *Connected Society: Unlocking Rural Coverage—Enablers for Commercially Sustainable Mobile Network Expansion*. London: GSMA.

Guida, J. and Crow, M. (2009) 'E-Government and E-Governance'. In T. Unwin (ed.), *ICT4D: Information and Communication Technology for Development*. Cambridge: Cambridge University Press, pp. 283–320.

Gurstein, M. (2011) 'Open Data: Empowering the Empowered or Effective Data Use for Everyone?' *First Monday*, 16(2). <http://dx.doi.org/10.5210/fm.v16i2.3316>.

Haas, H. (2013) 'High-Speed Wireless Networking Using Visible Light'. *SPIE*, 10.1117/2.1201304.004773. <http://citeseerx.ist.psu.edu/viewdoc/download?doi=10.1.1.570.9789 &rep=rep1&type=pdf>.

Habermas, J. (1971) 'Technology and Science as "Ideology"'. In J. Habermas, *Toward a Rational Society: Student Protest, Science and Politics*. Boston, MA: Beacon Press, pp. 81–122.

Habermas, J. (1974) *Theory and Practice*. London: Heinemann.

Habermas, J. (1978) *Knowledge and Human Interests*, 2nd edn. London: Heinemann.

Habermas, J. (1981) 'Modernity versus Postmodernity'. *New German Critique*, 22, pp. 3–14.

Habermas, J. (1984) *The Theory of Communicative Action, Volume 1: Reason and the Rationalisation of Society*. Boston, MA: Beacon Press.

Habermas, J. (1987) *The Theory of Communicative Action, Volume 2: Lifeworld and System*. Cambridge: Polity Press.

Habermas, J. (1996) *Between Facts and Norms: Contributions to a Discourse Theory of Law and Democracy*. Cambridge, MA: MIT Press.

Hague, W. (2011) 'Foreign Secretary's Closing Remarks at the London Conference on Cyberspace'. <https://www.gov.uk/government/speeches/foreign-secretarys-closing-remarks-at-the-london-conference-on-cyberspace>.

Hall, C., Scott, C., and Hood, C. (2000) *Telecommunications Regulation: Culture, Chaos and Interdependence Inside the Regulatory Process*. London: Routledge.

Hampton, J. (1986) *Hobbes and the Social Contract Tradition*. Cambridge: Cambridge University Press.

Hanna, N. K. with Summer, R. (2015) *Transforming to a Networked Society: Guide for Policy Makers*. Gaithersburg: Sriban.

Hansen, N., Postmes, T., Bos, A., and Tovote, A. (2009) 'Does Technology Drive Social Change? Psychological, Social and Cultural Effects of OLPC among Ethiopian Children'. <http://www.gg.rhul.ac.uk/ict4d/NinaandTom.pdf>.

Hardin, G. (1968) 'The Tragedy of the Commons'. *Science*, 162(3859), pp. 1243–8.

Harraway, D. (1985) 'Manifesto for Cyborgs: Science, Technology, and Socialist Feminism in the 1980s'. *Socialist Review*, 80, pp. 65–108.

Harraway, D. (1991) *Simians, Cyborgs and Women: The Reinvention of Nature*. New York: Routledge.

Harris, J. (2005) 'Great Promise, Hubris and Recovery: A Participatory History of Development Studies'. In U. Kothari (ed.), *A Radical History of Development Studies: Individuals, Institutions and Ideologies*. London and Cape Town: Zed Books and David Philip, pp. 17–46.

Hassan, B. and Unwin, T. (2017) 'Student Mobile Identity in Pakistan: On, In and Through the Phone'. *Information Technologies & International Development* (under review).

Hearn, G., Tacchi, J., Fogh, M., and Lennie, J. (2009) *Action Research and New Media*. New York: Hampton Press.

Heeks, R. (2008) 'ICT4D 2.0: The Next Phase of Applying ICT for International Development'. *Computer*, 41(6), pp. 26–33.

Heeks, R. (2010) 'ICT4D Journal Ranking Table'. <https://ict4dblog.wordpress.com/2010/04/14/ict4d-journal-ranking-table>.

Heeks, R. (2013) 'Development Studies Research and Actor-Network Theory'. Manchester: Centre for Development Informatics, Actor-Network Theory for Development Working Paper Series, Paper No.1. <http://www.seed.manchester.ac.uk/medialibrary/IDPM/working_papers/cdi_ant4d/ANT4DPaper1Heeks.pdf>, accessed 26 May 2016.

Held, D. (1980) *Introduction to Critical Theory: Horkheimer to Habermas*. Oakland: University of California Press.

Hilbert, M. (2016) 'Big Data for Development: A Review of Promises and Challenges'. *Development Policy* Review, 34(1), pp. 135–74. <http://doi.org/10.1111/dpr.12142>.

Hill, R. (2014) *The New International Telecommunication Regulations and the Internet: A Commentary and Regulatory History*. Heidelberg: Springer.

Hilty, L. M. and Aebischer, B. (eds.) (2015) *ICT Innovations for Sustainability*. Cham: Springer International.

Hersent, O., Boswarthick, D., and Elloumi, O. (2012) *The Internet of Things: Key Applications and Protocols*. Chichester: Wiley.

Hobbes, T. (1996) *Leviathan*, edited with an introduction by J. C. A. Gaskin. Oxford: Oxford University Press (first published 1651).

Hofmann, J. (2016) 'Multi-Stakeholderism in Internet Governance: Putting a Fiction into Practice'. *Journal of Cyber Policy*, 1(1), pp. 29–49.

Hogan Lovells (2014) *Data Privacy Regulation Comes of Age in Asia*. Hong Kong: Hogan Lovells. <http://www.hoganlovells.com/en/publications/data-privacy-regulation-comes-of-age-in-asia>.

Hollow, D. (2008) 'Low-Cost Laptops for Education in Ethiopia'. <http://www.gg.rhul.ac.uk/ict4d/workingpapers/Hollowlaptops.pdf>.

Hollow, D. (2010) 'Evaluating ICT for Education Initiatives in Africa'. PhD thesis, Royal Holloway, University of London.

Horkheimer, M. (1972) *Critical Theory*. New York: Seabury Press.

Howard, M. C. and King, J. E. (1985) *The Political Economy of Marx*, 2nd edn. London: Longman.

Howard, P. N. (2015) *Pax Technica: How the Internet of Things May Set Us Free or Lock Us Up*. New Haven, CT: Yale University Press.

Hulme, D. and Edwards, M. (eds.) (1997) *NGOs, States and Donors: Too Close for Comfort*. Basingstoke: Macmillan.

Human Rights Commission Pakistan (2016) *State of Human Rights in 2015*. Islamabad: Human Rights Commission Pakistan.

Hunt, J. (2012) 'Gender and Development'. In D. Kingsbury, J. McKay, J. Hunt, M. McGillivray, and M. Clarke, *International Development: Issues and Challenges*. Basingstoke: Palgrave Macmillan, pp. 272–301.

Ibáñez Colomo, P. (2012) *European Communications Law and Technological Convergence: Deregulation, Re-Regulation and Regulatory Convergence in Television and Telecommunications*. Alphen aan den Rijn: Kluwer Law International.

ICANN (2016) 'A Quick Look at ICANN'. Los Angeles: ICANN. <https://www.icann.org/en/system/files/files/quick-look-icann-01nov13-en.pdf>.

ICANNWiki (2014) NETmundial. <https://icannwiki.com/NETmundial>.

IGF (2016) 'Policy Options for Connecting and Enabling the Next Billion—Phase II'. IGF 2016 Community Intersessional Programme. <http://www.intgovforum.org/cms/documents/policy-options/796-connectingthenextbillion-framework-phase-ii-v7/file>.

IGF Best Practice Forum's Consultants (2016) 'Contributions Taking Stock of IGF 2015 and Looking Ahead to IGF 2016'. <http://www.intgovforum.org/cms/documents/igf-meeting/igf-2016/takingstock/694-contribution-from-igf-best-practice-forums-bpfs-consultants>.

IICD (2004) *The ICT Roundtable Process: Lessons Learned from Facilitating ICT-Enabled Development*. The Hague: IICD. <http://www.bibalex.org/search4dev/files/287832/118715.pdf>.

IIMB and CDP (2014) *ICT Sector's Role in Climate Change Mitigation: An Analysis of Climate Change Performance and Preparedness of 320 Global ICT Companies*. New Delhi and Bangalore: CDP and IIMB. <https://www.cdp.net/CDPResults/CDP-ICT-sector-report-2014.pdf>.

*info*Dev (2009) *A Model for Sustainable and Replicable ICT Incubators in Sub-Saharan Africa*. Washington, DC: *info*Dev.

Inglis, T. (1997) 'Empowerment and Emancipation'. *Adult Education Quarterly*, 48(1), pp. 3–17.

Internet Watch Foundation (2015) *Annual Report 2015*. Cambridge: Internet Watch Foundation.

ISOC (2015) *Internet Society Global Internet Report 2015: Mobile Evolution and Development of the Internet*. Reston: Internet Society.

ITU (2005) *WSIS Golden Book*. Geneva: ITU.

ITU (2012) *Assessment Framework for Environmental Impact of ICT*. Geneva: ITU. <https://www.itu.int/dms_pub/itu-t/oth/4B/04/T4B0400000B0008PDFE.pdf>.

ITU (2013) *Universal Service Funds and Digital Inclusion for All*. Geneva: ITU.

ITU (2014) *WSIS+10 Outcome Documents*. Geneva: ITU.

ITU (2015a) *Report 2015 by the m-Powering Development Advisory Board: m-Powering Development Initiative*. Geneva: ITU.

ITU (2015b) *Advancing Sustainable Development Through Information and Communication Technologies: WSIS Action Lines Enabling SDGs*. Geneva: ITU.

itublog (2014) 'Engaging Civil Society in the ICT Sector'. *itublog*, 23 October. <https://itu4u.wordpress.com/2014/10/23/engaging-civil-society-in-the-ict-sector>.

ITU-*info*Dev (regularly updated) *ITU-infoDev ICT Regulation Toolkit*. <http://www.ictregulationtoolkit.org/en/home> (first published 2004).

ITU and Cisco (2016) *Harnessing the Internet of Things for Global Development*. Geneva: ITU.

Jamni, M., Kinshuk, and Khribi, M. K. (eds.) (2016) *Open Education: From OERs to MOOCs*. Berlin: Springer.

Janssen, M., Charalabidis, Y., and Zuiderwijk, A. (2012) 'Benefits, Adoption Barriers and Myths of Open Data and Open Government'. *Information Systems Management*, 29(4), pp. 258–68.

Jay, M. (1973) *The Dialectical Imagination: A History of the Frankfurt School and the Institute of Social Research 1923–1950*. London: Heinemann.

Jigsaw Consult (2014) 'MBRSLP Research 2013–2014'. <http://smartlearning.gov.ae/wp-content/uploads/2014/09/MBRSLP-research-2013-2014.pdf>.

Kabeer, N. (2015) 'Gender, Poverty, and Inequality: A Brief History of Feminist Contributions in the Field of International Development'. *Gender and Development*, 23(2), pp. 189–205.

Kalvet, T. (2007) *The Estonian Information Society: Developments Since the 1990s*. Tallinn: PRAXIS Center for Policy Studies and Tallinn University of Technology.

Kaplan, F. (2016) *Dark Territory: The Secret History of Cyber War*. New York: Simon & Schuster.

Kappeler, A. and Nemoz, M. (2010) 'Public–Private Partnerships in Europe—Before and During the Recent Financial Crisis'. European Investment Bank Economic and Financial Report 2010/04. <http://www.eib.org/epec/resources/efr_epec_ppp_report1.pdf>.

Keith, N. W. (1997) *International Development: Globalism, Postmodernity, and Difference*. Thousand Oaks, CA: Sage.

Kelly, T. and Firestone, R. (2016) *How Tech Hubs are Helping to Drive Economic Growth in Africa*. Washington, DC: World Bank (World Development Report Background Paper 102957). <http://documents.worldbank.org/curated/en/626981468195850883/pdf/102957-WP-Box394845B-PUBLIC-WDR16-BP-How-Tech-Hubs-are-helping-to-Drive-Economic-Growth-in-Africa-Kelly-Firestone.pdf>.

Kinyanjui, P. E. (2007) 'Development of NEPAD E-Schools Initiative'. In Commonwealth Secretariat (ed.), *Commonwealth Education Partnerships*. Cambridge: Nexus, pp. 179–85. <http://www.cedol.org/wp-content/uploads/2012/02/179-185-2007.pdf>.

Kirkpatrick, D. (2011) *The Facebook Effect: The Inside Story of the Company that is Connecting the World*. New York: Simon & Schuster.

Kleine, D. (2013) *Technologies of Choice: ICTs, Development, and the Capabilities Approach*. Cambridge, MA: MIT Press.

Kleinwächter, W. (2004) 'Beyond ICANN vs ITU: How WSIS Tried to Enter the New Territory of Internet Governance'. *Gazette: The International Journal for Communication Studies*, 66(3–4), pp. 233–51.

Kleinwächter, W. (2012) 'WCIT and Internet Governance: Harmless Resolution or Trojan Horse?' *CircleID: Internet Infrastructure*, 17 December. <http://www.circleid.com/posts/20121217_wcit_and_internet_governance_harmless_resolution_or_trojan_horse>.

Kothari, U. (ed.) (2005) *A Radical History of Development Studies: Individuals, Institutions and Ideologies*. London and Cape Town: Zed Books and David Philip.

Kramer, R. M. (2009) 'Rethinking Trust'. *Harvard Business Review*, June, pp. 69–77.

Kshetri, N. (2010) *The Global Cybercrime Industry: Economic, Institutional and Strategic Perspectives*. Heidelberg: Springer.

Kummer, M. (2013) 'Multistakeholder Cooperation: Reflections on the Emergence of a New Phraseology in International Cooperation'. <https://www.internetsociety.org/blog/2013/05/multistakeholder-cooperation-reflections-emergence-new-phraseology-international>.

Lanier, J. (2011) *You Are Not a Gadget: A Manifesto*. London: Penguin.

Laprise, J. and Musiani, F. (2015) 'Internet Governance'. In R. Mansell and P. H. Ang (eds.), *The International Encyclopedia of Digital Communication and Society*. Chichester: Wiley-Blackwell, pp. 1–9. <http://onlinelibrary.wiley.com/doi/10.1002/9781118767771.wbiedcs141/pdf>.

Leiner, B. M., Cerf, V. G., Clark, D. D, Kahn, R. E, Kleinrock, L., Lynch, D. C., Postel, J., Roberts, L. G., and Wolff, S. (2012) *Brief History of the Internet*. Reston: Internet Society. <http://www.internetsociety.org/brief-history-internet>.

Lennie, J. and Tacchi, J. (2013) *Evaluating Communication for Development: A Framework for Social Change*. London: Routledge Earthscan.

Lewis, D. (2002) 'Civil Society in African Contexts: Reflections on the Usefulness of a Concept'. *Development and Change*, 33(4), pp. 569–86.

Ligh, M. H., Adair, S., Haststein, B., and Richard, M. (2011) *Malware Analyst's Cookbook and DVD: Tools and Techniques for Fighting Malicious Code*. Indianapolis: Wiley.

Lillemose, J. and Kryger, M. (2015) 'The (Re)invention of Cyberspace'. *Kunstkritikk*. <http://www.kunstkritikk.com/kommentar/the-reinvention-of-cyberspace>.

Lipsey, R. G. and Chrystal, K. A. (1995) *An Introduction to Positive Economics*, 8th edn. Oxford: Oxford University Press.

Livingstone, D. (2015) *Transhumanism: The History of a Dangerous Idea*. USA: Sabilillah Publications.

Locke, J. (1987) *Two Treatises of Government*, ed. R. Ashcraft. London: Allen & Unwin (originally published 1689).

McAfee (2014) *Net Losses: Estimating the Global Cost of Cybercrime. Economic Impact of Cybercrime II*. Santa Clara: McAfee.

McCarthy, T. (1978) *The Critical Theory of Jürgen Habermas*. London: Hutchinson.

Mackenzie, D. and Wajcman, J. (eds.) (1999) *The Social Shaping of Technology*, 2nd edn. Philadelphia: Open University Press.

MacLean, D. (ed.) (2004) *Internet Governance: A Grand Collaboration*. New York: UN ICT Task Force.

McMichael, P. (2012) *Development and Social Change: A Global Perspective*, 5th edn. Thousand Oaks, CA: Pine Forge.

Maitland, D. (1984) *The Missing Link: Report of the Independent Commission for World Wide Telecommunication Development*. Geneva: ITU.

Malcolm, J. (2008) *Multi-Stakeholder Governance and the Internet Governance Forum*. Perth: Terminus Press.

Malcolm, N. (2016) *Agents of Empire: Knights, Corsairs, Jesuits and Spies in the Sixteenth-Century Mediterranean World*. London: Penguin.

Malone, M. S. (2014) *The Intel Trinity: How Robert Noyce, Gordon Moore, and Andy Grove Built the World's Most Important Company*. New York: HarperCollins.

Mann, D. and Sutton, M. (1998) 'Netcrime'. *British Journal of Criminology*, 38(2), pp. 210–29.

Mansell, R. and Ang, P. H. (eds.) (2015) *The International Encyclopedia of Digital Communication and Society*, 3 vols. Chichester: Wiley-Blackwell.

Mansell, R. and Wehn, U. (1998) *Knowledge Societies: Information Technology for Sustainable Development*. Oxford: Oxford University Press.

Martens, J. (2007) *Multistakeholder Partnerships: Future Models of Multilateralism*. Berlin: Friedrich Ebert Stiftung.

Marx, K. (1976) *Capital, Volume 1*. Harmondsworth: Penguin (originally published 1867).

Mercer, C. (2002) 'NGOs, Civil Society and Democratization: A Critical Review of the Literature'. *Progress in Development Studies*, 2(1), pp. 5–22.

Mercer, C. (2003) 'Performing Partnership: Civil Society and the Illusions of Good Governance in Tanzania'. *Political Geography*, 22, pp. 741–63.

Miao, F., Mishra, S., and McGreal, R. (eds.) (2016) *Open Educational Resources: Policy, Costs and Transformation*. Paris and Burnaby: UNESCO and COL.

Microsoft (2015) 'Microsoft's White Space Free WiFi Projects are Annoying Indian Telecos'. <http://mspoweruser.com/microsofts-white-space-free-wifi-projects-are-annoying-indian-telecos>.

Milanovic, B. (2003) 'The Two Faces of Globalization: Against Globalization as We Know It'. *World Development*, 31(4), pp. 667–83.

Millennium Project (2006) 'Goals, Targets and Indicators'. <http://www.un millenniumproject.org/goals/gti.htm>.

Milward-Oliver, G. (ed.) (2005) *Maitland +20: Fixing the Missing Link*. Bradford on Avon: Anima.

Mingay, S. and Pamlin, D. (2008) *Assessment of Global Low-Carbon and Environmental Leadership in the ICT Sector*. Stamford, CA: Gartner and WWF. <http://www.wwf.se/source. php/1298320/WWF_Gartner-Assessment_of_global_lowcarbon_IT_leadership.pdf>.

Ministry of Foreign Affairs, Republic of Korea (2013) 'Seoul Framework for and Commitment to Open and Secure Cyberspace'. <http://www.mofat.go.kr/english/visa/images/res/SeoulFramework.pdf>.

Momsen, J. H. and Townsend, J. (1987) *Geography of Gender in the Third World*. London: Hutchinson.

Moody, G. (2002) *Rebel Code and the Open Source Revolution*. New York: Basic Books.

Mueller, M. (1999) 'ICANN and Internet Governance: Sorting through the Debris of "Self-Regulation"'. *info*, 1(6), pp. 497–520.

Mueller, M. (2014) 'What Did the WCIT Really Do? A Review'. *Internet Governance Project*, 13 March. <http://www.internetgovernance.org/2014/03/13/what-did-the-wcit-really-do-a-review>.

Musiani, F., Cogburn, D. L., DeNardis, L., and Levinson, N. S. (eds.) (2016) *The Turn to Infrastructure in Internet Governance*. New York: Palgrave Macmillan.

Naughton, J. (1999) *A Brief History of the Future: The Origins of the Internet*. London: Phoenix.

Naughton, J. (2012) *From Gutenberg to Zuckerberg: What You Really Need to Know About the Internet*. London: Quercus.

Naughton, J. (2016) 'The Evolution of the Internet: From Military Experiment to General Purpose Technology'. *Journal of Cyber Policy*, 1(1), pp. 5–28.

Neeson, J. M. (1993) *Commoners: Common Right, Enclosure and Social Change in England, 1700–1820*. Cambridge: Cambridge University Press.

NETmundial (2014) 'NETmundial Multistakeholder Statement'. <http://netmundial.br/wp-content/uploads/2014/04/NETmundial-Multistakeholder-Document.pdf>.

News24 (2013) 'Brazil to Host Internet Governance Summit', 10 October. <http://www.news24.com/Technology/News/Brazil-to-host-internet-governance-summit-20131010>.

Next Generation Mobile Networks (2015) *NGMN 5H White Paper*. Frankfurt: Next Generation Mobile Networks.

Norton (2016) 'Online Harassment: The New Zealand Woman's Experience'. <https://phoenix.symantec.com/Norton/nz/online-harassment-experience-women/assets/OnlineHarassmentNZ_Women%202016_FA_WEB.pdf>.

NTIA (2014) 'NTIA Announces Intent to Transition Key Internet Domain Name Functions'. <https://www.ntia.doc.gov/press-release/2014/ntia-announces-intent-transition-key-internet-domain-name-functions>.

NTIA (2016) 'Fact Sheet on NTIA's Assessment of the IANA Stewardship Transition Proposal'. <https://www.ntia.doc.gov/other-publication/2016/fact-sheet-ntias-assessment-iana-stewardship-transition-proposal>.

Nwana, H. S. (2014) *Telecommunications, Media and Technology (TMT) for Developing Economies: How to Make TMT Improve Developing Economies in Africa and Elsewhere for the 2020s*. London: Gigalen Press.

O'Boyle, E. J. (1999) 'Toward an Improved Definition of Poverty'. *Review of Social Economy*, 57(3), pp. 281–301.

OECD (2014) 'Focus on Inequality and Growth—December 2014'. <http://www.oecd.org/social/Focus-Inequality-and-Growth-2014.pdf>.

OECD (2015a) *In It Together: Why Less Inequality Benefits All*. Paris: OECD.

OECD (2015b) *Students, Computers and Learning: Making the Connection*. Paris: OECD Publishing.

OECD (2016) 'Are There Differences in How Advantaged and Disadvantaged Students Use the Internet?' *PISA in Focus*, 64. <http://www.keepeek.com/Digital-Asset-Management/

oecd/education/are-there-differences-in-how-advantaged-and-disadvantaged-students-use-the-internet_5jlv8zq6hw43-en#.V7GjFLWM-d1#page1>.

Osibanjo, O. and Nnorom, I. C. (2007) 'The Challenge of Electronic Waste (E-Waste) Management in Developing Countries'. *Waste Management and Research*, 25, pp. 489–501.

Owen, G. and Savage, N. (2015) *The Tor Dark Net*. London: CIGI and Chatham House. Global Commission on Internet Governance, Paper Series No. 20, September. <https://www.ourinternet.org/sites/default/files/publications/no20_0.pdf>.

Oxfam (2016) *An Economy for the 1%: How Privilege and Power in the Economy Drive Extreme Inequality and How This Can be Stopped*. Oxford: Oxfam.

Patrinos, H. A., Barrera-Osorio, F., and Guáqueta, J. (1999) *The Role and Impact of Public–Private Partnerships in Education*. Washington, DC: World Bank.

Pavlik, J. V. (2005) 'Understanding Convergence and Digital Broadcasting Technologies for the 21st Century'. *NHK Broadcasting Studies*, 4, pp. 131–58.

Phillips, W. (2015) *Mapping the Relationship Between Online Trolling and Mainstream Culture*. Cambridge MA: MIT Press.

Pietrosemoli, E. and Zennaro, M. (eds.) (2013) *TV White Spaces: A Pragmatic Approach*. Trieste: The Abdul Salam International Centre for Theoretical Physics. <http://wire less.ictp.it/tvws/book/tvws.pdf>.

Pon, B. (2016) *Winners and Losers in the Global App Economy*. London: Caribou Digital and Mozilla.

Porterfield, J. (2013) *Niklas Zennstrom and Skype*. New York: Rosen Classroom.

Prasad, R. (2014) *5G: 2020 and Beyond*. London: River Publishers.

Pratt, B., Hailey, J., Gallo, M., Shadwick, R., and Hayman, R. (2012) 'Understanding Private Donors in International Development'. INTRAC Policy Briefing Paper 31. <http://www.intrac.org/data/files/resources/747/Briefing-Paper-31-Understanding-private-donors-in-international-development.pdf>.

Prescott, D. and Stibbe, D. (2015) *Unleashing the Power of Business: A Practical Roadmap to Systematically Engage Business as a Partner in Development*. Oxford: The Partnering Initiative. <http://www.thepartneringinitiative.org/wp-content/uploads/2015/07/Unleash ing-the-Power-of-Business_Roadmap_full_forweb.pdf>.

Privacy International (2013) 'Data for Development: The New Conflict Resource?' <https://www.privacyinternational.org/node/414>.

Proenza, F. J. (ed.) (2015) *Public Access ICT Across Culture: Diversifying Participation in the Network Society*. Cambridge, MA: MIT Press.

Qiang, C. Z.-W. and Rossotto, C. M. (2009) 'Economic Impacts of Broadband'. In World Bank, *Information and Communications for Development 2009: Extending Reach and Increasing Impact*. Washington, DC: World Bank, pp. 35–50. <https://issuu.com/world.bank.publications/docs/9780821376058>.

Raiti, G. C. (2006) 'The Lost Sheep of ICT4D Research'. *Information Technologies and International Development*, 3(4), pp. 1–7.

Ralston, A., Reilly, E. D., and Hemmendinger, D. (2000) *Encyclopedia of Computer Science*, 4th edn. Chichester: Wiley.

Ranis, G., Vreeland, J. R., and Kosacj, S. (eds.) (2006) *Globalization and the Nation State: The Impact of the IMF and the World Bank*. London: Routledge.

References

Ravallion, M. (1997) 'Can High-Inequality Developing Countries Escape Absolute Poverty?' *Economics Letters*, 56(1), pp. 51–8.

Ravallion, M. (2001) 'Growth, Inequality and Poverty: Looking Beyond Averages'. *World Development*, 29(11), pp. 1803–15.

Rawls, J. (1971) *A Theory of Justice*. Cambridge, MA: Harvard University Press.

Reason, P. and Bradbury, H. (eds.) (2008) *The Sage Handbook of Action Research: Participatory Inquiry and Practice*, 2nd edn. London: Sage.

Rodine-Hardy, K. (2013) *Global Markets and Government Regulation in Telecommunications*. Cambridge: Cambridge University Press.

Rodriguez, J. (2015) *Fundamentals of 5G Mobile Networks*. Chichester: Wiley.

Rostow, W. (1960) *The Stages of Economic Growth: A Non-Communist Manifesto*. Cambridge: Cambridge University Press.

Rousseff, D. (2014) 'NETmundial—Dilma Rousseff's Opening Speech'. <http://netmundial.br/wp-content/uploads/2014/04/NETMundial-23April2014-Dilma-Rousseff-Opening-Speech-en.pdf>.

Rubin, R. (2015) 'U.S. Companies are Stashing $2.1 Trillion Overseas to Avoid Taxes'. *Bloomberg News*. <http://www.bloomberg.com/news/articles/2015-03-04/u-s-companies-are-stashing-2-1-trillion-overseas-to-avoid-taxes>.

Sachs, J. (2005) *The End of Poverty: How We Can Make it Happen in Our Lifetime*. London: Penguin Books.

Sachs, W. (ed.) (1992) *The Development Dictionary: A Guide to Knowledge as Power*. London: Zed Books.

Samarajiva, R. (2012) 'Facebook = Internet?' <http://lirneasia.net/2012/05/facebook-internet>.

Schmidt, E. and Rosenberg, J. (2015) *How Google Works*. London: John Murray.

Schwab, K. (2016) *The Fourth Industrial Revolution*. Cologny: World Economic Forum.

Selinger, M. (2006) 'Developing an Understanding of Blended Learning'. In C. J. Bonk and C. R. Graham (eds.), *The Handbook of Blended Learning: Global Perspectives, Local Designs*. San Francisco: Wiley Pfeiffer, pp. 432–43.

Sen, A. (1983) 'Poor, Relatively Speaking'. *Oxford Economic Papers*, 35, pp. 153–69.

Sen, A. (1999) *Development as Freedom*. New York: Alfred A. Knopf.

Serianu (2015) *Kenya Cybersecurity Report 2015: Achieving Enterprise. Cyber Resilience Through Situational Awareness*. Nairobi: Serianu. <http://serianu.com/downloads/KenyaCyberSecurityReport2015.pdf>.

SIDA (2003) *Digital Empowerment: Information and Communication Technology for Democratic Governance and Social Development—A Strategy for ICT for Development (ICT4D)*. Stockholm: SIDA.

Singer, P. W. and Friedman, A. (2014) *Cybersecurity and Cyberwar: What Everyone Needs to Know*. Oxford: Oxford University Press.

Singh, P. (1995) *The Naxalite Movement in India*. New Delhi: Rupa.

Skouby, K. E. and Williams, I. (eds.) (2014) *The Africa Mobile Story*. Aalborg: Rover Publishers.

Skovdal, M. and Cornish, F. (2015) *Qualitative Research for Development*. Rugby: Practical Action.

Smith, W. (1997) 'Utility Regulation: The Independence Debate'. *Public Policy for the Private Sector*, Note No. 127. <http://siteresources.worldbank.org/EXTFINANCIALSECTOR/Resources/282884-1303327122200/127smith.pdf>.

Söderberg, J. (2008) *Hacking Capitalism: The Free and Open Source Software Movement*. Abingdon: Routledge.

Sofaer, A. D., Clark, D., and Diffie, W. (2010) 'Cyber Security and International Agreements'. In Committee on Deterring Cyberattacks: Informing Strategies and Developing Options, National Research Council (eds.), *Proceedings of a Workshop on Deterring Cyberattacks: Informing Strategies and Developing Options for U.S. Policy*. Washington, DC: National Academic Press, pp. 179–206.

Song, S. (2013a) 'Television White Spaces Spectrum in Africa: The Story So Far in 2013'. *Many Possibilities*. <https://manypossibilities.net/2013/06/tv-white-spaces-in-africa>.

Song, S. (2013b) 'The Open Data Cart and Twin Horses of Accountability and Innovation'. *Many Possibilities*. <https://manypossibilities.net/2013/06/the-open-data-cart-and-twin-horses-of-accountability-and-innovation>.

Song, S. (2016) 'Resolving the Free Basics Paradox'. *Many Possibilities*. <https://manypossibilities.net/2016/02/resolving-the-free-basics-paradox>.

Souter, D. (2005) 'Then and Now: What Would Be the Remit of a Modern-Day Maitland Commission?' In G. Milward-Oliver (ed.), *Maitland +20: Fixing the Missing Link*. Bradford on Avon: Anima, pp. 3–20.

Souter, D. (2012) *Assessing National Internet Governance Arrangements: A Framework for Comparative Assessment*. London: ICT Development Associates for the Internet Society.

Souter, D. with Jagun, A. (2007) *Whose Summit? Whose Information Society? Developing Countries and Civil Society at the World Summit on the Information Society*. Melville, South Africa: Association for Progressive Communications.

Southwood, R. and Tijani, B. (2012) 'Nigeria: Bosun Tijani, Co-Creation Hub Talks Innovation and Social Entrepreneurs'. *allAfrica*. <http://allafrica.com/view/resource/main/main/id/00031754.html>.

Special Representative of the Secretary-General on Violence against Children (2014) *Releasing Children's Potential and Minimizing Risks: ICTs, the Internet and Violence Against Children*. New York: The Special Representative of the Secretary-General on Violence against Children.

Spratt, S. and Baker, J. (2015) *Big Data and International Development: Impacts, Scenarios and Policy Options*. Falmer: Institute of Development Studies, Evidence Report No. 163. <http://opendocs.ids.ac.uk/opendocs/bitstream/handle/123456789/7198/ER163_BigDataandInternationalDevelopment.pdf;jsessionid=468B67A0E69DCDC65977403D2FEC9EA0?sequence=1>.

Steurer, R., Langer, M. E., Konrad, A., and Martinuzzi, A. (2005) 'Corporations, Stakeholders and Sustainable Development I: A Theoretical Exploration of Business–Society Relations'. *Journal of Business Ethics*, 61, pp. 263–81.

Steyn, J. and Johansen, G. (eds.) (2011) *ICTs and Sustainable Solutions for the Digital Divide: Theory and Perspectives*. Hershey: Information Science Reference.

Strickling, L. (2016) 'Reviewing the IANA Transition Protocol'. <https://www.ntia.doc.gov/blog/2016/reviewing-iana-transition-proposal#.VuRmzAOZ91M.facebook>.

Stross, R. (2008) *Planet Google: One Company's Audacious Plan to Organize Everything We Know*. New York: Free Press.

Sutinen, E. and Tedre, M. (2010) 'ICT4D: A Computer Science Perspective'. In T. Elomaa, H. Mannila, and P. Orponen (eds.), *Algorithms and Applications: Essays Dedicated to Esko Ukkonen on the Occasion of his 60th Birthday* (Volume 6060 in the series Lecture Notes in Computer Science). Berlin: Springer-Verlag, pp. 221–31.

Swanson, A. (2014) 'Eight Innovative Industries China Does Better Than Anywhere Else'. *Forbes Asia*, 30 November. <http://www.forbes.com/sites/anaswanson/2014/11/30/eight-innovative-industries-china-does-better-than-anywhere-else/#1c014716618a>.

Tacchi, J., Lennie, J., and Wilmore, M. (2010) 'Critical Reflections on the Use of Participatory Methodologies to Build Evaluation Capacities in International Development Organisations', 8th World Congress 2010: Participatory Action Research and Action Learning, 6–9 September, Melbourne, Australia. <https://www.researchgate.net/profile/June_Lennie/publication/228394865_Critical_reflections_on_the_use_of_participatory_methodologies_to_build_evaluation_capacities_in_international_development_organisations/links/0deec524e43ce1bffa000000.pdf?origin=publication_list>.

Tacchi, J. A., Slater, D., and Hearn G. N. (2003) *Ethnographic Action Research: A User's Handbook*. New Delhi: UNESCO.

Tafazolli, R. (ed.) (2006) *Technologies for the Wireless Future: Wireless World Research Forum (WWRF), Volume 2*. Chichester: Wiley.

Tar, Z. (1977) *The Frankfurt School: The Critical Theories of Max Horkheimer and Theodore W. Adorno*. New York: Wiley.

Tennyson, R. (2011) *The Partnering Toolbook*, 4th edn. Oxford: The Partnering Initiative (IBLF). <http://thepartneringinitiative.org/wp-content/uploads/2014/08/Partnering-Toolbook-en-20113.pdf>.

The Partnering Initiative (2003) *Driving Effective Collaboration for a Sustainable Future*. <http://www.thepartneringinitiative.org>.

Thompson, A. (ed.) (2007) *The Media and the Rwanda Genocide*. London: Pluto Press.

Thompson, E. P. (1991) *The Making of the English Working Class*. Harmondsworth: Penguin.

Tiles, M. and Oberdiek, H. (1995) *Living in a Technological Culture: Human Tools and Human Values*. New York: Routledge.

Touré, H. et al. (2014) *The Quest for Cyberconfidence*. Geneva: ITU.

Townsend, D. (2015) 'Universal Access and Service Funds in the Broadband Era: The Collective Investment Imperative'. Alliance for Affordable Internet. <http://a4ai.org/wp-content/uploads/2015/03/A4AI-USAFs-2015_Final-v.2.pdf>.

Toyama, K. (2015) *Geek Heresy*. New York: Public Affairs.

Trucano, M. (2015) 'Universal Service Funds & Connecting Schools to the Internet around the World'. *Edutech, a World Bank Blog on ICT Use in Education*, 26 February. <http://blogs.worldbank.org/edutech/universal-service-funds-connecting-schools-internet-around-world>.

Tucker, A. B. (2004) *Computer Science Handbook*, 2nd edn. London: Chapman & Hall/CRC Press.

UK Government Web Archive (2007) 'Imfundo Research Programme'. <http://webarchive.nationalarchives.gov.uk/+/<http:/www.dfid.gov.uk/research/imfundo.asp.

UK Public Administration Select Committee (2011) 'Government and IT—"A Recipe for Rip-Offs": Time for a New Approach'. <http://www.publications.parliament.uk/pa/cm201012/cmselect/cmpubadm/715/71505.htm>.

UK Treasury Commons Select Committee (2011) *Treasury—Seventeenth Report: Private Finance Initiative, Conclusions and Recommendations*. <http://www.publications.parliament.uk/pa/cm201012/cmselect/cmtreasy/1146/114608.htm>.

UN (n.d.) 'Millennium Development Goals Indicators'. <http://mdgs.un.org/unsd/mdg/host.aspx?Content=indicators/officiallist.htm>.

UN (2015) *Transforming our World: The 2030 Agenda for Sustainable Development A/RES/70/1*. New York: United Nations. <https://sustainabledevelopment.un.org/content/documents/21252030%20Agenda%20for%20Sustainable%20Development%20web.pdf>.

UN (2016) 'Sustainable Development Knowledge Platform'. <https://sustainabledevelopment.un.org/?menu=1300>.

UNDP (2015) *Human Development Report 2015: Work for Human Development*. New York: United Nations Development Programme.

UNESCO (2013) *UNESCO Global Report. Opening New Avenues for Empowerment: ICTs to Access Information and Knowledge for Persons with Disabilities*. Paris: UNESCO.

UNESCO (2015) *Fostering Digital Citizenship Through Safe and Responsible Use of ICT: A Review of Current Status in Asia and the Pacific as of December 2014*. Bangkok: UNESCO (APEID-ICT in Education, UNESCO Asia-Pacific Regional Bureau of Education).

UNESCO and COL (2015) *Guidelines for Open Educational Resources (OER) in Higher Education*, 2nd edn. Paris and Vancouver: UNESCO and COL.

UNGA (2011) *Report of the Special Rapporteur on the Promotion and Protection of the Right to Freedom of Opinion and Expression, Frank La Rue, A/HRC/17/27*. <http://www2.ohchr.org/english/bodies/hrcouncil/docs/17session/A.HRC.17.27_en.pdf>.

UNGA (2015) 'Resolution Adopted by the General Assembly on 16 December 2015'. *70/125 Outcome Document of the High-Level Meeting of the General Assembly on the Overall Review of the Implementation of the Outcomes of the World Summit on the Information Society, A/RES/70/125*. <http://workspace.unpan.org/sites/Internet/Documents/UNPAN96078.pdf>.

Universidad Rey Juan Carlos y Fundación EHAS (eds.) (2010) *Actas de las Jornadad Internacionales en Investigación en TIC para el Desarrollo Humano*. Madrid: Universidad Rey Juan Carlos y Fundación EHAS.

University of Cambridge Computer Laboratory (1999) 'EDSAC 99'. <https://www.cl.cam.ac.uk/events/EDSAC99/reminiscences>.

UNODC (2012) *The Use of the Internet for Terrorist Purposes*. New York: United Nations Office on Drugs and Crime in collaboration with the United Nations Counter-Terrorism Implementation.

Unwin, D. J. and Maguire, D. J. (1990) 'Developing the Effective Use of Information Technology in Teaching and Learning in Geography: The Computers in Teaching Initiative Centre for Geography'. *Journal of Geography in Higher Education*, 14(1), pp. 77–82.

Unwin, T. (1992) *The Place of Geography*. Harlow: Longman.

References

Unwin, T. (ed.) (1994) *Atlas of World Development*. London: Wiley.

Unwin, T. (1998) 'Ideas of Europe'. In T. Unwin (ed.), *A European Geography*. Harlow: Addison Wesley, Longman, pp. 1–16.

Unwin, T. (2003) 'What is Imfundo? A Message from the Team Leader'. <http://web. archive.org/web/20031102094704/<http://imfundo.digitalbrain.com/imfundo/web/ imfundo/about>.

Unwin, T. (2004) 'Beyond Budgetary Support: Pro-Poor Development Agendas for Africa'. *Third World Quarterly*, 25(8), pp. 1501–23.

Unwin, T. (2005) *Partnerships in Development Practice: Evidence from Multi-Stakeholder ICT4D Partnership Practice in Africa*. Paris: UNESCO.

Unwin, T. (2007) 'No End to Poverty'. *Journal of Development Studies*, 45(3), pp. 929–53.

Unwin, T. (ed.) (2009) *ICT4D: Information and Communication Technology for Development*. Cambridge: Cambridge University Press.

Unwin, T. (2010) 'ICTs, Citizens, and the State: Moral Philosophy and Development Practices'. *Electronic Journal on Information Systems in Developing Countries*, 44(1), pp. 1–16.

Unwin, T. (2011) 'On Publishing in ICT4D'. <https://unwin.wordpress.com/2011/01/ 02/on-publishing-in-ict4d>.

Unwin, T. (2013) 'The Internet and Development: A Critical Perspective'. In W. Dutton (ed.), *The Oxford Handbook of Internet Studies*. Oxford: Oxford University Press, pp. 531–54.

Unwin, T. (2014) 'Prolegomena on Human Rights and Responsibilities'. <https://unwin. wordpress.com/2014/09/01/prolegomena-on-human-rights-and-responsibilities>.

Unwin, T. (2015) 'Multistakeholder Partnerships'. In R. Mansell and P. H. Ang (eds.), *The International Encyclopedia of Digital Communication and Society*. Chichester: Wiley, pp. 634–44.

Unwin, T. and Day, B. (2005) 'Dos and Don'ts in Monitoring and Evaluation'. In D. A. Wagner, B. Day, T. James, R. B. Kozma, J. Miller, and T. Unwin, *Monitoring and Evaluation of ICT in Education Projects: A Handbook for Developing Countries*. Washington: *info*Dev, pp. 65–72.

Unwin, T. and Wong, A. (2012) *Global Education Initiative: Retrospective on Partnerships for Education Development 2003–2011*. Cologny: World Economic Forum.

Vaccaro, A. (2006) 'Privacy, Security, and Transparency: ICT-Related Ethical Perspectives and Contrasts in Contemporary Firms'. In E. Trauth, D. Howcroft, T. Butler, B. Fitzgerald, and J. DeGross (eds.), *Social Inclusion: Societal and Organizational Implications for Information Systems*. IFIP International Federation for Information Processing, Volume 208. Boston, MA: Springer, pp. 245–58.

Vise, D. A. (2005) *The Google Story*. New York: Bantam Dell.

VisionMobile (2014) *Developer Economics Q3 2014: State of the Developer Nation*. London: VisionMobile. <http://www.visionmobile.com/product/developer-economics-q3-2014>, accessed 19 February 2016.

VisionMobile with Ericsson (2012) *The Telco Innovation Toolbox: Economic Models for Managing Disruption and Reinventing the Telco*. London: VisionMobile in Association with Ericsson.

Vogel, I. (2012) *Review of the Use of 'Theory of Change' in International Development.* London: DFID. <http://r4d.dfid.gov.uk/pdf/outputs/mis_spc/DFID_ToC_Review_VogelV7.pdf>.

Wagner, D. A., Day, B., James, T., Kozma, R. B., Miller, J., and Unwin, T. (2005) *Monitoring and Evaluation of ICT in Education Projects: A Handbook for Developing Countries.* Washington: *info*Dev. <http://www.infodev.org/infodev-files/resource/In fodevDocuments_9.pdf>.

Walden, I. (ed.) (2009a) *Telecommunications Law and Regulation,* 3rd edn. Oxford: Oxford University Press.

Walden, I. (2009b) 'Telecommunications Law and Regulation: An Introduction'. In I. Walden (ed.), *Telecommunications Law and Regulation,* 3rd edn. Oxford: Oxford University Press, pp. 3–22.

Walsham, G. (2001) *Making a World of Difference: IT in a Global Context.* Chichester: Wiley.

Walsham, G. (2012) 'Are We Making a Better World with ICTs? Reflections on a Future Agenda for the IS Field'. *Journal of Information Technology,* 27, pp. 87–93.

Wanmali, S. (1981) *Periodic Markets and Rural Development in India.* New Delhi: BR.

Warner, M. and Sullivan, R. (2004) *Putting Partnerships to Work: Strategic Alliances for Development between Government, the Private Sector and Civil Society.* Sheffield: Greenleaf.

Weigel, G. and Waldburger, D. (eds.) (2004) *ICT4D—Connecting People for a Better World.* Berne and Kuala Lumpur: Swiss Agency for Development and Cooperation and Global Knowledge Partnership.

Weimann, G. (2006) *Terror on the Internet: The New Arena, the New Challenges.* Washington, DC: United States Institute of Peace.

WGIG (2005) 'Report of the Working Group on Internet Governance', Château de Bossey, June. <http://www.wgig.org/docs/WGIGREPORT.pdf>.

White House (2011) *International Strategy for Cyberspace.* Washington, DC: President of the United States. <https://www.whitehouse.gov/sites/default/files/rss_viewer/inter national_strategy_for_cyberspace.pdf>.

WikiLeaks (ed.) (2015) *The WikiLeaks Files: The World According to US Empire.* London: Verso.

Williams, F. (2015) *Green Giants: How Smart Companies Turn Sustainability into Billion-Dollar Businesses.* New York: AMACOM.

Williams, G. H. (2004) 'Evaluating Participatory Development: Tyranny, Power and (Re)politicisation'. *Third World Quarterly,* 25(3), pp. 557–78.

Williamson, J. (ed.) (1990) *Latin American Adjustment: How Much has Happened?* Washington, DC: Institute for International Economics.

Wireless World Research Forum (2015) *5G Vision, Enablers and Challenges for the Wireless Future.* Zurich: Wireless World Research Forum. <http://www.wwrf.ch/files/wwrf/content/files/publications/outlook/Outlook16.pdf>.

Wittel, A. (2016) *Digital Transitions.* Saarbrücken: Lambert Academic Publishing.

World Bank (2012) *Information and Communications for Development 2012: Maximising Mobile.* Washington: World Bank/*info*Dev.

World Bank (2016a) *World Development Report 2016: Digital Dividends.* Washington, DC: World Bank.

World Bank (2016b) *Open Data for Sustainable Development*. Washington, DC: World Bank. <http://pubdocs.worldbank.org/en/999161440616941994/Open-Data-for-Sustainable-Development.pdf>.

World Economic Forum (2012) *Big Data, Big Impact: New Possibilities for International Development*. Cologny: World Economic Forum.

World Economic Forum (2016) *Internet for All: A Framework for Accelerating Internet Access and Adoption*. Cologny: World Economic Forum, prepared in collaboration with The Boston Consulting Group. <http://www3.weforum.org/docs/WEF_Internet_for_All_Framework_Accelerating_Internet_Access_Adoption_report_2016.pdf>.

WSIS (2005) 'Tunis Agenda for the Information Society'. WSIS-05/TUNIS/DOC/6 (Rev. 1)-E. <http://www.itu.int/net/wsis/docs2/tunis/off/6rev1.html>.

Yeo, A. W. (2015) *Leveraging Research and Innovation in ICTs for Socio-Economic Development in Malaysia*. Sarawak: UNIMAS.

Zennaro, M. and Bagula, A. (2015) 'IoT for Development (IoT4D)'. *IEEE Newsletter*, July. <http://iot.ieee.org/newsletter/july-2015/iot-for-development-iot4d.html>.

Zetter, K. (2014) *Countdown to Zero Day: Stuxnet and the Launch of the World's First Digital Weapon*. New York: Crown.

Zetter, K. (2016) 'Everything We Know about Ukraine's Power Plant Hack'. *Wired*, 20 January. <https://www.wired.com/2016/01/everything-we-know-about-ukraines-power-plant-hack>.

Zittrain, J. (2009) *The Future of the Internet: And How to Stop It*. London: Penguin.

Zook, M. A. (2005) *The Geography of the Internet Industry: Venture Capital, Dot-Coms and Local Knowledge*. Oxford: Blackwell.

Index